ACHIEVING DIGITAL TRANSFORMATION THROUGH ANALYTICS AND AI

Digital Transformation: Accelerating Organizational Intelligence

Print ISSN: 2811-0552
Online ISSN: 2811-0560

Series Editor: Jay Liebowitz *(Rollins College, USA)*

According to a report released by Veritis in 2021 "the global digital transformation market size is anticipated to reach USD 1009.8 billion by 2025 from USD 469.8 billion in 2020. The demand for digital transformation services is expected to rise at a Compound Annual Growth Rate (CAGR) of around 16.5% over the forecast period from 2021 to 2025. The growing adoption of digital technologies, including Artificial Intelligence (AI), cloud computing, big data, the Internet of Things (IoT), and Machine Learning (ML), is driving the growth of the digital transformation market." To be competitive in today's fast-changing marketplace, organizations need to apply the "alphabet" of digital transformation.

The focus of the book series is unique and will cover the various perspectives on organizational digital transformation, namely business & management, technology, legal and ethics, and social aspects.

Published:

Vol. 8 *Achieving Digital Transformation through Analytics and AI*
edited by Jay Liebowitz

Vol. 7 *Digital Transformation and Society*
edited by Jay Liebowitz

Vol. 6 *Strategic Risk, Intelligence and Digital Transformation*
by Eduardo Rodriguez

Vol. 5 *Digital Transformation for Entrepreneurship*
edited by Susanne Durst and Aive Pevkur

Vol. 4 *Digital Strategies and Organizational Transformation*
edited by G Reza Djavanshir

Vol. 3 *Doing Well and Doing Good: Human-Centered Digital Transformation Leadership*
by Cheryl Flink, Liora Gross and William Pasmore

Vol. 2 *Digital Transformation Demystified*
by Frank Granito

Vol. 1 *Digital Transformation for the University of the Future*
edited by Jay Liebowitz

More information on this series can be found at https://www.worldscientific.com/series/dtaoi

Digital Transformation
Accelerating Organizational Intelligence
– Volume 8

ACHIEVING DIGITAL TRANSFORMATION THROUGH ANALYTICS AND AI

Edited by

Jay Liebowitz
Rollins College, USA

World Scientific

NEW JERSEY • LONDON • SINGAPORE • BEIJING • SHANGHAI • HONG KONG • TAIPEI • CHENNAI

Published by

World Scientific Publishing Co. Pte. Ltd.
5 Toh Tuck Link, Singapore 596224
USA office: 27 Warren Street, Suite 401-402, Hackensack, NJ 07601
UK office: 57 Shelton Street, Covent Garden, London WC2H 9HE

Library of Congress Control Number: 2024046645

British Library Cataloguing-in-Publication Data
A catalogue record for this book is available from the British Library.

Digital Transformation: Accelerating Organizational Intelligence — Vol. 8
ACHIEVING DIGITAL TRANSFORMATION THROUGH ANALYTICS AND AI

ISBN 978-981-12-9646-8 (hardcover)
ISBN 978-981-12-9647-5 (ebook for institutions)
ISBN 978-981-12-9648-2 (ebook for individuals)

For any available supplementary material, please visit
https://www.worldscientific.com/worldscibooks/10.1142/13939#t=suppl

Desk Editors: Nambirajan Karuppiah/Catherine Domingo Ong

Typeset by Stallion Press
Email: enquiries@stallionpress.com

Printed in Singapore

Jan 2025

To Isar—

A great colleague

and friend—

Am Yisrael Chai—

Best—

Joe

To all those AI explorers over the past almost 70 years who contributed to today's AI worldwide appeal.

https://doi.org/10.1142/9789811296475_fmatter

Foreword

The present reality reflects the imminent arrival of digital transformation facilitated by analytics and AI. This transformation isn't just confined to corporate environments; it's poised to revolutionize education as well. The capabilities of AI tools like ChatGPT and Deep Learning surpass those of humans in processing vast amounts of educational data encompassing behavioral patterns, academic performance, and assessments with unparalleled speed and efficiency. In an era where truth is often distorted and falsehoods masquerade as reality, AI-powered chatbots now assume the role of investigators, scrutinizing sources, preemptively identifying inaccuracies before they propagate. The imperative for fact-checking in today's socio-political landscape has catalyzed a democratization of data access, where computational linguistics has supplanted rhetorical maneuvers. Achieving digital transformation entails democratizing access to data beyond the confines of select IT professionals and data analysts, empowering individuals with comprehensible, actionable insights for effective data analysis and interpretation. The symbiotic relationship between business and education is bolstered by the synergy between artificial intelligence and data analytics. Notably, digital transformation in education is driven more by business than vice versa, with teaching and learning paradigms increasingly molded by AI, catering to personalized classroom experiences and student preferences. The journey toward achieving digital transformation through analytics and artificial intelligence is an ever-evolving narrative of continuous adaptation.

Jay Liebowitz's latest endeavor, *Achieving Digital Transformation through Analytics and Artificial Intelligence (AI)* navigates the complex landscape of extracting business value from these transformative AI tools. What insights and trust are requisite for realizing digital transformation? Just as education and business sectors converge to revolutionize pedagogy through AI and data analytics-driven instruction, the AI and analytics communities must foster improved communication and collaboration. The proliferation of extensive datasets, previously exclusive to higher education institutions, now extends to K-12 establishments adapting swiftly to post-pandemic learning environments. This paradigm shift in learning methodologies heralds the advent of code generation, dashboard creation, and report generation as integral components of the educational reform agenda. The ethos of AI and analytics, encompassing technology, processes, culture, and leadership traits, constitutes the cornerstone of "today's" educational reform landscape. This future is poised to harness predictive, prescriptive, diagnostic, and descriptive analytics, bolstering agility through timely data-driven decision-making, facilitated by the convergence of aptitude and opportunity. Individuals can be digitally augmented, fortified, and empowered to navigate the intricacies of a technologically driven world with enhanced prowess and intelligence, courtesy of artificial intelligence and analytics.

The forthcoming challenges in achieving transformation through artificial intelligence and analytics across organizations, educational institutions, and broader society underscore the imperative of cultivating a digitally adept talent pipeline capable of devising innovative solutions to counter the ever-evolving threats and opportunities posed by AI. In this era of digital interconnectedness and interdependence, education reform must parallel business advancements in cultivating a cadre of professionals and students adept at managing and optimizing digital talent pipelines. Such an achievement would epitomize a triumph for educational and economic progress alike.

Llewellyn Simmons
Director of Academics/Education Consultancy, Bermuda
National Education Institute, Bermuda

https://doi.org/10.1142/9789811296475_fmatter

Preface

Artificial Intelligence (AI) has evolved dramatically from an emerging concept to a fundamental force in digital transformation (DX), reshaping sectors from healthcare and finance to manufacturing and education. This book compiles insights from experts at the forefront of industry innovation, offering a rich tapestry of perspectives from diverse fields and academic settings. It explores the intricate details and broader implications of integrating AI and Analytics into DX, positioning itself as an essential guide for thought leaders navigating this complex landscape.

Recent studies by the World Economic Forum and PwC highlight AI and automation's potential to transform approximately 1.1 billion jobs by 2030. This transformation, though disruptive economically, also opens unprecedented opportunities to amplify human potential, revolutionize organizational structures, and foster greater creativity and innovation through strategic AI and DX initiatives.

Current Landscape and Future Trajectory

Over the past decade, the DX landscape has sky-rocketed, driven by the proliferation of smart devices, social media, reduced computing costs, and increased data generation. The landmark release of OpenAI's ChatGPT in November 2022 marked a pivotal moment, achieving the fastest technology adoption in history with one million downloads in a single week. Projections suggest that by 2027, global spending on digital transformation will approach $4 trillion, with the U.S. alone investing over $1 trillion, according to sources (Statista, McKinsey, and Gartner).

AI's role in redefining operational efficiencies, enhancing creativity, and transforming decision-making processes is becoming increasingly significant.

Looking ahead, GenAI and Large Language Models (LLMs) will continue to dominate digital transformation initiatives. It is estimated that in the next year, nearly every U.S. industry will increase its AI project spending by 25%.[1]

Future Trends and Predictions

As we look to the future, 10 key trends are poised to shape the trajectory of digital transformation, all of which include the application of AI:

1. **Productivity and measured outcomes:** The focus will shift from identifying and scaling use cases and application deployment to capturing value (e.g., productivity gains and revenue growth) across all sectors.
2. **Humans in the loop:** There will be a growing emphasis on ensuring human oversight in AI-driven systems. Think — humans in the feedback loop of all systems where LLMs or GenAI is being used.
3. **Continued investment:** Anticipated annual increases of 25% in digital AI transformation budgets.
4. **Reskilling and upskilling:** Reinvigorating the skills gap with personalized learning and upskilling initiatives that provide employees with new pathways and the confidence to learn new skills.
5. **Build vs. buy:** The debate between developing in-house solutions vs leveraging third-party platforms will intensify with managers trying to balance data lakes and cloud platforms getting bigger alongside the growth request for third-party apps and on-premise solutions.
6. **Accountability and governance:** A push toward stronger governance, AI councils and "responsible" AI policies will continue. (I highly recommend reading the WH Executive order on Safe, Secure, and Trustworthy Development and Use of Artificial Intelligence released on October 30, 2023).

[1]The Rise of Generative AI Across Enterprises — Wharton Professor, Stefano Puntoni and GBK Collective, October, 2023.

7. **Transparency and bias:** Organizations should proactively address model and data bias by implementing robust validation processes, promoting diversity in training datasets, and fostering transparency in AI development to ensure equitable and accurate outcomes.
8. **Data and privacy:** Increase focus on data management and literacy as data become a pivotal organizational asset. Data will continue to grow as a balance sheet asset and is the fuel for company revenue growth. However, curated and unbiased data will be the most valuable.
9. **Change management and organizational restructuring:** Look for the adoption of more "agile" work teams that will adapt to dynamic project handling and organizational boundaries that will be dismantled; plus, a shift away from traditional hierarchical structures toward flatter organization charts. Middle management will have the greatest changes and challenges.
10. **Leadership:** The role of leaders in articulating vision and fostering a culture of innovation will be more crucial than ever.

In the coming years, AI integration will become seamless within operational frameworks. The potential discourse is shifting toward responsible AI usage and potential organization responsibility for AI deployment. This book, through a myriad of expert insights, underscores AI's profound role in reshaping business and societal landscapes. I encourage leaders and practitioners across industries to use these insights to harness AI and Analytics thoughtfully and ethically in their transformation journeys, setting the stage for a future where AI's promise is fully realized.

As we increasingly integrate AI and specifically, GenAI (LLMs), into the DX roadmap, the focus will intensify on transforming data, skills, and processes. The themes of transformation, speed, and scale will dominate, determining which companies excel not only by adopting the latest tools but also by carefully integrating these technologies into their strategic roadmaps.

Mary Purk
Executive Director, AI at Wharton

https://doi.org/10.1142/9789811296475_fmatter

About the Editor

Dr. Jay Liebowitz is the Professor of Business Innovation and Industry Transformation and the Director of a new AI-EDGE Center in the Crummer Graduate School of Business at Rollins College. He has recently served as the inaugural Executive-in-Residence for Public Service at Columbia University's Data Science Institute. He was previously a Visiting Professor in the Stillman School of Business and the MS-Business Analytics Capstone & Co-Program Director (External Relations) at Seton Hall University. He previously served as the Distinguished Chair of Applied Business and Finance at Harrisburg University of Science and Technology. Before HU, he was the Orkand Endowed Chair of Management and Technology in the Graduate School at the University of Maryland University College (UMUC). He served as a Full Professor in the Carey Business School at Johns Hopkins University. He was ranked one of the top 10 knowledge management researchers/practitioners out of 11,000 worldwide and was ranked #2 in KM Strategy worldwide according to the January 2010 *Journal of Knowledge Management*. At Johns Hopkins University, he was the founding Program Director for the Graduate Certificate in Competitive Intelligence and the Capstone Director of the MS-Information and Telecommunications Systems for Business Program, where he engaged over 30 organizations in industry, government, and not-for-profits in capstone projects.

Prior to joining Hopkins, Dr. Liebowitz was the first Knowledge Management Officer at NASA Goddard Space Flight Center. Before NASA, Dr. Liebowitz was the Robert W. Deutsch Distinguished Professor of Information Systems at the University of Maryland-Baltimore County,

Professor of Management Science at George Washington University, and Chair of Artificial Intelligence at the U.S. Army War College.

Dr. Liebowitz is the Founding Editor-in-Chief of *Expert Systems With Applications: An International Journal* (published by Elsevier; ranked as a top-tier journal; Thomson Impact Factor from June 2021 is 8.665). He is a Fulbright Scholar, IEEE-USA Federal Communications Commission Executive Fellow, and Computer Educator of the Year (International Association for Computer Information Systems). He has published over 45 books and a myriad of journal articles on knowledge management, analytics, financial literacy, intelligent systems, and IT management. Dr. Liebowitz served as the Editor-in-Chief of *Procedia-CS* (Elsevier). He is also the Series Book Editor of the *Data Analytics Applications* book series (Taylor & Francis), as well as the Series Book Editor of the new *Digital Transformation: Accelerating Organizational Intelligence* book series (World Scientific Publishing). In October 2011, the International Association for Computer Information Systems named the "Jay Liebowitz Outstanding Student Research Award" for the best student research paper at the IACIS Annual Conference. Dr. Liebowitz was the Fulbright Visiting Research Chair in Business at Queen's University for the Summer 2017 and a Fulbright Specialist at Dalarna University in Sweden in May 2019. He is in the Top 2% of the top scientists in the world, according to a 2019 Stanford Study. As of 2021, he is the Visiting Distinguished Professor at the International School for Social and Business Studies in Slovenia. His recent books are as follows: *Data Analytics and AI* (Taylor & Francis, 2021), *The Business of Pandemics: The COVID-19 Story* (Taylor & Francis, 2021), *A Research Agenda for Knowledge Management and Analytics* (Elgar Publishers, 2021), *Online Learning Analytics* (Taylor & Francis, 2022), *Digital Transformation for the University of the Future* (World Scientific, 2022), and *Cryptocurrency Concepts, Technology, and Applications* (Taylor & Francis, April 2023), *Pivoting Government Through Digital Transformation* (Taylor & Francis, 2024), and *Developing the Intuitive Executive: Using Analytics and Intuition for Success* (Taylor & Francis, 2024). His latest book, *Regulating Hate Speech Created by Generative AI*, was published by Taylor & Francis in the fall of 2024. He has lectured and consulted worldwide.

https://doi.org/10.1142/9789811296475_fmatter

Editor's Note

In 2020, I published two articles on the "ABCDE's for Digital Transformation" [https://pubsonline.informs.org/do/10.1287/LYTX.2020.04.02/full/] and the "Other Half of the Digital Transformation Alphabet" [https://pubsonline.informs.org/do/10.1287/LYTX.2020.05.01/full/]. I recognized early on that if organizations were going to succeed, they needed to move from digitization to digitalization to digital transformation. Since 2018, you started to see the emergence of research articles being published on digital transformation, with Germany playing a major role as one of the key drivers of Industry 4.0 [https://www.sciencedirect.com/science/article/pii/S2405844023000415]. Certainly, some of the main advancements in the digital transformation field have resulted from the use of Analytics and Artificial Intelligence (AI). And, as we all know, digital transformation isn't just about technology, it involves people/culture, process, leadership, change management, and the like.

Due to the rapid emergence of the development and use of Analytics and AI in organizations, I wanted to focus this book on these aspects related to digital transformation. We are in the midst of the GenAI craze, with prompt engineering, large language models, and AI ethics playing key roles. According to estimates, about 329 million terabytes of data are created each day [https://explodingtopics.com/blog/data-generated-per-day] or approximately 120 zettabytes per year. IDC's "Data Age 2025" report states that "if you were to store 120 zettabytes on DVDs, your stack of DVDs would be long enough to circle Earth 152 times" [https://www.seagate.com/files/www-content/our-story/trends/files/Seagate-WP-DataAge2025-March-2017.pdf]. With this overabundance of data, in all types of forms, the use of Analytics and AI are essential techniques to help organizations make sense of their digital transformation efforts.

In this book volume, we are fortunate to have the contributions of leading individuals worldwide in various sectors. I am also very grateful to Mary Purk at Wharton and Lew Simmons in the Ministry of Education in Bermuda for their thoughtful Preface and Foreword, respectively. I am also very appreciative to World Scientific and their associates who are an integral part of my *Digital Transformation: Accelerating Organizational Intelligence* book series [https://www.worldscientific.com/series/dtaoi].

I hope this book provides some new insights to help you on your digital transformation journey.

Jay Liebowitz
Winter Park, FL, USA

https://doi.org/10.1142/9789811296475_fmatter

List of Contributors

Lillian Maria Araujo de Rezende Alvares
University of Brasilia, Brazil

Ben Apple
Naval Surface Warfare Center, Carderock Division, USA

Oren Eilam
Consultant and Author, Israel

Roy Gelbard
Head of Information Systems Program
Bar-Ilan University, Israel

Neil Hamlett
Uncertainty Research, LLC, USA

Patrick Held
University of Bayreuth, Germany

Tim Heubeck
Chair of International Management
University of Bayreuth, Germany

Musammat Tahmina Khanom
University of the Cumberlands, USA

Noam Koriat
Bar-Ilan University, Israel

Jay Liebowitz
Crummer Graduate School of Business
Rollins College, USA

Anna Lissitz
Data Analytics
McDaniel College, USA

Peter McAlindon
Crummer Graduate School of Business
Rollins College, USA

Tereza Raquel Merlo
Department of Information Science
University of North Texas, USA

Arthur Murray
Applied Knowledge Sciences, Inc., USA

Edgard Costa Oliveira
University of Brasilia, Brazil

Mary Purk
Wharton/University of Pennsylvania, USA

Robert Scavilla
FourFront, USA

Marc Schmitt
Siemens AG, Germany

Washington Luís Ribeiro de Carvalho Segundo
Brazilian Institute of Information in Science and Technology, Brazil

Trisha Shields
Naval Surface Warfare Center, Carderock Division, USA

Llewellyn Simmons
Bermuda National Education Institute
Bermuda

Marcel Garcia de Souza
Brazilian Institute of Information Science and Technology, Brazil

https://doi.org/10.1142/9789811296475_fmatter

Contents

https://doi.org/10.1142/9789811296475_0001

Chapter 1

Digital Transformation through AI, Machine Learning, and Analytics

Robert Scavilla

FourFront, Glenside, PA, USA

1. Background

Evolution has taught us that the species most likely to persist are those that fight for survival and adapt to changes in environmental conditions. Those that are too weak become prey and those too dominant lose their ability to defend themselves from predators. Similarly, the survival of a business is influenced by its ability to adapt to its environment and successfully compete for market share.

Throughout history, business transformation has been largely driven by the need to adapt to external changes: technological, economic, social, or environmental. To stay viable, businesses must constantly be on the lookout for disruptors that will cause a shift in market demand and fulfillment. Being content with a business model that works could be the death of a business. A classic example: In 1975, an engineer at Kodak built the first digital camera. Kodak's leadership rejected it, fearing it would destroy their existing business model. It eventually did because competitors came in and cashed in on the opportunity, leaving Kodak so far behind they couldn't catch up.

Significant business transitions have occurred throughout history including steam power replacing horses, electricity and internal combustion engines replacing water and manual power, the desktop computer and of course, the Internet. The latter two transitions certainly caused the following: (1) resistance to change, (2) buzzwords and curiosity, and finally, (3) panic from fear of missing out followed by a poor transition plan.

The integration of artificial intelligence (AI), machine learning (ML), and Big Data analytics into business processes represents the latest phase of transformation, enabling more informed decision-making, automation, and personalized customer experiences. Although AI has been used as a business tool for years, it wasn't until more recently that consumer-grade computing power increased sufficiently enough to run the resource-intensive algorithms used for neural networks. Early adopters who were technical enough used open-source AI libraries such as TensorFlow to build ML applications for prediction as well as classification, natural language processing (NLP), and image recognition tools.

As with the desktop computer and the Internet, many early adopters of AI have positioned themselves well to take advantage of the increased efficiencies AI can offer; however, the AI transition is only at the beginning of the bell curve. It will take years for innovation and business adoption to come into balance. This doesn't mean that the use of AI will stagnate over time, rather it means the role AI plays in business will be better defined and change will be more about improving the AI infrastructure that exists within a business as opposed to introducing it.

Business transformation often involves migrating from traditional business processes that have been the foundation of success to embracing innovative practices that are yet being refined. Success will be based on how well you plan.

Many organizations going through digital transformation think success comes from advanced algorithms or Big Data. However, this approach is mistaken. As AI technology becomes more common, success won't depend on data scientists. Instead, those who understand business and can merge it with technology to create a practical AI vision will lead the way.

2. What is Digital Transformation for Business?

Digital transformation for business refers to the process of integrating digital technology into all areas of a business, fundamentally changing how it operates and delivers value to customers. It involves a cultural shift that requires organizations to continually challenge the *status quo*, experiment, and get comfortable with failure. This transformation goes beyond simply adopting new technologies; it also involves rethinking existing business models, processes, and strategies to improve efficiency, enhance customer experience, and drive innovation in a rapidly evolving digital economy.

2.1. *Get comfortable with failure*

Why does digital transformation require comfort with failure? With rapid technological advancements and changing customer expectations, organizations that can learn from failure are more capable of pivoting and adapting their strategies to produce successful outcomes. Embracing failure as a part of the digital transformation process enables businesses to innovate, learn, and adapt more effectively. It fosters a culture of experimentation, resilience, and continuous improvement, which are all essential for navigating the challenges and opportunities of the digital age.

Digital transformation often involves exploring new technologies, processes, and business models. When businesses are not afraid to try new things, they are more likely to discover breakthrough innovations and solutions that can significantly enhance their competitive edge.

3. Common Challenges in Digital Transformation

Businesses undergoing digital transformation often face a variety of challenges. These challenges can vary widely depending on the industry, the size of the business, and the level of digital preparedness already in place. However, some common hurdles include the following:

- **Cultural resistance:** Many organizations face internal resistance to change. Employees and sometimes management may be accustomed to traditional ways of working and may resist adopting new technologies or processes. Overcoming this resistance requires effective change management strategies, including communication, education, and involvement of staff in the transformation process.
- **Lack of digital skills:** Digital transformation requires a workforce with digital skills, including data analytics, digital marketing, and

cybersecurity, among others. Finding and retaining talent with these skills can be difficult, particularly in highly competitive markets.

- **Data management and integration issues:** Businesses often struggle with managing and integrating data from various sources. Legacy systems and siloed data can hinder the effective use of data analytics, making it challenging to derive actionable insights.
- **Security and privacy concerns:** With an increase in digital operations comes the heightened risk of cyber threats. Protecting sensitive data and ensuring privacy in compliance with regulations such as GDPR and CCPA is a significant challenge for businesses.
- **Budget constraints:** Digital transformation can require significant investment in new technologies, training, and possibly even new personnel. Balancing these costs with expected benefits can be challenging, especially for small- and medium-sized enterprises (SMEs).
- **Technology selection and implementation:** Choosing the right technologies that align with business goals and then successfully implementing them can be complex and risky. Organizations must navigate a rapidly evolving tech landscape, make informed decisions, and manage the implementation process while avoiding operational disruptions.
- **Aligning digital strategy with business goals:** Ensuring that the digital transformation strategy aligns with overall business objectives is crucial. Misalignment can lead to wasted resources and missed opportunities.
- **Scalability and flexibility issues:** As businesses grow, their digital infrastructure needs to scale and adapt. Solutions that work well initially may not meet the needs of an expanding business, requiring ongoing adjustments to technology and strategy.
- **Customer experience challenges:** Digital transformation initiatives often aim to improve customer experience. Understanding customer needs and behaviors in a digital context, and then designing experiences that meet or exceed expectations, can be difficult.
- **Measuring return on investment (ROI):** Finally, measuring the ROI of digital transformation efforts can be challenging. The benefits may not always be immediately apparent, and they can be difficult to quantify in terms of traditional financial metrics.

The key to these challenges is to start with a progressive plan and get buy-in from those who can affect the success of the project.

4. How is AI Being Used to Support Digital Transformation?

AI is increasing the speed at which businesses transform their operations, create new value propositions, and innovate. AI is allowing more sophisticated decision support than what was previously possible, especially for smaller businesses. AI applications are becoming easier to use and integrate with existing systems, leading to increased efficiency. Some key ways AI is being used in businesses as part of digital transformation include the following:

- **Data analysis and insights:** AI algorithms analyze vast amounts of data to uncover patterns, trends, and insights that were previously difficult or impossible to detect. This can inform strategic decisions, optimize operations, and uncover trends.
- **Prediction:** ML is being used to find patterns in historical data that can be used to predict future trends with confidence.
- **Customer service and experience:** AI-powered chatbots and virtual assistants are being used to provide 24/7 customer service, offering quick responses to inquiries and personalized assistance. This improves customer satisfaction and frees up human agents to handle more complex issues.
- **Personalization:** Businesses use AI to deliver personalized experiences to customers, from customized product recommendations on e-commerce sites to personalized content on streaming platforms. This personalization enhances customer engagement and loyalty.
- **Supply chain optimization:** AI is used to forecast demand, optimize inventory levels, and improve logistics. It can predict supply chain disruptions and suggest alternative strategies, making supply chains more resilient and efficient.
- **Marketing and sales:** AI tools analyze customer behavior and preferences to optimize marketing campaigns and sales strategies, enabling businesses to target the right audience with the right message at the right time. AI technologies can help predict customer churn, enhance conversion rates, and enable effective upselling strategies. Moreover, AI can perform automated customer segmentation using unsupervised learning techniques, which group customers based on their behaviors and preferences without pre-labeled categories.

- **Cybersecurity:** AI enhances cybersecurity by identifying and responding to threats in real time. It can detect patterns indicative of cyber attacks, automatically block suspicious activities, and even predict future threats based on data analysis.
- **Human resources (HR):** In HR, AI is used for tasks such as screening resumes to identify the best candidates, automating administrative tasks, and even analyzing employee sentiment to improve workplace culture.
- **Process automation:** Robotic process automation (RPA) combined with AI (intelligent automation) streamlines business processes, automating routine tasks and freeing up human employees to focus on more complex and strategic work.
- **Product and service innovation:** AI drives innovation by enabling the development of new products and services, such as AI-based health diagnostics, autonomous vehicles, and smart home devices.
- **Operational efficiency:** AI optimizes operational processes, reducing waste, saving time, and cutting costs. For example, predictive maintenance in manufacturing can prevent equipment failures and minimize downtime.

4.1. *AI definitions*

AI is an umbrella term. It encompasses all digital systems that use calculations on input data to estimate a likely output. Some common types of AI include the following:

- **Large Language Models (LLM):** An advanced artificial intelligence system trained on vast amounts of data capable of completing tasks not explicitly trained to do using a technique known as Self Supervised Learning.
- **Natural Language Processing (NLP):** NLP entails the ability of a machine to understand the context of a language. Automated chatbots are an example of NLP applications.
- **Machine Learning (ML):** ML involves the ability to predict a future value based on historical data applied to present data:
  - **Regression ML:** Regression algorithms are used to predict continuous numerical values. Regression is used to estimate a numerical output, referred to as continuous outcome variables. A regression ML model can predict the relationship between advertising spend and sales volume, or house features and the price the house would sell for.

- ○ **Classification ML:** Logistic regression algorithms such as Sigmoid are typically used to classify data into binary (true/false, yes/no) categories. Classification is used to analyze medical data for tasks, such as determining whether a tumor is benign or malignant or whether an email is spam.
- **Deep learning (DL):** DL uses a series of nodes in an attempt to simulate how the human brain analyzes problems. DL is used in applications, such as vision for driverless vehicles, weather predictions, calculating outcomes for defense strategies, and image recognition.

Before getting into the details, it will be helpful to define a few common terms:

- It is common to consider **features** of a dataset as the input to a model and **labels** of the same dataset as the model's output. In ML, labels are what the model predicts.
- When data are **tagged**, it means there is a description of what the data represent. In a spreadsheet, the column header would be the tags.
- Within regression models, there are two popular AI techniques: **unsupervised** learning and **supervised** learning, which will be described in more detail in the following:
  - ○ **Unsupervised learning** is where the data are not tagged and the machine must learn on its own. Unsupervised ML models are used to discover patterns without any explicit guidance or instruction. This type of ML is more resource-intensive. It is ideal for finding unknown correlations in data features and for clustering data based on correlations. An example of unsupervised ML is data clustering. This is where the system finds similarities in data records and organizes them into groups.
  - ○ **Supervised learning** is where the training data are tagged, implying that the data contain both inputs (**features**) and correct outputs (**labels**). The algorithm is then trained to learn the features that correlate to labels so that by inputting a set of features, the system can predict output values.

4.2. *Deeper insight*

Supervised ML is perhaps the most relevant subset of AI for use in business analytics. An example of supervised training would be a house price predictor. The training data would be a labeled dataset of home sales

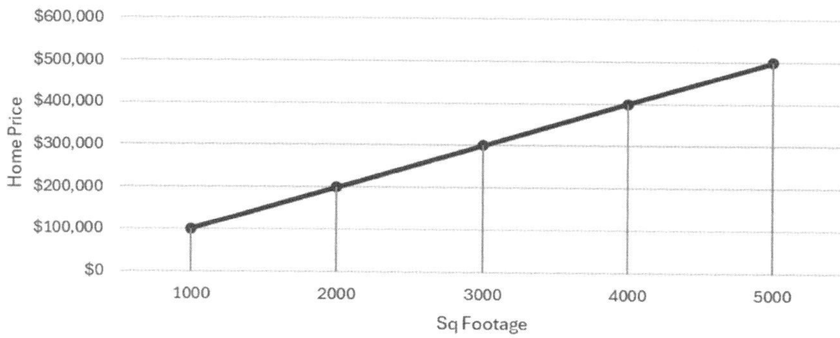

Figure 1. *X,Y* in lockstep.

containing features, such as property size, number of bedrooms and bathrooms, and living space. The dataset would also contain the price (label) the house sold for.

The first step in building a supervised model is to plot the data on an *X,Y* axis and look at it. In a perfect world, the data would be linear, implying the *X* and *Y* values are in lockstep, as shown in Figure 1. This isn't typical, but if it did occur, by extending the line, the model would suggest that a house of 6,000 sq. ft. would sell for $600k and a house of 500 sq. ft. would sell for $50k. This line is said to have zero loss because each point of *Y* exactly matches each point of *X*.

More realistically, the data show an imperfect correlation between features and outcomes. To see the correlation between the feature and the label, it's best to analyze each feature independently to determine the correlation between the feature and the label. Figure 2 plots the price label vs. the square footage feature.

Creating correlation plots for each feature compared to the label will show the effect the feature has on influencing the label. A feature weight will be determined based on how closely the feature correlates to the value of the label. Features with higher correlations will be set to higher weights in the prediction algorithm.

In ML, the graph line that represents the least amount of distance between the plotted points is called the **cost line**. Figure 2 just shows a linear cost line; however, in regression models, polynomial, binomial, and quadratic functions are also popular choices for building functions to generate the best-fit cost line. The function that produces the cost line is

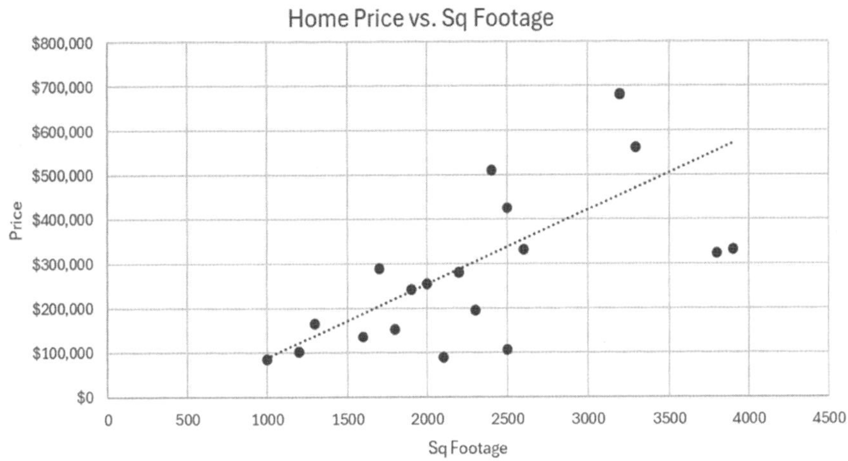

Figure 2. Home price vs. square footage.

called the **loss function**. The tuning of the loss function is called the **gradient descent**. The average distance between the data points and the cost line is used to calculate the **model confidence**. To generate the best predictions, it is necessary to fit the cost line with the lowest loss to the training data. Building the loss function that best represents the data is a subject for another time.

A **correlation matrix** shows the relationship between all of the feature values to the label. A feature can have a positive, inverse, or zero correlation. The stronger the correlation (positive or inverse), the more weight that feature should have in the prediction model. Those features with low or zero correlation can be omitted. It is important to note that when analyzing correlation, sometimes the relationship of multiple features combined has a stronger correlation to the label than the features had independently.

Entering house features into a well-trained model should yield a prediction of what the house will sell for along with a confidence score.

4.3. *Prerequisites to AI transition*

Most organizations can be graded regarding their ability to access data, analyze it, and create actionable recommendations from it. Whatever level your organization is, it's important to make sure you have the necessary data infrastructure in place to support AI. For AI to produce benefits, there needs to be an agreement on how data can be applied to support your organization, data supply, and an understanding of what the data can tell you.

- **A culture of data:** This involves an organizational mindset that values data-driven evidence over gut feelings or assumptions.
- **Data inventory:** This involves preparing a list of your internal data and how to access as well as knowing sources of external data that can be blended with internal data to enrich analytics throughout your organization.
- **Data potential:** It involves creating a list of ideal reports for managing your organization. This step requires you to imagine you have all the data in the world. From this, create a series of ideal reports for running your business. These reports may be hypothetical, but they allow you to draw up a suite of reports that would give you all possible insights into your business, market, and operations. Once you have identified this ideal suite of reports, you can use your data inventory to see what is possible to create.

4.3.1. *A culture of data*

To realize the benefits that AI can offer your organization, it is necessary to establish a culture of data where the organizational ethos prioritizes and values the use of data in all aspects of decision-making, strategy, and operations. It's not merely about having access to data or technology but about embedding data into the core of the organization's practices, behaviors, and mindset. This culture impacts how every employee, from top leadership to entry level, interacts with data and uses it as a fundamental resource for their work. Successful adoption of this culture requires the right technology, skills, and expertise in data analysis.

On top of this, it is necessary to foster an organizational mindset that values data-driven evidence over gut feelings or assumptions. It involves a commitment to using data as a foundational element in strategic planning, decision-making, and operational management. Adopting a culture of data within your company can enhance decision-making processes, drive innovation, and provide a competitive advantage.

Adopting a culture of data does not have to happen all at once. Typically at the beginning, it's better to gradually introduce data and then build processes incorporating data support into your operations. Getting everyone in an organization on board with a data-centric managerial style isn't always easy. You may find that you are working with people who have always done business a certain way and are resistant to adopting a data-driven approach. Initially, these people tend to look for where the data failed. However, as more people adopt data into their processes, the more evident the necessity for data will be.

4.3.2. *Data inventory*

In this data-rich world, it's tempting to dive straight into analysis. Yet, a crucial preliminary step is to map out what data are available to you and document how to access them. This involves not only taking stock of the data you already have but also identifying potential sources you have yet to tap into. This process is also useful for identifying what data you don't have. Such an assessment is foundational, ensuring that the reports you envision are grounded in both reality and ambition.

Most managers are familiar with their company's income statement, balance sheet, and statement of cash flow produced by the company's bookkeeping system. Typically, organizations have a lot more data than what may be obvious. These unknown data could be useful in providing decision support.

Taking inventory of your data sources sets the stage for how data can be used to support your organization. One typical place data are stored within an organization is the CRM. CRM data can be populated from website forms, phone calls, email requests, and even walk-ins, and often integrates with sales and operations data. A quick example of data sources is listed in the following:

Internal data sources:
- website data,
- operations/production data,
- transactional POS data,
- e-mail marketing metrics,
- customer profile data,
- records of customer interactions (email queries, support calls),

- online activity leading to a sale or conversion,
- customer feedback,
- phone logs,
- CRM data,
- energy metering,
- software log files,
- sensor data.

External data sources:

- open sources (data.gov),
- social media data (X, Instagram, Facebook, LinkedIn),
- paid sources,
- AWS (Amazon Web Services).

Steps to create a data inventory include the following:

1. **List all data sources:** Start by listing all the data sources you currently have. This includes internal systems, such as CRM, ERP, and HR systems, as well as external data sources, such as social media analytics, market research reports, and public databases.
2. **Document data characteristics:** For each data source, document the type of data, the format, the update frequency, and the data's current use cases. Note any software or tools needed to access and analyze this data.
3. **Evaluate data quality:** Assess the accuracy, completeness, timeliness, and relevance of each data source. This step will help you understand the reliability of the data for making decisions.
4. **Identify data owners and access permissions:** Determine who is responsible for managing each data source and who currently has access to the data. This helps in establishing clear data governance policies.
5. **Map data flows:** Understand how data flow within your organization. This includes how data are collected, stored, processed, and reported. Mapping these flows can help identify bottlenecks or inefficiencies.
6. **Assess compliance and security:** Ensure that data-handling practices meet legal and regulatory requirements, especially for sensitive or personal data. Assess the security measures in place to protect data from unauthorized access or breaches.

7. **Identify gaps and redundancies:** Look for areas where you might be missing critical data that could support decision-making or where you have redundant data that could be streamlined.
8. **Plan for improvement:** Based on your inventory, create a plan to address any gaps, improve data quality, enhance data governance, and ensure compliance and security. Consider how you might integrate disparate data sources for more comprehensive analyses.

With a thorough inventory of your data sources, you can better understand the resources at your disposal for creating decision-support reports and analytics. This inventory enables you to perform the following:

- **Prioritize data initiatives:** Focus on improving or integrating data sources that offer the most value to your decision-making processes.
- **Develop reporting and analytics:** Identify what types of reports and analytics you can produce with your current data and what additional data you might need to support further analyses.
- **Enhance data-driven culture:** Foster a culture that understands the value of data, encourages data literacy, and uses data in strategic and operational decision-making.

4.3.3. *Data potential*

Custom reports and data segmentation ensure that your data can portray different aspects of your business while meeting the requirements of the diverse audience within your organization.

Understanding data potential starts with the creative process of imagining an ideal suite of reports to run your business. While imagining, remove all barriers and don't worry about what data you have or don't have. For this exercise, assume you are given the key to all the world's data. This exercise will highlight both the data you have and the data gaps and will help identify a starting point for your report portfolio.

Designing an ideal suite of reports to run your business begins with clear business goals. Whether it's driving revenue growth, expanding into new markets, increasing operational efficiency, or elevating customer satisfaction, understanding your objectives is paramount to creating useful reports. Goals guide the creation of specific, measurable key performance indicators (KPIs) that can be used to track progress.

The types of reports that form the cornerstone of this ideal suite are as varied as the facets of your business. Operational reports offer a lens into day-to-day functioning, providing real-time insights into efficiency and productivity. Financial reports, from profit and loss statements to budget analyses, offer a window into the fiscal health of your enterprise. Meanwhile, customer insight reports delve into the behaviors and preferences of your clientele, offering a mirror to reflect their desires and expectations.

In parallel, market analysis reports offer a bird's-eye view of your market, identifying opportunities and threats within the broader landscape. Product and service performance reports zoom in on the heartbeat of your offerings, measuring their success and areas for enhancement. The human element of your enterprise includes employee and HR reports shedding light on the workforce and driving your business forward.

In today's age, where sustainability and social responsibility are increasingly at the forefront of strategic considerations, reports tracking environmental, social, and governance (ESG) goals highlight not just the profitability but the ethics of your operations.

Here is a step-by-step guide on how to approach this exercise:

1. **Define business objectives:**
   - Clearly articulate your business goals and objectives. Understanding what you aim to achieve (e.g., revenue growth, market expansion, and customer satisfaction improvement) will guide the types of reports and data you'll need.
2. **Identify KPIs:**
   - For each objective, identify specific, measurable KPIs that can track progress toward these goals. These KPIs will form the backbone of your reports. Note that KPIs track your business objectives.
3. **Create a list of ideal reports:**
   - Create as many reports as you can think of that would be beneficial to manage your organization.

4. **Identify the data you have and don't have:**
   - Although this scenario assumes access to all data, in Section 4.3.2, you mapped out what data you currently have and what data you can access. Now, list any gaps in data that might prevent you from fully understanding performance against your KPIs.
5. **Determine report types:**
   - **Operational reports:** These include daily or real-time reports that track operational efficiency and productivity.
   - **Financial reports:** These include weekly, monthly, and yearly financial reports, including profit and loss statements, balance sheets, cash flow statements, and budget vs. actuals.
   - **Customer insights reports:** These include analysis of customer behavior, preferences, satisfaction levels, and engagement across all touchpoints.
   - **Market analysis reports:** These include insights into market trends, competitor performance, and market share to identify opportunities and threats.
   - **Product/service performance reports:** These include detailed analytics on product sales, service uptake, customer feedback, and lifecycle.
   - **Employee and HR reports:** These include metrics on employee performance, satisfaction, turnover, and training effectiveness.
   - **Sustainability and social impact reports:** These include reports tracking sustainability efforts, social impact, and governance issues for businesses focusing on ESG goals.
6. **Envision advanced analytics and AI:**
   - With access to all data, create a list of what you would like to predict. Leverage ML and AI for predictive analytics, trend forecasting, and behavior analysis to not just report on past and present performance but also to anticipate future trends.
7. **Customization and segmentation:**
   - Customize reports for different audiences within your organization. For example, executive leadership may need high-level dashboards, while department heads may require more detailed reports.
   - Segment data to provide insights into different customer groups, product lines, or geographic regions, as relevant.

4.4. *Case studies with ML prediction examples*

4.4.1. *An online tire store*

Confronted with the challenges of the pandemic and supply chain disruptions, an online tire retailer needed to strike a balance between maintaining its business margins and ensuring prompt deliveries, particularly in an industry dominated by physical stores. The company's answer was a supply chain performance index powered by ML.

The performance index ranks suppliers for each order based on their predicted delivery performance. By integrating historical data, static variables, and carrier-related metrics, the model selects the most efficient supplier for each order. The model operates in several modes, such as velocity, margin, and customer satisfaction, and self-adjusts daily with new data.

Deliveries for distances under 100 miles improved by 2%, with only a minimal impact on margins. Customer satisfaction greatly benefited, with on-time deliveries well above industry standards, arriving either on the same day or the next at well above 90%. This boost in service level has driven higher conversion rates and increased customer lifetime value.

4.4.2. *A digital agency*

A digital marketing and analytics company that provides service to clients that have multiple bricks and mortar locations needed the ability to assess the effectiveness of advertising campaigns and determine how far customers were willing to travel to visit a location and what the cost for acquiring a customer was. It was also necessary to analyze how the proximity of competing stores affected customer acquisition.

Geospatial analytics needed to be integrated with web analytics. The challenge was determining whether digital ads reached the company's target audience within a suitable distance from each physical location and how much proximity and population density influence how far a customer would travel to a location. A secondary challenge was to calculate the opportunity cost of competitor's locations based on proximity. These data would also be used to help locate new locations for best performance.

The resulting system blended web analytics data, geospatial data, census data, and weather and population density data to determine features that affected location visitations. This enriched web analytics data allowed for analysis of the distance of each web visitor from the nearest store. Weather data are used to predict the impact on location visitation and sales based on weather type.

Analysis of the enriched data revealed that user conversion likelihood varied by location and depended on whether the store was in a rural or urban area. To address this variability, the company FourFront provided the capability to define an ideal target radius for each store based on population density. Using the target radius, the tool segments each user as either "in range" or "out of range" to accurately quantify and assess the traffic quality.

The resulting system is being used to optimize ad campaigns for better targeting and improve ROI on the client's ad spend. The system is also used to identify expansion opportunities, measure various trends, and improve ad targeting for e-commerce sites in underserviced areas. This solution emphasizes the importance of using data and analytics in making informed marketing decisions to optimize ROI.

4.5. *Wrap up*

Galápagos finches are a prime example of adaptation. These birds have adapted rapidly into a multitude of new forms when a change in their environment makes new resources available, creates new challenges, or opens new environmental niches. They essentially evolved into several species from a single ancestor. The speed and efficiency at which they adapted have been critical to their survival.

Your competitors will leverage AI to gain business advantages. Adapting with the changing AI landscape takes decisive action, a sizable investment of skills, time, and personnel, and the willingness to fail and grow from those failures. Those businesses with the ability to work with data stand to gain the most from the AI revolution.

https://doi.org/10.1142/9789811296475_0002

Chapter 2

A Theory and Methodology for AI-Based Digital Transformation

Neil Hamlett

Uncertainty Research, LLC, Vienna, VA, USA

1. Introduction: What This Is and Why It Interests Us

At the time of this writing, artificial intelligence (AI) commands inescapable popular attention. Predictions about its potential economic impacts range from transformative to modest (Acemoglu, 2024; Keynes, 2024). Its ubiquitous mass appeal incents "AI washing" by marketers in technology and other industries (Vanderford, 2023). In such environments, business decision makers must weigh the risks of messy adoption of not-ready-for-prime-time technologies against those of being left behind (Vinsel, 2023).

"At its most fundamental level, digital transformation is about the ability of organizations, its leaders, and employees to adapt to rapid changes wrought by evolving digital technologies" (Kane, 2017). Digitization — widespread computerization of business processes and activities — results from the "software-eating-the-world" phenomenon (Andreessen, 2011). AI provides the basis for many of the business functions that get digitized (Davenport, 2018).

1.1. *What do we mean by AI?*

Adoption of explicit definitions serves the rigor of discussion that follows. "There is no greater impediment to the advancement of knowledge than the ambiguity of words" (T. Reid, cited in Hubbard 2023). Although no general agreed-to definition exists (Brock, 2019), herein we base our AI definition on *Britannica*: "AI is the ability of a digital computer or computer-controlled robot to perform tasks commonly associated with intelligent beings" (Copland, 2024).

Davenport (2018) identifies three classes of AI-based functional capabilities. *Process automation* assists or replaces humans' task performance with technology. The technology might assist or augment humans' activities, or might autonomously replace them (Garbuio, 2019). AI searches produce *cognitive insights* — evidence of counterintuitive or unanticipated phenomena — by searching large datasets. *Cognitive engagement* allows humans to interact with technology on their own terms. Generative AI exemplifies the latter.

1.2. *Why digital transformation?*

Through digital transformation, organizations respond to competitive threats, carve out competitive advantages, or create new lines of business (Van Alstyne, 2021). This often involves standardization to create economies of scale. Moore (2004) cites the mantra, "standardize, centralize, automate."

Digital transformation contributes decisively to fulfilling Davenport's (2005) prediction about "the commoditization of business processes." Enterprise resource planning (ERP) systems provide this. Tech platforms drive global-scale digital transformation, thereby disrupting "'traditional' matchmaker businesses that have been operating platforms for connecting different groups of customers" (Evans, 2016).

Organizations apart from ERP providers and tech-platform operators digitally transform their operations within this context. They often seek to optimally align their differentiating capabilities with these sets of commoditized digital services (Kretschmer, 2020). In such cases, digital transformation initiatives pursue pointed strategic objectives.

1.3. *What do we mean by acceleration?*

Acceleration occurs when an organization achieves *innovation* ahead of the market. Three key salient points apply here. First, "define innovation as the creation of new productive knowledge" (Stoelhurst, 2021). Avoid conflating innovation with invention, the creation of novel technology. Innovation adds methods, techniques, and operating models to make inventions useful. Not every invention leads to new productive knowledge. New productive knowledge can similarly occur apart from novel inventions.

Second, inventions typically follow consistent trajectories to mainstream marketplace adoption. Gartner's hype cycle exemplifies one well-known representation. Murtha (2002) and Moore (2004) contain others. Widespread popular excitement, frequently accompanied by *inflated expectations*, accompanies new inventions (Martínez, 2024). The emergence of mainstream marketplace productive knowledge usually follows some time thereafter. Innovation — new productive knowledge — corresponds to Gartner's *slope of enlightenment*. The intervening period can span years to decades (Chui, 2023; Keynes, 2024; Swanson, 2004).

Acceleration, then, occurs when an organization innovates ahead of its marketplace peers. This requires a clear-eyed understanding of what emerging technologies can and cannot do at the time of their adoption. A firm grasp of the organization's own differentiators and weaknesses is also a must. Competitive advantages result. These may be enduring, but are more often transient (Barney, 2004; Suarez, 2005). Advantages based on productive knowledge are often replicable.

2. Six Principles of AI-Value Realization

The business literature contains a resounding consensus regarding the essential principles underlying AI-based innovation. This perspective often contrasts starkly with technology marketers' claims. We assume here that the former encapsulates empirical evidence about what works in practice.

Six key principles encapsulate this business literature consensus. The grouping here is neither exhaustive nor exclusive. The preponderance of the empirical evidence nonetheless maps to these big ideas.

2.1. *Start with a high-leverage business problem*

Lavallee (2010) counsels, "focus on the biggest and highest-value opportunities." O'Toole (2020) recommends, "Identify a small number of 'high-leverage' business problems that are tightly defined, promptly addressable, and will produce evident business value, and then focus on those to show business results." "Prioritize high-impact ideas that are reasonably feasible in terms of data availability, technology capability, and change management" (Kesari, 2024). Each of these perspectives applies concepts from Kotter (2012): build organizational confidence through quick, early wins.

Opportunities become clear through "Developing a theory of the problem and articulating hypotheses that logically flow from that theory" (Camuffo, 2014) clarifies which opportunities. Merrifield (2008) illustrates one such approach using a *business capability analysis*. AI-based innovation results from a disciplined, scientific approach involving deliberate experimental excursions from the operational *status quo* (Thomke, 2014).

2.2. *Frame analytics projects in terms of decisions*

Superior decision-making contributes significantly to competitive advantage (Blenko, 2010). "AI creates value by improving the quality of decisions" (Agrawal, 2022). Lavallee (2010) tells us, "start with the questions, *not the data*." We recognize key decisions — and their supporting questions — by following Thomke's (2014) discipline of business experimentation. Applying algorithmic alchemy to search for serendipity in large datasets only infrequently leads to value (Redman, 2018).

2.3. *Work data quality from the source*

Useful AI simply cannot occur without high-quality data (Christen, 2024). Ångström (2023) identifies data availability as a leading obstacle to AI adoption. Scientific practice clearly recognizes the limited utility of opportunistically aggregated data, not deliberately developed for the purpose that interests us (Cox, 2000). High-quality data ideally result from designing organizations and operations to produce them (Kretschmer, 2020; Redman, 2024). This principle even applies to generative AI (Davenport, 2024).

2.4. *Match the AI approach to the problem*

Although "deep learning" — AI based on complex artificial neural networks — attracts widespread popular attention, such approaches do not fit every business problem (Mims, 2023). Westerman (2024) recommends five *business* factors for AI approaches to business problems: the cost of being wrong; the need to explain results; the importance of results' repeatability; the veracity of data sources; and how well training datasets resemble "live" operational conditions.

These business criteria crucially influence the selection of AI technical approaches. Figure 1 summarizes the technical performance characteristics of common classes of machine-learning techniques. The essential point here is that each exhibits distinct sets of advantages and disadvantages. Matching these technical properties to the business factors above requires a deliberate, cautious AI-design methodology.

2.5. *Evaluate projects using business metrics*

We pursue AI-based digital transformation to improve business performance, typically quantified in terms of efficiency and effectiveness. Leaders must evaluate AI's business contributions accordingly (Siegel, 2024). Initial application of AI to an operational process represents an experiment (Thomke, 2014) by which we test hypotheses about business improvement opportunities (Camuffo, 2024). Translating between AI's

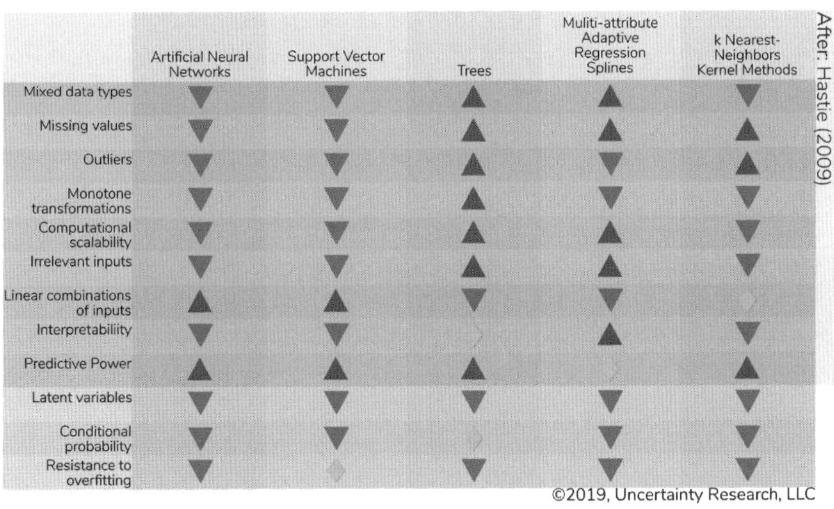

Figure 1. Various machine-learning methods exist, each with its distinct set of strengths and weaknesses.

technical performance characteristics — on which technologists focus — and business performance criteria requires an uncommon expertise (Davenport, 2013; Herring, 2019).

2.6. *Transform the business incrementally*

Digital transformation represents a whole-of-the-business endeavor. Kotter's (2012) *Leading Change* principles — emphasizing the gradual, progressive building of trust via small wins — prove indispensable. Trust represents a formidable barrier to AI adoption, in particular (Ångström, 2023; Chakravorti, 2024).

Davenport (2018) cautions, "don't start with moon shots." Lavallee (2010) advises leaders to "plan the whole, build the parts." Merrill (2019) recommends thinking about AI as "an operating expense, not a capital investment." Digital transformation occurs through a portfolio of small, short-duration projects. Each project addresses a thoughtfully scoped decision or an operational activity.

3. A Methodological Framework for AI-Value Creation

Digital transformation based on AI requires a scientific, systematic approach that addresses the whole organization (Kretschmer, 2020). In the previous section, we considered the key principles that substantially influence success in AI. We now turn our attention to a methodological framework.

Figure 2 depicts such a framework comprising three distinct facets. This methodology supports a portfolio approach for the design and management of a collection of AI implementation projects leading to digital transformation. Weill (2005) describes a governance framework for assembling and managing such a portfolio.

We use a hybrid of waterfall and agile paradigms to manage our portfolio of projects (Nieto-Rodriguez, 2023). The incremental rollout of business use cases resembles an agile approach. Each project delivers a clearly defined business capability — comprising technology and procedures — contributing to a distinct aspect of operational improvement. Consistent with an agile philosophy, we pursue this through a series of small, short-duration projects.

The technology infrastructure — the digital transformation's technical foundation — tends to follow a waterfall pattern. Our foundation for operations (Ross, 2006) must be technically and operationally stable. We seek a uniform, standardized computing infrastructure onto which we deploy digital operational components, "agents," in Kretschmer's (2020) terms.

3.1. *Framing business objectives: The Inescapable starting point*

Hoerl (2022) estimates the rate of data science project failure as high as 80%. Somewhat more optimistically, Ångström (2023) estimates a 30% success rate. Both identify scope definition as essential. Our framework for framing seeks to mitigate this obstacle.

In Figure 2, Kretschmer's (2020) approach to business problem framing contains concepts consistent with model-based systems engineering (MBSE) (Shevchenko, 2020, 2022). Merrifield's (2008) business capability analysis — also resembling the MBSE technique — shows specifically how specific stages of Kretschmer's framework might be performed. Hamlett (2007) illustrates operational modeling to identify "clusters."

Kretschmer's framework exemplifies a strong — but neither exhaustive nor exclusive — approach. Davenport (2013) describes an alternative approach more focused on analytics and decision-making. Fundamentally, business contribution framing must follow the scientific philosophy underlying the principles above, particularly by Camuffo (2024) and Thomke (2014).

3.2. *Technology realization through architecture and governance*

The technology facet shown in Figure 2 provides the *foundation for operations* for digital transformation (Ross, 2006). Getting this foundation right is essential. Its architecture must ultimately scale to support the entire enterprise.

Principles applicable to other large technical projects apply to building out the foundation for operations. Harford (2022) recommends, "keep things as simple as you can, using repeated modular elements and

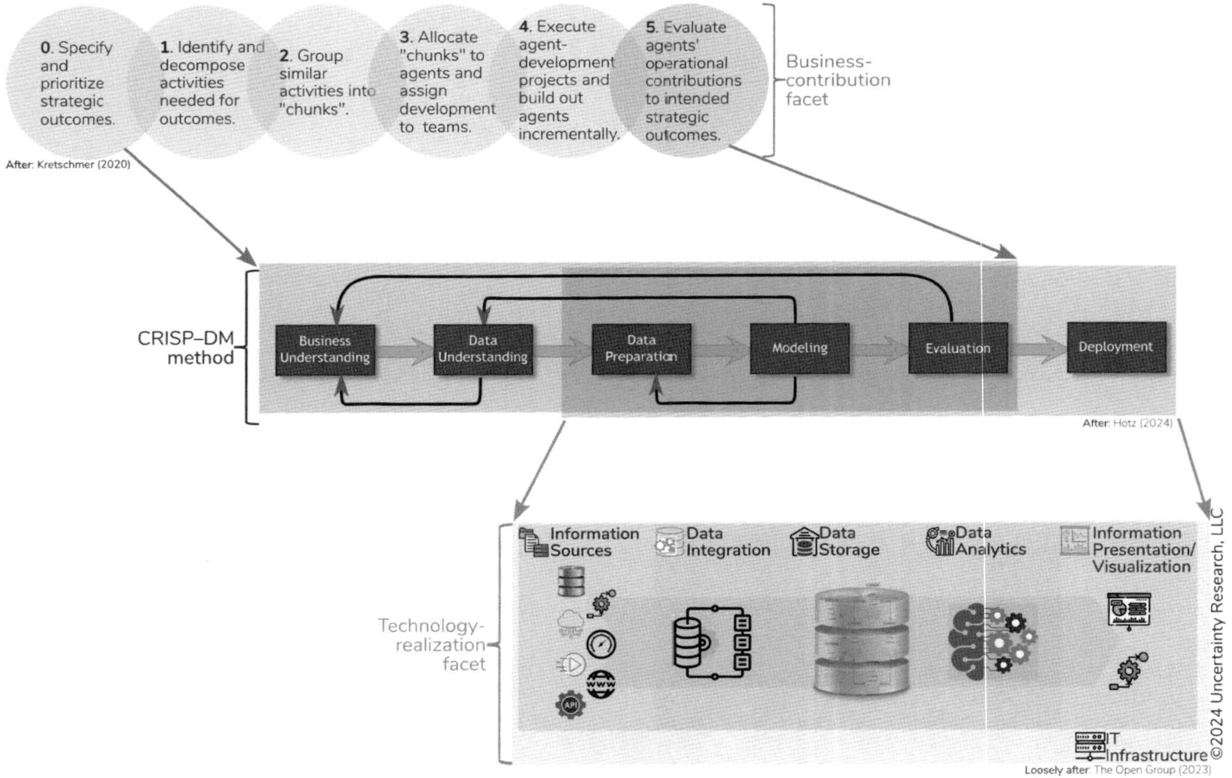

Figure 2. The CRISP-DM methodology (Saltz, 2022; Hotz, 2024) provides a disciplined, structured approach for incrementally realizing business-aligned AI functionality.

avoiding eye-catching firsts." Initially, organizations' foundations should consist of a relatively small set of general-purpose components.

Technology sales folk seek to persuade us to buy everything in their catalog, including lots of niche tools. Many technology practitioners define themselves by the diversity of tools with which they are conversant. Organizations nonetheless should strive to keep their technology portfolios as simple as possible for as long as possible.

3.3. *Using the CRISP-DM methodology* (*Hotz, 2023*) *as a structure for AI project portfolios*

The CRISP-DM methodology provides a framework for planning and executing distinct projects to digitize "chunks" of operational capabilities. Saltz (2022) compares a variety of data science project management approaches. Starting with business considerations — as opposed to jumping straight into the data — distinguishes CRISP-DM from many of the others. The business- and data-understanding stages drive attention to business contribution factors. The deployment stage accounts for the development of operational technology, aligning its capabilities with operational activities and deploying it onto our foundation for operations.

Holtz (2023) notes that CRISP-DM is not explicitly a project management approach. The framework in Figure 1 nonetheless provides ample structure from which to construct a work breakdown structure for each project in the portfolio. Each project produces a digitized business activity with accompanying operational procedures.

Individual projects are narrowly scoped so that they can be executed and evaluated quickly. "Take your time planning. When the plan is complete, execute it as quickly as possible" (Harford, 2022). O'Toole (2020) similarly emphasizes small, short-duration projects.

Think of each project as an experiment (Thomke, 2014). Expeditious project execution gives stakeholders frequent opportunities to assess progress and decide whether to continue or to exit, as appropriate (Camuffo, 2024). The systematic progression through short-duration, deliberately scoped experiments drives organizational learning.

Now, CRISP-DM emanates from the analytics industry. We most commonly associate this with Davenport's (2018) cognitive insights. A more expansive interpretation of what constitutes a "model" generalizes it to Kretschmer's "agents." These could similarly support automation or cognitive engagement activities. Its overarching approach to structuring work applies to any digitization activity. Judicious application leads to well-scoped, expeditiously executed projects.

4. How Figure 2's Framework Addresses AI-Success Principles

Figure 2 provides organizations with a systematic approach to address the AI-success principles from the business literature. The CRISP-DM method — by which the business and technical facets are aligned — features a structure that drives focus to business considerations. Table 1 contains a concise mapping.

Now, Hotz (2023) does not explicitly spell out the considerations in Table 1. This exhibit follows from a systems thinking approach, extending the CRISP-DM framework so that it aligns with the business literature consensus described above. In fact, no single framework contains prescriptive, exhaustive guidance for all situations. Each organization must adapt a framework along the lines of Figure 2 to its own circumstances.

5. Conclusion: Digital Transformation Is More Than Simply a Technology Problem

Digital transformation offers irresistible promise to improve business operations. No technology by itself however can obviate strategic, operational, and organizational challenges. Digital transformation paves the way to adopt operational and organizational models that are impractical without it.

Nonetheless, the introduction of digital transformation must be accompanied by leadership attention focused on these issues. For each project, "Identify a business owner who will lead the initiative, be accountable, and influence user involvement — from project design through execution and ongoing usage" (Kesari, 2024). Success is unlikely if digital transformation is left as a CIO thing.

The business literature contains a resounding consensus about prerequisites for AI success. As with digital transformation, AI provides a tool that can help address operational and organizational challenges. In the end, however, "AI is math, not magic" (Merrill, 2019). Within the

Table 1. Figure 2's framework based on the CRISP-DM provides a systematic approach to the AI-success factors emphasized in the business literature.

CRISP-DM stage	AI-success principles
Business understanding	• **Identify high-leverage business problems:** ○ Develop theories of the business. ○ Formulate hypotheses about operational and organizational opportunities for improvement. ○ Assemble opportunities into a portfolio of small, short-duration projects to test hypotheses. • **Frame analytics in terms of decisions:** Identify the decisions for which enhanced quality leads to differentiation. • **Evaluate using business metrics:** Clarify business metrics by which business improvements are characterized. • **Match AI approach to problem:** Identify AI approach factors needed to meet business objectives.
Data understanding	• **Frame analytics in terms of decisions:** Identify evidentiary standards for high-confidence decision-making. • **Work data quality from source:** Evaluate decisional suitability of available data.
Data preparation	• **Work data quality from source:** ○ Identify organizational- and operational-design opportunities to improve evidentiary quality. ○ Best-achievable decisional confidence given available data. ○ Curate available data to approach best-achievable evidentiary quality. • **Match AI approach to the problem:** Organize data to address technical needs of modeling approach.
Modeling	• **Match AI approach to the problem:** ○ Select technical approaches that support business factors. ○ Develop approach to translate the model's technical performance characteristics into business metrics.
Evaluation	• **Evaluate projects using business metrics:** ○ Review the business contribution based on the AI approach. ○ Determine whether business improvement hypotheses are confirmed. ○ Revise theories and plan next steps.

constraints of its fundamental limitations, it can help reduce uncertainty, improve efficiency, and advance the quality of decision-making.

Realization of these benefits must be accomplished via approaches that are systematic and scientific. Innovation — the creation of new productive knowledge — rarely occurs serendipitously. It results from deliberate, methodical hard work.

The framework in Figure 2 exemplifies such a scientific approach. The preceding discussion presents only broad strokes. It nonetheless demonstrates how principles from the business literature can be applied to the pursuit of digital transformation that improves an organization's competitive position.

References

Acemoglu, C. (2024). The simple microeconomics of AI. *Economic Policy*, National Bureau of Economics Research. Working Paper 32487. http://www.nber.org/papers/w32487.

Andressen, M. (2011). Why software is eating the world. *Wall Street Journal*, August 20, http://online.wsj.com/article/SB10001424053111903480904576512250915629460.html.

Ångström, R. (2023). Getting AI implementation right: Insights from a global survey. *California Management Review*, 66(1): 5–22.

Agrawal, A., Gans, J., & Goldfarb, A. (2022). From prediction to transformation. *Harvard Business Review*, November–December. https://hbr.org/2022/11/from-prediction-to-transformation.

Barney, J. B., Reeves, M. (2024, September). AI won't give you a sustainable advantage. *Harvard Business Review*. https://hbr.org/2024/09/ai-wont-give-you-a-newsustainable-advantage.

Blenko, M. W., Mankins, M., & Roger's, P. (2010). The decision-driven organization. *Harvard Business Review*, June. https://hbr.org/2010/06/the-decision-driven-organization.

Bonnet, D. (2022). The 3 stages of a successful digital transformation. *Harvard Business Review*, September 20. https://hbr.org/2022/09/3-stages-of-a-successful-digital-transformation.

Brock, J. K. & von Wangenheim, F. (2019). Demystifying AI: What digital transformation leaders can teach you about realistic artificial intelligence. *California Management Review*, 61(4): 110–134.

Camuffo, A., *et al.* (2024). A scientific approach to strategic decision-making: Large-scale replication and extension. *Strategic Management Journal*, 45(6): 1209–1237.

Chakravorti, B. (2024). AI's trust problem: Twelve persistent risks of AI that are driving skepticism. *Harvard Business Review*, May 3. https://hbr.org/2024/05/ais-trust-problem.

Chui, M., *et al.* (2023). The economic impacts of generative AI: The next productivity frontier. *McKinsey & Company*, June 14. https://www.mckinsey.com/capabilities/mckinsey-digital/our-insights/the-economic-potential-of-generative-ai-the-next-productivity-frontier.

Christen, P. & Schnell, R. (2024). When data science goes wrong: How misconceptions about data capture and processing causes wrong conclusions. *Harvard Data Science Review*, 6(1). https://doi.org/10.1162/99608f92.34f8e75b.

Copeland, B. (2024). Artificial intelligence. *Encyclopedia Britannica*, April 19. https://www.britannica.com/technology/artificial-intelligence.

Correani, A., *et al.* (2020). Implementing a digital strategy: Learning from the experience of three digital-transformation projects. *California Management Review*, 62(4): 37–56.

Cox, D. R. & Reid, N. (2000). *The Theory and Design of Experiments*. New York, NY: Taylor and Francis.

Davenport, T. H. (2005). The coming commoditization of business processes. *Harvard Business Review*, June. https://hbr.org/2005/06/the-coming-commoditization-of-processes.

Davenport, T. H. (2013). Keeping up with your quants. *Harvard Business Review*, July–August. https://hbr.org/2013/07/keep-up-with-your-quants.

Davenport, T. H. & Ronanki, R. (2018). AI for the real world. *Harvard Business Review*, February. https://hbr.org/2018/01/artificial-intelligence-for-the-real-world.

Davenport, T. H. & Tiwari, P. (2024). Is your company's data ready for generative AI? *Harvard Business Review*, March 26. https://hbr.org/2024/03/is-your-companys-data-ready-for-generative-ai.

Evans, D. S. & Schmalensee, R. (2016). The businesses that platforms are actually disrupting. *Harvard Business Review*, September 21. https://hbr.org/2016/09/the-businesses-that-platforms-are-actually-disrupting.

Garbuio, M. & Lin, N. (2018). Artificial intelligence as a growth engine for health care startups: Emerging business models. *California Management Review*, 61(2): 59–63.

Gartner Inc. (2018). Understanding Gartner's hype cycles. *Gartner Research*, August 20. https://www.gartner.com/en/documents/3887767.

Hamlett, N. (2007). IT outsourcing impacts on enterprise architecture. *IT Professiona*, 9(2): 34–40.

Harford, T. (2022). Mega projects often end up late and hideously over budget. Why? *Financial Times*, September 2. https://www.ft.com/content/6cabfac4-1faa-4730-90d0-e14b3f0ff817.

Hastie, T., Tibshirani, R., & Friedman, J. (2009). *Elements of Statistical Learning*. New York, NY: Springer.

Herring, L., *et al.* (2019). How to train someone to translate business problems into analytics questions. *Harvard Business Review*, February 11. https://hbr.org/2019/02/how-to-train-someone-to-translate-business-problems-into-analytics-questions.

Hoerl, R., Kuonen D., & Redman, T. C. (2022). Frame data science problems the right way from the start. *MITSloan Management Review*, April 14. https://sloanreview.mit.edu/article/framing-data-science-problems-the-right-way-from-the-start/.

Hotz, N. (2024). What is CRISP DM? *Data Science Process Alliance*, March 26. https://www.datascience-pm.com/crisp-dm-2/.

Hubbard, D. W. & Seierson, R. (2023). *How to Measure Anything in Cybersecurity Risk*. Wiley. https://doi.org/10.1002/9781119892335.

Kane, G. C. (2017). Digital transformation is a misnomer. *MITSloan Management Review*, August 7. https://sloanreview.mit.edu/article/digital-transformation-is-a-misnomer/.

Kesari, G. (2024, May 14). Building a data-driven culture: Three mistakes to avoid. *MITSloan Management Review*. https://sloanreview.mit.edu/article/building-adata-driven- culture-three-mistakes-to-avoid/.

Keynes, S. (2024). How to get big numbers when predicting AI's effect on growth. *Financial Times*, May 10. https://www.ft.com/content/8ee7fe88-ef5a-405a-9cac-914612fd4c89.

Kotter, J. P. (2012). *Leading Change*. Harvard Business Press. https://hbsp.harvard.edu/product/11116-PDF-ENG.

Kretschmer, T. & Khashabi, P. (2020). Digital transformation and organization design: An integrated approach. *California Management Review*, 62(4), 86–104.

Lavallee, S., *et al.* (2010). Big data, analytics, and the path from insights to value. *MITSloan Management Review*, December 21. https://sloanreview.mit.edu/article/big-data-analytics-and-the-path-from-insights-to-value/.

Lamar, E., *et al.* (2023). The value of digital transformation. *Harvard Business Review*, July 21. https://hbr.org/2023/07/the-value-of-digital-transformation.

Lamparth, M. & Schneider, J. (2024). Why the military can't trust AI. *Foreign Affairs*, April 29. https://www.foreignaffairs.com/united-states/why-military-cant-trust-ai.

Martínez, E. (2024). Re-evaluating GPT-4's bar exam performance. *Artificial Intelligence and Law*. https://doi.org/10.1007/s10506-024-09396-9.

Merrifield, R., Calhoun, J., & Stevens, D. (2008). The next revolution in productivity. *Harvard Business Review*, June. https://hbr.org/2008/06/the-next-revolution-in-productivity.

Merrill, D. (2019). What boards need to know about AI. *Harvard Business Review*, May 24. https://hbr.org/2019/05/what-boards-need-to-know-about-ai.

Mims, C. (2022). How to build AI that actually works for your business. *Wall Street Journal*, July 23. https://www.wsj.com/articles/how-to-build-ai-that-actually-works-for-your-business.

Moore, G. (2004). Darwin and the demon: Innovating within established organizations. *Harvard Business Review*, July–August. https://hbr.org/2004/07/darwin-and-the-demon-innovating-within-established-enterprises.

Murtha, T. P., Leeway, S. A., & Hart, J. A. (2002). *Managing New Industry Formation: Global Knowledge Formulation and Entrepreneurship in High Technology*. Stanford Business Press. https://wwwsup.stanford.edu/books/title/?id=1723

Nieto-Rodriguez, A. (2023). It's time to end the battle between waterfall and agile. *Harvard Business Review*, October 10. https://hbr.org/2023/10/its-time-to-end-the-battle-between-waterfall-and-agile.

O'Toole, T. (2020). What's the best approach to analytics? *Harvard Business Review*, March 20. https://hbr.org/2020/03/whats-the-best-approach-to-data-analytics.

Praslova, L. N. (2023). Today's most-critical workplace challenges are about systems. *Harvard Business Review*, January 10. https://hbr.org/2023/01/todays-most-critical-workplace-challenges-are-about-systems.

Ross, J. R., Weill, P., & Robertson, D. C. (2006). *Enterprise Architecture as Strategy: Creating an Architecture for Business Execution*. Boston, MA: Harvard Business School Press.

Redman, T. C. (2018). Are you setting your data scientists up to fail? *Harvard Business Review*, January 25. https://hbr.org/2018/01/are-you-setting-your-data-scientists-up-to-fail.

Redman, T. C. (2020). To improve data quality, start at the source. *Harvard Business Review*, February 10. https://hbr.org/2020/02/to-improve-data-quality-start-at-the-source.

Redman, T. C. & Hoerl, R. W. (2024). AI and statistics: Perfect together. *MITSloan Management Review*, April 16. https://sloanreview.mit.edu/article/ai-and-statistics-perfect-together/.

Saltz, J. (2022). What is a data-science workflow? *Data Science Process Alliance*, September 5. https://www.datascience-pm.com/data-science-workflow/.

Shevchenko, N. (2020). *An Introduction to Model-Based Systems Engineering (MBSE)*. Software Engineering Institute, Carnegie Mellon University, December 21. Retrieved May 9, 2024, from https://insights.sei.cmu.edu/blog/introduction-model-based-systems-engineering-mbse/.

Shevchenko, N. (2022). *Modeling capabilities with Model-Based Systems Engineering (MBSE)*. Software Engineering Institute, Carnegie Mellon University, November 28. https://doi.org/10.58012/5mgc-q360.

Siegel, E. (2024). What AI projects should know about measuring AI project value. *MITSloan Management Review*, February 7. https://sloanreview.mit.edu/article/what-leaders-should-know-about-measuring-ai-project-value/.

Stoelhurst, J. W. (2021). Value, rent, and profit: A stakeholder resource-based theory. *Strategic Management Journal*, 44(6): 1488–1513.
Suarez, F. F. & Lanzolla, G. (2005). The half-truth of first-mover advantage. *Harvard Business Review*, April. https://hbr.org/2005/04/the-half-truth-of-first-mover-advantage.
Swanson, E. B. (2024). Technology entrepreneurship is more than one might think. *Information and Organization*, 34(2). https://doi.org/10.1016/j.infoandorg.2024.100512.
The Open Group (2023). Information architecture: Business intelligence and analytics. *TOGAF® Series Guide*, August. https://pubs.opengroup.org/togaf-standard/bi-analytics/.
Thomke, S. & Manzi, J. (2014). The discipline of business experimentation. *Harvard Business Review*, December. https://hbr.org/2014/12/the-discipline-of-business-experimentation.
Unruh, G. & Kiron, D. (2017). Digital transformation on purpose. *MITSloan Management Review*, November 7. https://sloanreview.mit.edu/article/digital-transformation-on-purpose/.
Van Alstyne, M. W. & Parker, G. G. (2021). Digital transformation changes how companies create value. *Harvard Business Review*, December 17. https://hbr.org/2021/12/digital-transformation-changes-how-companies-create-value.
Vanderford, R. (2023). SEC head warns against 'AI washing', a high-tech version of 'greenwashing'. *Wall Street Journal*, December 5. https://www.wsj.com/articles/sec-head-warns-against-ai-washing-the-high-tech-version-of-greenwashing.
Vinsel, L. (2023). Don't get distracted by the hype around generative AI. *MITSloan Management Review*, May 23. https://sloanreview.mit.edu/article/dont-get-distracted-by-the-hype-around-generative-ai/.
Weill, P. & Ross, J. W. (2005). A matrixed approach to designing IT governance. *MITSloan Management Review*, January 15. https://sloanreview.mit.edu/article/a-matrixed-approach-to-designing-it-governance/.
Westerman, G., Ramsbotham, S., & Farranoto, C. (2024). Find the AI approach that fits the problem you're trying to solve. *Harvard Business Review*, February 24. https://hbr.org/2024/02/find-the-ai-approach-that-fits-the-problem-youre-trying-to-solve. Giatectatem et lautas anderovidi con prat fugiam, volorerum fuga. Ut latempo riaspel luptamenda essum re con conet harcienda sum quiae nimo et et pa sanditam, sequi tectur restrum aut eos molor sum fuga. Neque ipsame cusapel in percient omnia simil moleni sam fugia quis a vellam qui ullumquam, omnia qui cus imus inimusamus, corernatiur?
Ximi, que velene provid min cumquid qui nonet ut eaquas explatemos aut voluptatem solorit mo ex et faccat doloreh endelit laborru ptatem quaessi maiorem a se sum ent estium quid quia corepra essuntur? Quis esci seque nis saperferis ea iligenit ipisquas quid moloreicimet dolore, quis nita il milluptatur sitaquist alit veligenis mi, ne volore vent ulliqui delique audipsusda vel eum

https://doi.org/10.1142/9789811296475_0003

Chapter 3

The Missing Link in Digital Transformation: "What About Us Humans?"

Arthur J. Murray

Applied Knowledge Sciences, Inc. Boyce, VA, USA

As technology continues to evolve at an accelerated pace, many are expressing fears of a rapidly approaching "singularity," a point at which computer intelligence will exceed human intelligence. That is certainly a valid concern when considering the extremely slow pace of human evolution, especially when compared with the continued impact of Moore's law on information and computer technology (ICT), particularly regarding AI.

This chapter addresses this concern by weighing the pros and cons of the present and future capacities of both the technology/AI side and the human side, and how a more blended approach of the two can result in greater overall benefit than either side could achieve alone. In particular, we examine two ways that human evolution can be enhanced in ways that address shortfalls in AI and machine learning (AI/ML). These are (1) human deep learning (as opposed to the widely popular machine learning) and (2) applying a principle of Group Theory from mathematics to greatly expand our human capacity for sense making and discovery through a series of transformations in how we perceive and make sense of the world. But first, let's start with a brief overview of some key drivers that are helping to feed the imbalance.

1. Key Drivers of Digital Transformation: "The Five V's"

Let's call it runaway *informationflation*. The broad literature covers several key trends in data and information, the most common of which involve rapidly increasing volume, velocity, and variety, along with concerns regarding veracity and value. These are collectively referred to as "the five V's."

The first V, *Volume*, refers to the nearly exponential increase in the amount of data and information produced on a daily basis. The total volume of available information currently stands at around 120 zettabytes. Some estimate that sometime in the middle of this decade, we'll have access to essentially all of the data we'll ever need, which is expected to be in the range of 300 zettabytes.

Given that a zettabyte (10^{21} bytes) is one trillion gigabytes, it's not hard to imagine how users, especially decision makers, can become quickly overwhelmed. And that information is being made available at increasingly faster data rates (the second V, *Velocity*). Recent advances have produced fiberoptic data rates up to 22.9 petabits per second ($\sim 2.3 \times 10^{19}$ bps).

Given the increasing volume and speed, the next challenge is how to sort it all out in ways that make sense within a given context, which is the third V, *Variety*. This is becoming particularly important given the emergence of misinformation, disinformation, and AI-driven "deep fake." Decision makers at all levels, from government leaders to individuals, need to determine what's real and what isn't. That's the fourth V, *Veracity*.

Even if we somehow succeed in making it through the first four filters, we're still left with the fifth V, *Value*. This is perhaps the most important because even if the information is accurate, so much of what's coming at us is junk and garbage, or simply irrelevant to the situation at hand. A good illustration is the story of a hot air balloonist who gets blown far off course by high winds and ends up stuck in a tree. Having totally lost his sense of orientation, he spots a passer-by and asks, "excuse me, can you please tell me where I am?" The person responds by saying, "you're in a balloon stuck in a tree." Completely accurate yet totally useless information.

If we look at this example through a knowledge management lens, we can take it a step further and think about how to ferret out that which is accurate, apply it to solve a problem or respond to an opportunity, and even use or modify it to create additional value.

In today's global, knowledge-intensive business environment, these challenges will continue to accelerate, as will our reliance on AI and related technologies. As we're bombarded with ever-increasing amounts of data and information, we'll inevitably end up asking: Where's the knowledge in all of this?

2. The Growing Imbalance between the Human and the Digital

On the digital side, the unrelenting growth in the volume of data has been enabled by the decade-long consistent application of Moore's law, in which bandwidth and computational capacity tend to double approximately every 18–24 months. This has led many to conclude that we're getting very close to the point at which AI will exceed human intelligence, at least when compared to the computational and storage capacity of the human brain. This is being referred to as artificial general intelligence (AGI).

If this trend continues, many expect AGI to further evolve into something on the order of an artificial super intelligence (ASI). This includes a possible worst-case scenario of machines taking over, even to the point at which humans are seen as a threat and need to be exterminated. This is the dreaded "singularity" as depicted in dystopian science-fiction movies such as "*The Terminator*" (see Figure 1).

A more rational (and hopefully more likely) outcome is that we will need to more aggressively address a major frustration of the Information Age, often expressed as *we're drowning in data and starved for knowledge* (see Figure 2). The reason knowledge is so important is that it delivers

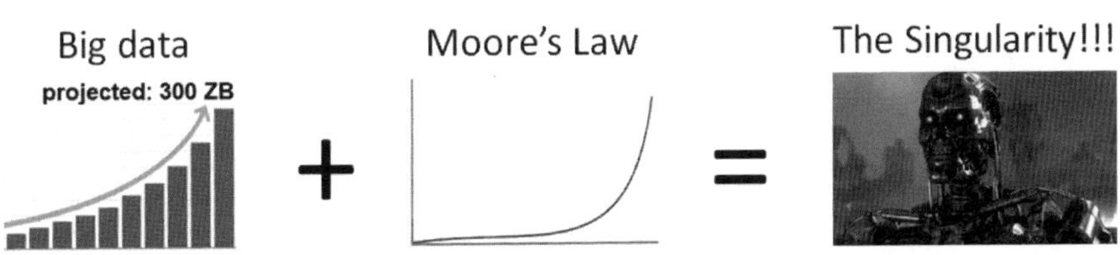

Figure 1. The ultimate "dark-side" scenario of AI evolution.

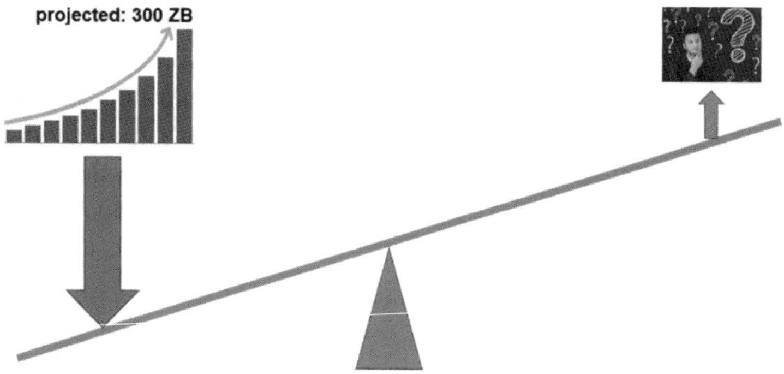

Figure 2. The imbalance between massive growth in data and information vs. human knowledge based mainly on intuition and judgment.

actionable information. Or more formally, knowledge is *the capacity to take effective action in varied and uncertain situations* (Bennet & Bennet, 2004, p. 5), in other words, making better decisions, including observing, generating, evaluating, selecting, and executing courses of action.

This imbalance is documented in a recent study. Out of 743 decision makers surveyed, 50% said that when making decisions, the necessary information simply wasn't available. Around 40% said that the quality of data that was available was not good enough to be used. Even when the right information was available, 32% said that it wasn't presented in a way that could be effectively applied. Interestingly, 58% of the respondents said that they based at least half of their decisions on gut feel or experience, rather than on data or information (Bange *et al.*, 2014).

With the introduction of generative AI (GenAI) platforms such as ChatGPT, Gemini, and others, this imbalance becomes even more pronounced. According to a recent survey, overreliance on GenAI was cited by 43% of respondents as the top ethical concern. The study defined overreliance as "accepting incorrect inputs or outputs generated by AI, and then relying heavily on them." This exceeded all other concerns, including privacy and data security (41%), job displacement (36%), misuse of generated AI content (29%), and the lack of transparency in data usage (21%) (Wilson, 2023).

Regarding the fear of job displacement, Forrester Research, Inc. estimates that by 2030, 2.4 million jobs will be lost to GenAI. However, they predict that in the same time frame, 11.8 million jobs will be enhanced by this technology, which is far more jobs than it will replace (Curran, 2023). In addition, according to the U.S. Bureau of Labor Statistics, data scientist positions will continue to be among the fastest-growing jobs between 2022 and 2032, with a projected 35% increase in job openings during that period (Bureau of Labor Statistics, 2024).

Overreliance on machine knowledge raises an important question: Are decision makers better off sticking with their gut intuition instead of blindly following the advice of GenAI and data science? As shown in Figure 3, there are several possible "points of failure" in the flow of information from data collection through post-decision. At the input side, the five V's raise the question: Are you using the correct data as inputs? Given the data are correct, very often, the analytical process occurs in a "black box" of undocumented or poorly documented algorithms, or worse yet, within the many "hidden layers" of complex neural networks. Are the outputs of those algorithms correct, and are they the proper inputs to be fed into the proper decision processes? Are those decision processes well understood and documented? Finally, how much consideration is given to the consequences of those decisions over the short-, intermediate-, and long-term?

To answer these questions, we turn our attention back to good old-fashioned human expertise and wisdom and see how best we can cultivate and incorporate it into personal and organizational knowledge flows.

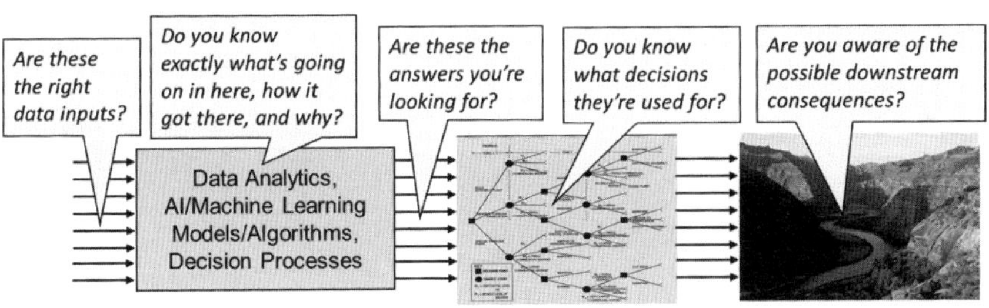

Figure 3. Increased dependency on AI and automation = increased risk and vulnerability.

3. Restoring Balance: Using Human Strengths to Offset Technology Weaknesses

Figure 4 illustrates the contrast between human and machine capacities to support learning and decision-making. The human side falls under the broad category of natural systems; the machine side consists of purely computational systems. Natural systems exhibit unique traits, such as autopoiesis, self-awareness, understanding, foresight, and consciousness. These in turn contribute to the human capacity for sense making, as well as the innate desire to ask and reflect on questions, similar to Einstein's thought process when he wondered: "*What is it like to ride on a beam of light?*" Humans also have traits that can be both beneficial and detrimental, such as bias (of which there are many different types), and emotions, especially fear.

On the machine side, whether a connectionist or symbolic processing approach is used, the basic architecture is purely computational and ultimately binary (at least until quantum computing becomes mainstream, which opens up an entirely different dynamic). Even then, machines treat everything (inputs, processes, and outputs) as raw data, without any emotional attachment, ethical concern, or regard for whether or not the results make sense in the real world.

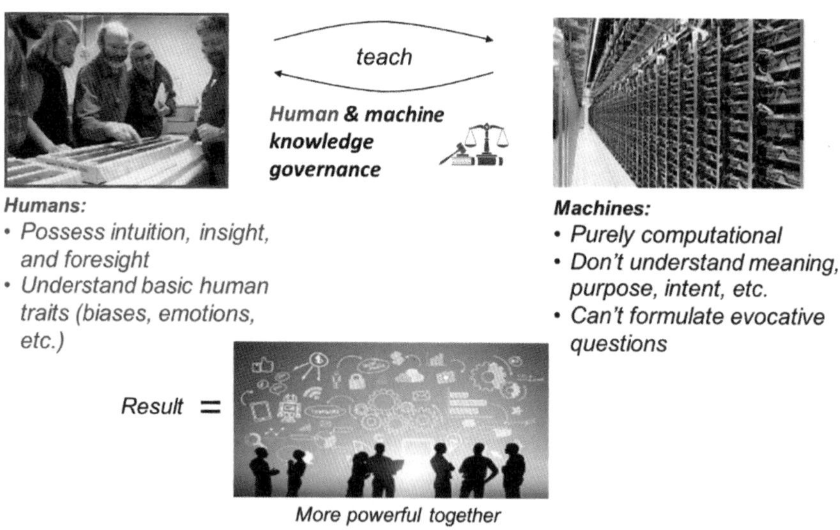

Figure 4. A possible end state for the integration of human and machine knowledge.

Given this, it should follow that in a fast-changing, complex world, a combination of both humans and machines working together provides the best chance for improvement. This was borne out in a study of the failures associated with the design of the Boeing 737-MAX Roll Command Alerting System (RCAS), which resulted in two crashes killing 346 people. The study involved the analysis of the internal Boeing emails related to the project, along with a large corpus of documents consisting of industry standards and lessons learned from 17 major US Department of Defense and NASA projects. The data were analyzed by two distinct groups: one consisting solely of human subject matter experts and the other consisting of a suite of AI tools performing a variety of functions, such as pattern and anomaly detection, identifying trends in sentiment over time, case-based reasoning, and others. The results were not entirely unexpected. The humans found errors, problems, and opportunities that the machines missed, and the machines discovered patterns and anomalies that the human experts missed (Murray, 2020).

Incorporating double- and triple-loop learning allowed human experts to fill gaps on the machine side and vice versa. The end result was an integrated system capable of producing more contextually accurate and effective results than either side could alone. Still, an important issue remains. With the machine side continuing to make exponential advances, how can the human side ever hope to keep up? What's the human equivalent of Moore's law?

The most common metrics used to gauge human progress are life expectancy, such as tracked by The World Bank, and the UN Human Development Index (HDI) (see Figure 5). Except for a sudden drop resulting from the global COVID-19 pandemic, life expectancy has been on a steady uptrend for most of the past century. With the introduction of several life-extending technologies including gene and stem cell therapies (along

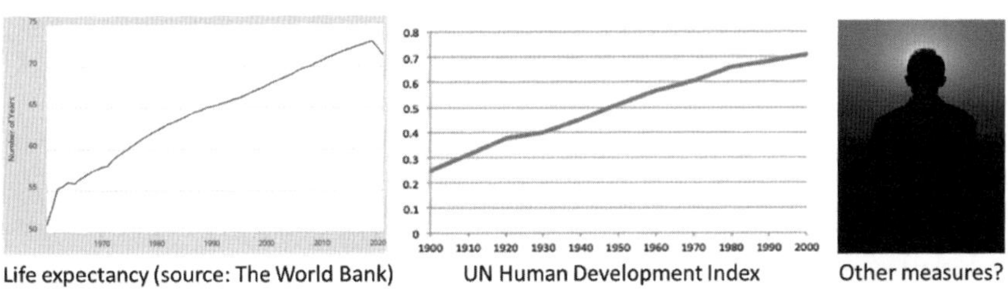

Figure 5. Research question: What attributes best define future human evolution?

Table 1. Mapping the five V's of data and information to knowledge and learning.

Metrics	Knowledge and learning characteristics
Volume	Ability to learn more
Velocity	Ability to learn more rapidly
Variety	Ability to learn a wide range of topics, their associations and interdependencies
Veracity	Ability to discern truth from falsehood
Value	Ability to focus on that which has the greatest potential positive impact on society

with the absence of a major war or another global pandemic), the upward trend will likely resume. The same can be expected regarding the HDI, although it is beginning to level off due to the negative impacts of climate change, socioeconomic pressures including increased debt burdens, and depletion of resources, including fresh water. Still, these metrics do not paint a complete picture. For the purposes of tracking, more complex and intangible human evolutionary cofactors such as the growth/contraction of human knowledge, awareness, and even consciousness, additional metrics are needed, which we pose as a question for further investigation.

At a minimum, with regard to enhancing knowledge workers' performance, we need to (1) examine what roles human analysts, experts, and decision makers play both now and in a highly digitized future; (2) determine what changes need to occur in order for the human workforce to assume and carry out these roles with ever-increasing efficiency and effectiveness.

Human transformation involves learning. Therefore, as a starting point, we can assert that the same characteristics that define the five V's of data and information also apply to knowledge. Table 1 assigns each of the five V's of information to human learning.

The question is where to start? The answer lies in returning to our deep learning roots as humans.

4. A Brief History of Deep Learning

A Google search of deep learning returns over 5.4 billion results, the vast majority of which associate deep learning with machines. Surprisingly, the top-ranked result, a link to https://www.ibm.com/topics/deep-learning, acknowledges its human origins. On their deep learning web page, IBM defines deep learning as *a subset of machine learning that uses multi-layered neural networks, called deep neural networks, to simulate the complex decision-making power of the human brain. Some form of deep learning powers most of the artificial intelligence (AI) in our lives today.*

If we refine the search by using the keywords "human deep learning," almost all 8,000 URLs returned point to content that addresses how humans can make better use of machine deep learning. This fails to recognize the innate capacity of humans to perform deep learning naturally. For our purposes, human deep learning occurs at a deep structure, or engram level, of memory. This is based on a vastly rich yet mostly forgotten body of work.

Much of this was the work of the late Karl Pribram, whose holonomic model posited a stratified structure in which stable memory elements are formed at the level of conscious awareness (surface learning), while base elements of memory (engrams) occur at a deep level, separated by an epistemic gap (Pribram, 1991, 1996, 1997). Many of Pribram's 700 published papers can be found at https://karlpribram.com/data-papers/.

4.1. *An early model of human deep learning: Indigenous knowledge preservation and transfer*

For over 15,000 years, Indigenous Alaskans have been accumulating, handing down, applying, and refining a vast treasure trove of wisdom, experience, and knowledge. Much of this tradition reflects a strong connection with nature, an example of how natural, living systems are tied to deep structure in ways that machines could never experience (Langlois, 2018).

For example, in the fall of 2012, a few native Alaskans emphatically warned that the coming winter was going to be extreme in terms of heavy snowfall, low temperatures, and high winds. No number of weather stations, climate and weather datasets, or predictive models could confirm this. Their prediction was solely based on intuitive sense and observing "large amounts of fat on caribou" to an extent never before seen. Clearly, the caribou also sensed the imminent shift in weather patterns. Their sudden voracious appetite provided sufficient data to validate the humans' trepidation. That year, Alaska experienced one of its worst winters ever, with a total snowfall of 134.5, "topping the old record of 132.6" set in the winter of 1954 (Wendler *et al.*, 2013, p. 7).

How did they know this with such a strong sense of certainty? They did in part because, as indigenous inhabitants of this beautiful yet extremely hostile wilderness, they didn't develop the capacity for survival, including predicting sudden changes in weather patterns, by being chained to a desk in a classroom, or by plowing through volumes of text and diagrams, sequentially reciting facts from one chapter after another. Rather, they acquired this ability, starting in early childhood, through various combinations of traditional visual arts, singing, movement, dance, and storytelling (ANHC, 2023). But most importantly, by actually going into the wilderness, hunting wild game, and foraging for berries. All excellent examples of experiential learning and whole-brain thinking. As the University of Alaska Anchorage Professor and Alaskool Co-Founder Paul Ongtooguk puts it, *Legends, oral traditions and stories give us a glimpse into how important it was in traditional Alaska Native societies to learn to share with others, to work hard, and to value wisdom* (Ongtooguk, n.d.).

This approach to learning is strongly evident in Inuit village schools, where education tends to be more cyclical than sequential and involves actively engaging in knowledge sharing with the local community. Knowledge is imparted using methods suited to each situation, such as context-rich stories enhanced through kinesthetic and sensory experience, as opposed to regurgitating facts and figures on standardized tests.

This is exactly the type of education reform we're going to need if we are to have any hope of responding to the tough challenges ahead. And if you don't think native Alaskans know how to solve hard problems, consider their extraordinary ability to hunt bowhead whales in the unforgiving icy waters off the northern coast (Hess, 2012). In addition to the life-and-death split-second decision-making that traditional whale hunting demands, the whale hunters found themselves at odds with sophisticated government data indicating the need for them to curtail their hunting due to dangerously low bowhead population levels. The hunters' natural sense told them otherwise. Eventually, the government relented, admitting that their analysis was off by an order of magnitude. Machine-based modern science got it wrong and the natives, relying on intuition and tacit knowledge, got it right.

The same mindsets can be found in the Diné culture, which spans a vast region of the Americas, including the Navajo, Apache, and other nations (Lerma, 2017; Greyeyes, 2022).

There's an important lesson to be learned here. In order to get knowledge to flow while drowning in a tidal wave of data, we should consider, at least on occasion, stepping away from our computer screens and mobile devices and re-discover what we did when all we had was each other, a team of dogs (or horses and mules), and a few knives and spears. As we build our future, let's pay heed to the old traditions. They worked well when we were struggling for our physical survival. As the five V's accelerate to the point of overwhelming both us and our machines, and as we're beginning to exhaust some of our most precious resources, we should look very closely at what wisdom we might draw from indigenous peoples in all parts of the world. This is worth considering especially given how they have been able to survive for many thousands of years in some of the most inhospitable environments on earth.

While not everyone may be willing or able to go out into the wilderness and expand their consciousness by becoming one with nature, there are other ways to develop, implement, and enhance human deep learning. Let's first review the fundamental principles of human deep learning, including deep structure. Then we'll take a look at two very different human deep learning approaches that are slowly making their way into practice in both education and business.

4.2. *Deep structure and its relationship to human deep learning*

At this point, you're probably wondering: What exactly is deep structure, and how might we tap into it? By deep structure, we mean the most basic, foundational laws, principles, and basic elements that give rise to what we observe at the surface level. Much of this work is based on a collaborative effort between American and Russian semioticians during the 1980s and 1990s (Pospelov, 1991; Coombs & Sulkoski, 1996). This is an excellent example of the need for knowledge preservation: bodies of seemingly obscure and esoteric knowledge produced decades ago simply might not have been ready at the time, but could save a tremendous amount of trial-and-error and repeated effort when re-visited and applied at a later date. This has been an ongoing project at the Harvard Law School Library Innovation Lab's Long Data Project, which uses open-source time capsule encryption software to help make newly released knowledge more durable and robust so it can be re-released at a specified moment in time (Rabin & Thorpe, 2006). The planned release date can be decades, centuries, or millennia down the road. No more "here today, gone tomorrow."

A major characteristic of deep structure is *time invariance*. In the era of big data, with innumerable zettabytes swirling around, it's easy to lose sight of the fact that there are time-invariant structures lying deep underneath. Atoms are one such basic, time-invariant element. Subjected to the natural laws of valence (also time-invariant), atoms can only be combined into molecules in certain ways. Yet, an almost infinite variety of valid combinations are possible. New compounds continue to emerge from our chemical and metallurgical laboratories on almost a daily basis. But it's the knowledge of deep structure that separates the study of chemistry today from the study of alchemy in the past.

You could also liken deep structure to the relatively small set of phonemes from which all human speech and language is constructed. Root sounds, when combined in ways that are syntactically and semantically correct, make sense. Other combinations which violate the rules of syntax and grammar make no sense. Unless of course, the combination represents a new type of expression, in which case the rules of syntax and grammar are modified (as in double-loop learning).

In the knowledge sciences, we refer to this type of system as a second-order cybernetic system. It simply means that unlike a first-order system in which the rules are "hard-wired" (such as a simple thermostat or the tax tables in an accounting system), a second-order cybernetic system can self-modify its rules as conditions change. In more advanced systems, the underlying rules can even be modified in anticipation of changes that may occur in the future. Sadly, this knowledge of deep structure and its accompanying rules of association have slowly been forgotten as we've amassed our vast data-rich, knowledge-poor digital library known as the Internet.

It's important to remember that in deep structure, things don't always line up according to a neatly organized set of rules. There are nonlinear structures present, including multiple states that a single basic element can exhibit at the same instant, much like elementary particles in quantum physics. These occur because deep structure, especially with regard to human cognition, is stratified (Challis & Velichkovsky, 1999). Two or more discrete states can be present at the same time.

4.3. *Re-wiring the brain for alignment with deep structure: Self-directed inquiry*

Like nature, the brain has an underlying deep structure. At the root of human memory are basic elements called engrams. Education based in large part on rote memorization and standardized testing is an anachronistic one-size-fits-all artifact of the Industrial Age. This has resulted in engrams that have been hard-wired into a first-order system. Today's online, computer-based training further exacerbates this condition. This is in sharp contrast to self-directed inquiry, which was the preferred approach to education prior to the 19th century (Long & Ashford, 1976).

The challenge for preparing tomorrow's workforce for a massively complex, rapidly changing world is to determine how best to re-introduce neural plasticity into education. One way to accomplish this is by making a major paradigm shift from rote learning to *guided self-discovery* (Murray, 2016a).

The idea is simple. When you discover things for yourself, or with a tutor, instructor, or mentor acting as your guide, it "sticks." You gain a deeper understanding of each topic and how to apply it in real life, even in entirely new situations. The end goal is not only to make the whole process completely automatic but also to make school, work, and life a continuing journey of discovery and learning.

This self-discovery process is a learning cycle consisting of the following six steps: think; observe; enumerate; express; assess; adjust. Feel free to try these steps, and hopefully make them a part of your learning habits:

1. **Think of an idea:** Anything. Most new discoveries simply start as an idea in someone's mind. Be sure to give it a name or a label.
2. **Observe that idea directly if you can, or through a book, a video, computer simulation, or demonstrated by an instructor or coach:** If there's no other way, then picture it in your mind. Not only visually but also using all of your feelings, senses, imagination, and emotions. Try to think like Einstein did when he asked himself, "*What would it be like to ride along a beam of light?*"
3. **Mentally enumerate what you've observed, in short, 30- to 60-second intervals:** In other words, think of the various aspects of what you're observing. Be sure to make each aspect totally different from the others. We call this process *descriptive enumeration.*
4. **Express in your own handwriting what you've observed and experienced:** Not by typing on an electronic device, but writing by hand using a paper and a pencil (you can digitally scan it later on). Writing by hand helps re-establish the almost-forgotten practice of whole-brain thinking. Now read what you've written. Refine and adjust. Repeat and re-iterate, steadily building your own personal

body of knowledge and idea bank. Consider using other natural modalities of expression, such as mind-mapping, art, music, poetry, dance…even cooking! Organize the knowledge into a representation space to help connect your topics and ideas in new and interesting ways. Organize it visually so you can easily navigate and expand it. Share it with others.

5. **Assess your progress by periodically stepping back and reviewing what you've expressed:** Let your handwritten notes and other forms of expression be your teacher. They'll give you insights into how deeply you're learning a particular topic. They'll also help you identify what learning behaviors, positive and negative, are in play and what adjustments, if any, you'll need to make (see Step 6).
6. **Based on your assessment, think about how you can adjust your deep learning approach:** It could be sharpening your powers of observation. Or taking steps to overcoming your fear of or disdain for a particular subject, or anything else that might be holding you back. Better yet, awaken the child in you by always asking, "*Why? Why? Why?*" Keep track of what topics are known and how well, what topics aren't known, and what topics need further exploration.

Keep repeating these six steps. You can't change how you learn with the click of a button. It takes time and effort. But the rewards are well worth it. Some of the reported benefits include the following:

- making sense of and gaining greater understanding in a soundbite world,
- increased powers of observation,
- improved ability to connect the dots and see the big picture,
- help in breaking old learning habits,
- building and growing a more enriching personal body of knowledge,
- improved means of communicating newly acquired knowledge so others may benefit.

Now, let's take a look at how this deep learning approach has dramatically transformed a particular group of freshman college students in their attitude to and performance in mathematics, moving from disdain and apprehension to fully understanding and applying it.

4.4. *Human deep learning applied to freshman college mathematics*

The modern-day application of human deep learning to mathematics education had its beginnings in 1911 at the University of Pennsylvania. There, Dr. R. L. Moore developed what eventually became known as the Moore Method, a means of applying a process of guided self-discovery to the subject of mathematics. He went on to apply and refine that method at the University of Texas from 1920 to 1969, including founding a separate and distinct Mathematics Department focused solely on his method (Parker, 2005; Coppin, 2009).

Dr. Paul S. Prueitt, Associate Professor of Mathematics and Chair of the A.S. Mathematics Degree program at Diné College in Tsaile, Arizona, USA, has picked up the baton and over the past several decades, has continued to expand, refine, and apply the Moore Method in a variety of cultural environments, including historically black, tribal, socio-economically disadvantaged, and special needs educational institutions. In addition to the self-directed inquiry approach described in the previous section, several other key aspects have been applied. Some of the more noteworthy differences from traditional mathematics pedagogy include the following:

- Students have the freedom to choose from, or wander among, a list of topics, provided they alternate between topics with which they feel comfortable and topics that are uncomfortable (the inability to do this in most classrooms is a major source of frustration, especially for students with ADHD).
- Allowing periods of "focus on, focus off" (this especially had a positive impact on students on the autism spectrum; previously forced to "*pay attention!*" they were instead given opportunities to take a break, do whatever they want, and return to the topic later on).
- Rather than being graded on their answers to standard questions, exams consist of "blank paper tests" in which students use handwritten narratives to demonstrate their understanding of a particular topic (see Figure 6).

The transformations have been dramatic, typically resulting in more than double the percentage of students passing freshman math classes, especially among non-STEM majors, the rate of which in recent cases went from 30% to 80%.

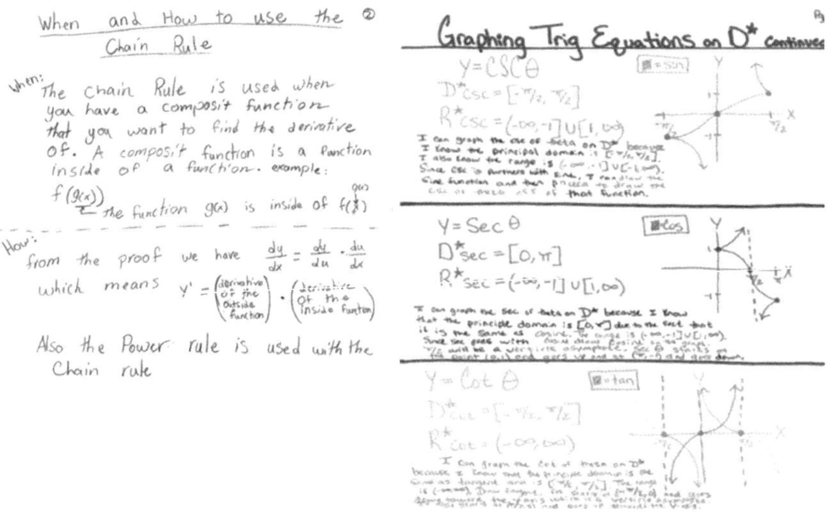

Figure 6. Blank paper test examples (including the use of colors to deepen understanding).

Similar successes were achieved in tribal colleges, where there is a tendency for strong apprehension regarding Western ways of thinking, especially with regard to STEM subjects. But attitudes changed when students were challenged to self-discover basic mathematics principles present deep within their culture and traditions. For example, the Navajo have a very specific ritual for properly orienting a teepee, including the placement of rocks at specific distances and angles. The same idea was extended to the Navajo concept of everything in nature consisting of four primary elements: rain, light, air, and pollen. It is no longer necessary, or even worth trying, to force old Western Industrial Age principles when people can tap into deep structure by seeing how it directly relates to their culture and tradition. Instead of somebody telling them what's going to be on the test and what they have to memorize, students are figuring out foundational principles by their own observation of how those principles are revealed in their culture and natural environment.

Expressing their newly acquired knowledge in handwriting or drawing not only stimulates whole-brain thinking but also provides a tool for the instructor to notice subtle learning behaviors (positive and negative) through various sentiment indicators (fear, apprehension, confidence, etc.) as evidenced in both the linguistic content as well as the nature and style of the markings (e.g., thin and light vs. dark and intensive). No more numerical scores. Rather, the focus shifts toward answering the question: Is learning happening, and if not, why not?

To date, anonymous and de-individualized data have been collected from a population of over 600 freshman college mathematics students (Prueitt, 2017, p. 118; 2020). Listed below are average responses to survey questions posed to students based on a Likert scale (−2, −1, 0, +1, +2). Students were also given the opportunity to provide comments and feedback. Table 2 provides a sample of those comments as they relate to various aspects of the human deep learning methods applied.

The methods used were different from what I expected.

Strongly Disagree Dis-agree No Opinion Agree Strongly Agree

____1.2____________

These methods were at first difficult to understand.

Strongly Disagree Dis-agree No Opinion Agree Strongly Agree

________________________________0.4____________________

Eventually I did understand what was expected in this class.

Strongly Disagree Dis-agree No Opinion Agree Strongly Agree

____1.2___________

My understanding of the curriculum in this course was improved more than I expected, and because of the pedagogy.

Strongly Disagree Dis-agree No Opinion Agree Strongly Agree

____1.4____________

*I do **NOT** believe that these methods should be used in this type of course.*

Strongly Disagree Dis-agree No Opinion Agree Strongly Agree

____________________–0.6______________________________

I would like to see these methods developed as part of an effort to improve non-STEM major mathematics offerings.

Strongly Disagree Dis-agree No Opinion Agree Strongly Agree

____1.25___________

Table 2. Human deep learning applied to freshman mathematics: Student feedback.

	Deep learning aspect	Student response/feedback
Positive	Freedom to choose topics	*I was able to explore higher-level mathematics like I was exploring a new land. I didn't have the essence of a harsh red pen at my back.*
		The math narratives were a hard concept for me to grasp. But once I understood how to do them, I really enjoyed and appreciated them. Not only did they allow me to have freedom with what I choose to write but they also made my knowledge on the subjects deeper. I enjoyed how we were not overworked like in some other math classes.
	Freedom to take a break ("focus on, focus off")	*Grasping and juggling concepts, equations, properties, and formulas is difficult for me. But the approach to this class allowed me to be engaged due to being able to learn at my pace, and the understanding that I learn differently than others.*
		Having a class that respects 'Focus on Focus off' is a breath of fresh air. I feel that I do that every day, whether I want to or not. So, in having this class, I feel as though I have come out on top when it comes to learning mathematics.
	Guided self-discovery	*This class made me try harder that I have ever tried in a math class. I found myself pretty good at math, I always liked math, and I felt like I always understood it. But this class has tested my math skills.*
		One other part of this method I want to address is the connection that this allows for between instructor and student. Due to [sic] the incredibly individualized nature of each student's work, it enables the instructor to get to know the student and get to familiarize themselves with the student's learning styles and, possibly the most important part, lets the teacher acknowledge how much the student understands the material in other ways besides simply just a test score and assignment scores.
		This course has allowed me reflection [sic]. You have allowed me the ability to get to know what I actually know and reflect on previous experiences in math and also how I view my life a little. You always had a welcoming and happy yet challenging environment to your classes and, though I may not have been awake for one or two sessions, your class was actually a class I looked forward to being in.

Table 2. (*Continued*)

	Deep learning aspect	Student response/feedback
	Overcoming fear/disdain for mathematics	*Mathematics has always been a word that made my heart beat fast. I was never able to look at mathematics as a journey; I always looked at it as something that resembled a walk in a quicksand pool. I used to feel stuck in mathematics. Yet, this semester, everything changed.* *Through this course, I was able to find that the wall I put up whenever I was learning a difficult concept was just a window I needed to crawl through. I figured out that the unknown is one of the greatest places to explore.* *Thank you, for helping me see mathematics in a new light.*
Negative	Dissatisfaction with the approach	*With this system, we are to do twice the work for little to no yield.* *I enjoyed/hated this class.*
	Resistance to change	*Perception regarding deep thinking: I am a creature of habit, especially when it comes to math. I was alarmed and upset when he discussed how he wanted our homework to be in narratives.* *Deep learning is something that is very difficult to adjust to. It requires students to think about the course a lot more outside of class.* *A lot of kids do not like it because it does not fit with common curriculum, and they do not like to struggle with concepts.* *Deep learning methods are far more difficult than what was done in high school.* *I never expected to take a math class where I wrote more than I did in English, yet here we are.*

4.5. *Diving into deeper realms: How to "think like a Rishi"*

All knowledge consists of three and only three distinct components: (1) an observer; (2) that which is observed; (3) the process of observation. In more general terms, a subject, an object, and a process, i.e., how the subject and object interact (see Figure 7). All three need to be present. Anything more is unnecessary and fundamentally incorrect. Anything less and the knowledge is fragmented and incomplete, which often gets us into trouble. This time-invariant threefold structure exists throughout

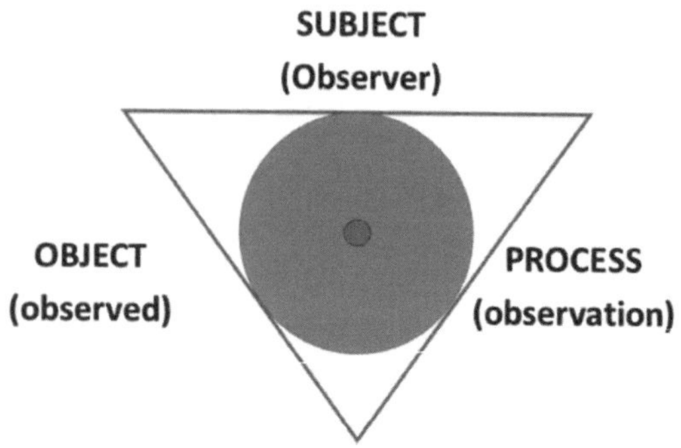

Figure 7. The time-invariant threefold structure of knowledge.

many different cultures and civilizations, from the Vedas as revealed by the Rishis ("seers") of ancient Bharat to the indigenous elders and medicine men in the Americas to modern systems thinking.

Consider, for example, the contrast between Eastern and Western philosophies. In Eastern thought, the subjective aspect of knowledge has primacy. You'll hear expressions like "the inner self." Internal, subjective experience. In its most extreme forms, all externality is suspect, not to be trusted. Truth resides only within. In the West, however, knowledge is typically approached from the opposite direction. In applying the scientific method, for example, subjectivity is frowned upon in the interest of purely "objective" science.

In Eastern approaches, the goal is to have the observer completely free of any influence of what's being observed. In the West, the flip side is true. The object of observation must be totally "blind" to the observer. Only recently in quantum physics, with principles such as entanglement, have people begun to accept that such isolation is impossible. That you cannot observe something without changing it and without it changing you the observer at least in some way. That's the interaction, or middle part of this threefold structure coming into play, with all the three acting as one.

This is what we referred to earlier when we talked about how many of the world's great thinkers reflexively looked back on their handwritten notes. Reflexivity is a key part of the interplay between a subject and an object. Observer, observed, and observation. To focus only on the subject and not the object, or vice versa, and not include the interaction between the two results in fragmented, incomplete knowledge. And with that comes errors, sometimes minor, sometimes catastrophic.

# 1	subject	→	process	→	object
# 2	object	→	process	→	subject
# 3	process	→	subject	→	object
# 4	subject	→	object	→	process
# 5	process	→	object	→	subject
# 6	object	→	subject	→	process
	(S)		(P)		(O)

Figure 8. The dihedral group of order six perspectives of subject, process, object.

This brings us to an excellent example of how deep structure combined with a foundational principle from Group Theory in mathematics can activate previously hidden and forgotten perspectives, leading to new insights and discoveries. That foundational mathematical principle is known as the dihedral group of order six. The practical application of this method, developed by mathematician Thomas J. McCabe (the discoverer of cyclomatic complexity and the McCabe complexity metric in software), is still in its early stages, yet has already been applied successfully in the areas of business entrepreneurship and incubation, secondary education (Murray, 2016b), and knowledge management.

Here's how it works. A dihedral group of order six means that there are six and only six ways the three elements of Subject, Process, and Object (S, P, O) can be ordered (*transformations* in mathematical terms), each resulting in a different frame of reference or perspective (see Figure 8). Let's briefly examine each.

#1: Subject → Process → Object

This perspective is essentially "home base," the familiar ordering of subject-verb-object that you learned in grammar school. This represents your view of the world as the observer, through your eyes and other senses, along with your beliefs and biases.

#2: Object → Process → Subject

In this transformation, you the subject, and the object (person or thing) with which you are interacting, switch places. This, along with perspective #6, is one of two empathy-based transformations. This is how a highly empathic individual tends to view the world, through the eyes of others.

#3: Process → Subject → Object

Here, the observer and process switch places. This tends to be characteristic of someone who is "process-oriented."

4: Subject → Object → Process

From this shift in perspective, you the subject remain the observer, thinking about what the world would look like if the process and object switched places. In other words, how you, the observer, would view the process (the new object of observation) through the lens of the object (the new process).

5: Process → Object → Subject

This is one of the two double transformations. In this case, the process becomes the subject, the subject becomes the object, and the object becomes the process.

6: Object → Subject → Process

This is the other double transformation, in which the subject becomes the process, the process becomes the object, and the object becomes the subject. Here, the empathic person tries to understand what the person they are trying to help (or the thing they are trying to improve) is going through. What's their situation? What's their environment like? How can it be changed for the better? You'll hear this type of person talking about "walking a mile" in someone else's shoes.

Since perspectives #1 and #4 view the world through the observer, i.e., a subjective perspective, we call them ego-based perspectives. People who view the world mainly through this type of lens tend to be very autocratic, seeking to impose their will on both the process and the object. For example, many Apple insiders recall that Steve Jobs was so intense in this regard they referred to him as viewing the world through what they called a "reality distortion field." Being grounded in these two perspectives, he transformed not only entire industries such as computers, phones, and music (Subject → Process → Object) but also the engineering and design processes that went into producing those products (Subject → Object → Process).

Similarly, perspectives #2 and #6 are empathy-centered. They try to see the world through the eyes of others, seeking total harmony with everyone (Object → Process → Subject). They see themselves as an instrument for world change and improving people's lives (Object → Subject → Process).

Perspectives #3 and #5 are process-centric. People in this category often focus on the journey, and their experiences along the way, whether good or bad (Process → Subject → Object). They seem to have an explanation for everything and tend to get frustrated when they can't find one (Process → Object → Subject). Trial lawyers tend to master these two types. For example, a lawyer representing the plaintiff will closely examine what the situation looks like (including pros and cons) when the legal process is viewed from the perspective of the plaintiff (Process → Subject → Object). That same attorney will do the same from the standpoint of the defendant (Process → Object → Subject), looking for strengths and weaknesses that can either be exploited or should be avoided. This is usually what's going on when you see court cases endlessly bogged down in procedural matters. Politics often works in much the same way.

Here's why these six transformations are so important. Depending upon your personal profile, you tend to view the world from only one or two perspectives. If that's the case, then you're missing out on four or more different ways of looking at things, along with the added insights, innovations, and breakthroughs that come from a more expanded view. Countless critical decisions may be impacted.

Now think of what could happen if you expanded your awareness in such a way that you could view the world from all six perspectives. The same goes for your workgroup. Your family. Legislative bodies. Nations. The world.

This gives you only a very small glimpse into the world of deep structure. The threefold structure of observer, observed, and observation is one such invariant. It represents a stable structure underneath to help people better understand the root causes of what might be perceived as uncontrolled chaos on the surface.

5. The Way Forward: An Integrated Human/Machine Approach to Digital Transformation

Pushing the evolution envelope on the human side is hard, very hard, as many of our students and workshop participants have expressed. Yet in the same vein as "no pain, no gain," many also express their satisfaction, even excitement, especially when their extra effort results in new discoveries and insights.

Blending human and machine intelligence doesn't mean, as some are predicting, implanting chips and other machine interfaces directly into our brains. Rather, we envision something more along the lines of Figure 4, a two-sided approach where, as in the Boeing 737-MAX study mentioned earlier, humans and machines teach each other, exploiting the strengths and offsetting the weaknesses of each.

The architecture that was used in that study, as well as in our research going forward, is shown in Figure 9. Just as ChatGPT and other large language model (LLM)-based GenAI platforms crawl the web, ingesting nearly everything, an enterprise-level human/AI system will ingest a relatively smaller, curated corpus of relevant documents. These documents, along with emails, text messages, and other discourse, and various structured datasets, are provided as inputs (the left-hand side of Figure 9).

Using a layered ontology as a reference, entity/association extraction and other analytics are performed on the input stream (the middle of Figure 9). The primary output is a graph database, with a visual interface such as a knowledge graph, which can be queried in natural language using GenAI or other retrieval mechanisms. Responses are reviewed by one or more subject matter experts, and adjustments to the reference ontology, graph database, and LLM are made as needed. These adjustments include prompt engineering, retrieval augmented generation

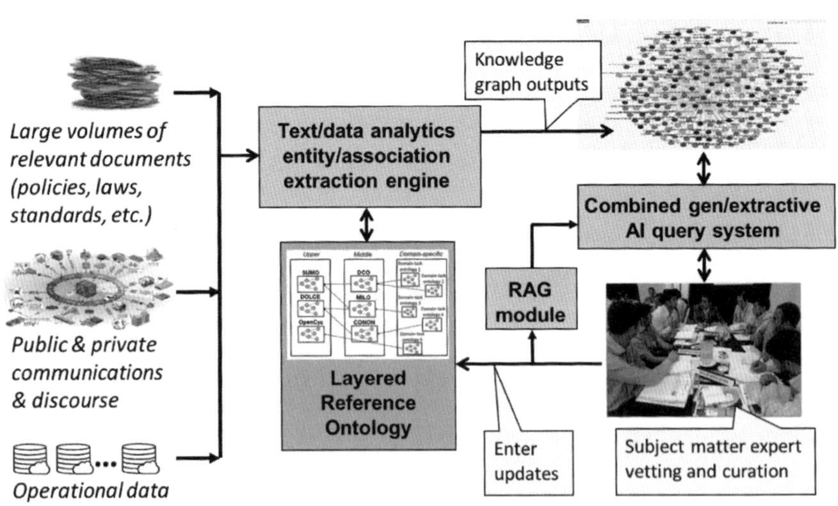

Figure 9. Two-sided human/machine top-level architecture.

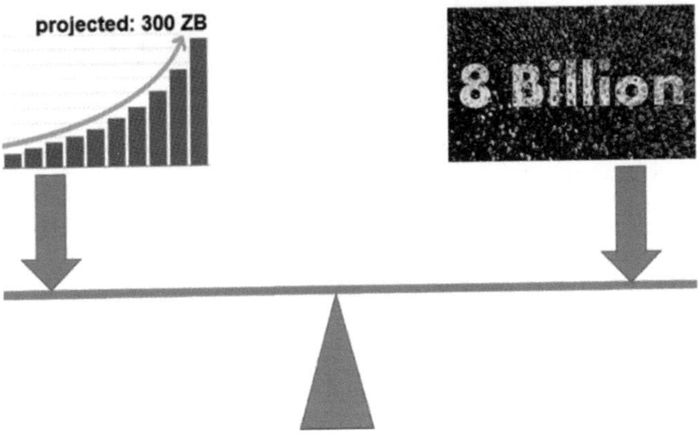

Figure 10. Tapping 8 billion human minds to restore balance in a tech-heavy world.

(RAG), and refinement of definitions, synonyms, and other means of improving the semantic understanding of the system (the right-hand side of Figure 9).

With technology racing ahead, perhaps it's time to dust off, review, and even revive some of the work which when published was very much ahead of its time (Penrose, 1994; Scardigli, 2022). With over 8 billion human minds with a far deeper knowledge base, history, and culture to tap into, there's no reason why we can't begin to tip the scales and make the best use of both artificial and natural systems (Figure 10).

References

ANHC Staff (2023). Honoring indigenous wisdom and heritage. *Alaska Native Heritage Center*, November 3.

Bennet, A. & Bennet, D. (2004). *Organizational Survival in the New World: The Intelligent Complex Adaptive System*, p. 5. Boston, MA: Elsevier.

Bange, C., Handford, M., & Janoschek, N. (2014). Information Culture: Leveraging the power of collective intelligence for better decision making. *BARC Institute*, May.

Bureau of Labor Statistics, U.S. Department of Labor (2024). *Occupational Outlook Handbook, Data Scientists.* April 17.

Challis, B. H. & Velichkovsky, B. M. (eds.) (1999). *Stratification in Cognition and Consciousness*. Amsterdam/Philadelphia: John Benjamins Publishing.

Coombs, M. J., Sulcoski, M. F., & Casti, J. L. (1996). Control mechanisms for complex systems: Issues of measurement and semiotic analysis. In:

Proceedings of the Workshop on Control Mechanisms for Complex Systems, Issues of Measurement and Semiotic Analysis, December 8–12, Las Cruces, New Mexico, USA.

Coppin, C. A., *et al.* (2009). *The Moore Method: A Pathway to Learner-Centered Instruction*. Washington, DC: Mathematical Association of America.

Curran, R. & Gownder, J. P. (2023). *The Generative AI Advantage: Embrace the Next Catalyst of Growth and Innovation Today*. Forrester Research Report, November 29.

Greyeyes, W. S. (2022). *A History of Navajo Nation Education: Disentangling our Sovereign Body*. Tucson, AZ: University of Arizona Press.

Hess, B. (2012). The movie, Big Miracle, and what I witnessed in real life, parts 1-13. *Logbook Wasilla Alaska blog*. http://www.logbookwasilla.com/logbookwasilla/2012/2/3/the-movie-big-miracle-and-what-i-witnessed-in-real-life-part.html.

Langlois, K. (2018). When whales and humans talk. *Hakai Institute*, April 3.

Lerma, M. (2017). *Guided by the Mountains: Navajo Political Philosophy and Governance*. New York, NY: Oxford University Press.

Long, H. B. & Ashford, M. L. (1976). Self-directed inquiry as a method of education in Colonial America. *The Journal of General Education*, 28(3): 245–255.

Murray, A. J. (2016a). *Deep Learning Manual: The Knowledge Explorer's Guide to Self-Discovery in Education, Work, and Life*. Boyce, VA: AKS Press vice Applied Knowledge Sciences Press.

Murray, A. J. (2016b). Preparing students to excel as knowledge workers: Three essential tools. Paper presentation at Kerala Forest Research Institute, Kerala, Bharat.

Murray, A. J. (2020). Human and machine knowledge-based project management: Detecting and responding to weak signals at the operational level. In: *DoD & Federal Knowledge Management Symposium*, December 2.

Ongtooguk, P. (n.d.). Alaska's cultures: Building a context for stories and traditions, Alaska history and cultural studies, Lake and Peninsula School District. *Alaska*. https://akhistory.lpsd.com/articles/article.php?artID=275. Accessed May 15, 2024.

Parker, J. (2005). *R. L. Moore: Mathematician and Teacher*. Mathematical Association of America Spectrum Series.

Penrose, R. (1994). *Shadows of the Mind: A Search for the Missing Science of Consciousness*. New York, NY: Oxford University Press.

Pospelov, D. A. (1991). *Situational Control: Theory and Practice*. Moscow: Nauka Publishers (in English).

Pribram, K. (1991). *Brain and Perception: Holonomy and Structure in Figural Processing*. New Jersey, NJ: Lawrence Erlbaum Associates.

Pribram, K. (1996). *The Deep and Surface Structure of Memory and Conscious Learning: Toward a 21st Century Model*. Brain Center, Radford University, February 20.

Pribram, K. (1997). Non-locality and localization: A holographic hypothesis about brain functioning in the processes of perception and memory. In: *Syrlergetics and Psychology, Issue 1: Methodological Issues*, Moscow, MGSU Union, pp. 156–183 (in Russian).

Prueitt, P. S. (2017). *Deep Learning Manual, Volume II: Foundations*, p. 118. Boyce, VA: AKS Press vice Applied Knowledge Sciences Press.

Prueitt, P. S. (2020). *Deep Learning Manual, Volume III: Design Principles*. Boyce, VA: AKS Press vice Applied Knowledge Sciences Press.

Rabin, M. O. & Thorpe, C. (2006). *Time-Lapse Cryptography*. Harvard University School of Engineering and Applied Sciences, Technical Report TR-22-06, 20 December.

Scardigli, F. (ed.) (2022). *Artificial Intelligence vs. Natural Intelligence*. Cham, Switzerland: Springer.

Wendler, G., Moore, B., & Galloway, K. (2013). *The Climate of Alaska for 2012*, p. 7. Alaska Climate Research Center, Geophysical Institute, University of Alaska Fairbanks.

Wilson, J. (2023). Over-reliance on generative AI top ethical concern for workers. *HR Reporter*, September 6.

https://doi.org/10.1142/9789811296475_0004

Chapter 4

Accelerating Business Model Development and Organizational Decision-Making through the Use of AI and Intuition

Peter McAlindon

Crummer Graduate School of Business, Rollins College, Winter Park, FL, USA

1. Introduction

Digital transformation involves the comprehensive integration of digital technology into all operational aspects of a business, fundamentally changing how the business operates and delivers value to customers. For startups, this transformation is not merely about adopting new technologies but creating a digital-first culture that leverages these technologies to drive business strategy, innovation, efficiency, and growth. By embracing digital technologies and integrating them into all aspects of their operations, startups can enhance operational efficiency, facilitate customer engagement, drive innovation, and gain a competitive edge (Gupta & Bose, 2022; Lisa *et al.*, 2020). Digital transformation, or in some cases, reinvention, must address the value the startup provides to customers through its products and services. A clear strategy must identify where value is created, re-created, or destroyed (Tischlinger & Van Wordragan, 2019).

One of the key advantages of digital transformation for startups is the ability to streamline processes and automate routine tasks, leading to increased productivity and cost savings (Lisa *et al.*, 2020). This operational agility allows startups to respond swiftly to market changes and customer needs, a critical factor in the early stages of business development. Additionally, digital technologies enable startups to gather and analyze customer data, providing valuable insights for targeted marketing and product development strategies (Sreenivasan & Suresh, 2023). Getting this right is crucial in a startup as it allows for identifying, evaluating, and understanding what customers want or need. Finding the proper digital technologies and implementing a digital strategy can be surprisingly difficult in practice. Figure 1 illustrates this dynamic.

Moreover, digital transformation fosters an environment of innovation by providing tools and platforms that support creativity and experimentation (Brem *et al.*, 2021). By leveraging technologies such as artificial intelligence (AI), startups can develop unique products and services that disrupt traditional markets and populate new business models,

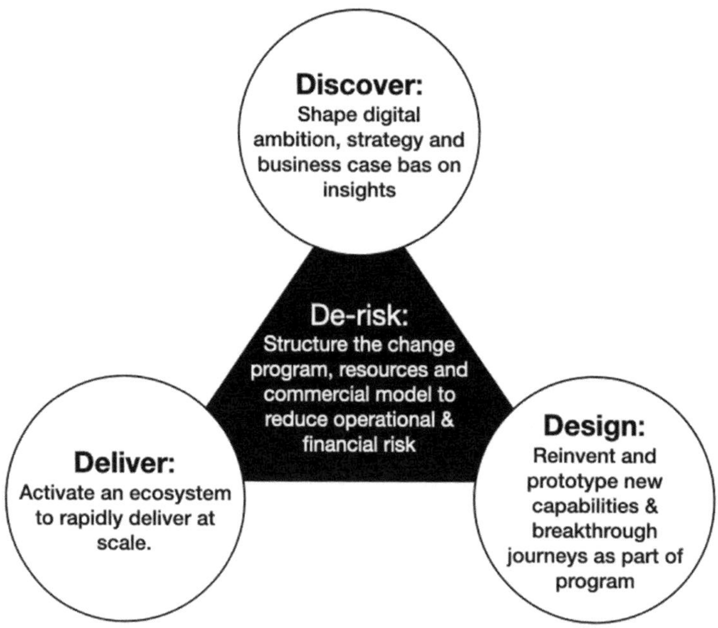

Figure 1. The 4Ds of digital transformation (Markovitch & Willmott, 2014).

giving them a competitive edge over established players (Weber *et al.*, 2022). No two entrepreneurial paths are the same, but the critical thinking skills needed for success are. From ideation to execution, the path of innovation is a complex journey that intertwines the waves of innovation (World Economic Forum, 2021; Chen, 2006; Daim *et al.*, 2006), the Gartner Hype Cycle (Adams, 2019; Ozgur & Steinert, 2016), Moore's (2014) *Crossing the Chasm*, models and frameworks like the Lean Startup (Ries, 2011), the Business Model Canvas (BMC) (Osterwalder *et al.*, 2010), and Wickman's (2012) Traction System and EOS. The hype cycle, a concept popularized by Gartner, illustrates the evolution of emerging technologies from their initial conception to widespread adoption. As entrepreneurs navigate this cycle, they must also confront the challenge of crossing the chasm, a critical transition point where a product moves from early adopters to the mainstream market. During the critical early adopter phase, the business model comes into play, serving as a roadmap for how the innovation will create, deliver, and capture value. The successful integration of these elements — understanding the overall waves of innovation, the Gartner Hype Cycle, strategically crossing the chasm, and developing a robust business model — is what often separates highly successful startups from the forgotten, paving the way for transformative innovations that reshape industries and further define the future of entrepreneurship.

This chapter discusses how to create digital transformations that best balance AI and intuition in the startup context and highlights the irreplaceable value of intuition in creating a business model for entrepreneurial success.

The goal is to aid in decision-making across all levels of the startup and build and iterate business models more quickly and accurately by leveraging the profound impact generative AI (GenAI) has on digital transformations for startups. It details how it serves as both a catalyst for growth and a forewarning for potential challenges that require strategic foresight and meticulous planning.

2. Startup Operating Environment

The failure rate of startups is notoriously high, with various data indicating that around 90% of startups ultimately fail (Startup Genome, 2019). This staggering statistic underscores the immense challenges and risks of launching and sustaining a successful startup venture. Some primary reasons for such high failure rates include lack of funding, lack of market need or product–market fit, intense competition, flawed business models, and team-related issues (CB Insights, 2019). Each failure point occurs primarily due to a lack of strategy, data, analytics, intuition, and a proper decision-making process.

In today's ever-accelerating startup environment, leveraging AI in decision-making is not just an advantage but a necessity. AI algorithms can process vast amounts of data, identify patterns, and predict outcomes with speed and accuracy far surpassing human capabilities. Such speed and accuracy allow organizations to make informed decisions quickly, optimize operations, and ultimately stay ahead in a competitive market. By integrating AI into their decision-making processes, startups can enhance efficiency and uncover innovative solutions to complex problems, driving growth and innovation forward.

However, startups operate in environments characterized by high uncertainty and limited data, conditions under which traditional AI systems, including GenAI, may not perform optimally. Human intuition, a cognitive process that elicits rapid responses based on experience and internal cues, provides a strategic advantage in such settings (Gobet & Philippe, 2009; Wonder & Blake, 1992; Julmi, 2019).

While AI offers unparalleled capabilities in processing data and providing insights, it cannot replace human intuition. Our intuitive abilities allow us to process information, emotions, and experiences quickly, making decisions that are not solely based on logic or data (Gore & Sadler-Smith, 2011). Research has shown that successful decision makers often rely on a combination of data and intuition to make sound judgments (Dane *et al.*, 2012; De Dreu, 2003). Therefore, startups need to cultivate a culture that values and encourages the use of intuition in decision-making. Such a culture can be achieved by fostering a diverse workforce, promoting open communication, and creating an environment that embraces creativity and risk-taking.

3. The Lean Startup and the Business Model Canvas

The Lean Startup methodology, pioneered by Eric Ries and influenced by Steve Blank's customer development framework, represents a paradigm shift in how startups are launched and managed. It advocates for developing a minimum viable product (MVP) — the simplest version of a product that allows the team to start the learning process as quickly as possible (Ries, 2011; Blank, 2013; Blank & Dorf, 2020). This concept challenges the conventional wisdom of product development which often involves long development cycles and the pursuit of product perfection before market introduction. Instead, the Lean Startup methodology encourages startups to launch early versions of their products to maximize learning through direct customer feedback (Blank, 2013).

This customer-centric approach is underpinned by continuous innovation and the iterative cycle of building, measuring, and learning directly from the customer. Startups test their hypotheses about the market and business model as they interact with customers, learning from these interactions and quickly iterating or pivoting in response to feedback (Ries, 2011; Blank, 2013). This method significantly reduces the risk and capital required by enabling startups to discover whether they are creating a viable business model before making, or seeking, large investments of time and money (Kakar, 2024).

Furthermore, the Lean Startup approach uses a set of metrics different from traditional business metrics, focusing instead on actionable metrics that guide decision-making and strategy adjustments in real time. These metrics are designed to provide real-time feedback that can be used to make informed decisions about whether to persevere in the current direction or pivot. Examples of these metrics include customer acquisition cost (CAC), customer lifetime value (LTV), churn rate, and revenue (Ries, 2011; Blank & Dorf, 2020). By focusing on these metrics, startups can make data-driven decisions that enhance their chances of long-term success. This focus on validated learning over intuition and "gut feeling" aligns with a more scientific approach to entrepreneurship, where decisions are made based on data derived from actual customer behavior rather than speculative forecasts.

The Business Model and its associated BMC are derived from the Lean Startup and represent a strategic management tool that has revolutionized how startups conceptualize and refine their business models. Developed by Osterwalder *et al.* (2010), the BMC offers a succinct yet comprehensive framework for understanding, designing, and iterating business models in a rapidly evolving market landscape.

At its core, the BMC is structured around nine key elements that collectively provide a holistic view of an organization's value proposition, customer segments, channels, customer relationships, revenue streams, key resources, key activities, key partnerships, and cost structure. This one-page overview enables businesses to articulate how they create, deliver, and capture value, fostering a deeper understanding of the intricate interdependencies within their operations. It is dynamic by nature, driven by data, and iterated until the business runs well.

The value proposition, positioned at the heart of the canvas, defines the unique benefits and solutions a company offers to its customers, distinguishing it from competitors (Osterwalder *et al.*, 2010). Customer segments and channels are critical in ensuring that the value proposition is effectively communicated and delivered to the intended audience. Meanwhile, customer relationships and revenue streams delineate how a business engages with its customers and generates income.

On the operational side, key resources, activities, and partnerships outline the essential assets, processes, and external collaborations that underpin the business model's execution. Lastly, the cost structure provides insight into the financial implications of the business model, highlighting the major expenses involved in creating and delivering value (Osterwalder *et al.*, 2010).

BMC's visual and intuitive design promotes collaborative discussion and strategic alignment within teams, making it an invaluable tool for aligning vision and operational strategies. It encourages iterative exploration and reevaluation of business models, enabling organizations to adapt and innovate in response to changing market dynamics and opportunities. Most importantly, it greatly benefits from GenAI models for helping establish the initial model and intuition for helping iterate it.

4. The Potential of AI, Intuition, and Business Model Development in Accelerating Decision-Making

Traditional decision-making processes often rely heavily on hierarchical structures and slow, deliberative practices that can hamper agility and responsiveness. These methods, while thorough, can lead to missed opportunities in a rapidly changing business environment where speed and flexibility are paramount. The linear approach of gathering information, analyzing data, and then making a decision may not be sufficient in contexts where immediate action is required. Furthermore, this conventional methodology might inhibit creativity and innovation, prioritizing risk aversion over bold, innovative moves. In contrast, leveraging AI, relying on intuitive judgment, and focusing on business model innovation can significantly enhance decision-making speed and quality. By adopting these modern approaches, startups can overcome the limitations of traditional decision-making processes and better position themselves for future success (Table 1).

The BMC is a blueprint for designing and analyzing business models. It offers a strategic lens through which startups can navigate the complexities of the modern business environment. Its adoption across diverse industries underscores its effectiveness in fostering strategic agility, customer-centric innovation, and sustainable growth.

Table 1. Benefits of AI integration in iterating a business model.

Real-time data analysis	AI-enabled systems can process and analyze vast amounts of data in real time, providing startups with up-to-date insights to make informed decisions quickly. This capability is particularly crucial for startups operating in fast-paced environments, where reacting to market changes promptly can mean the difference between success and failure.
Identifying patterns and trends	Humans have limitations in processing large amounts of data and identifying patterns and trends. Conversely, AI can analyze vast datasets efficiently and identify even the most subtle patterns or trends that could be crucial for making strategic decisions.
Predictive analytics	AI-driven predictive analytics enables businesses to accurately forecast future trends, risks, and opportunities. This foresight allows organizations to proactively plan and make decisions based on data-driven insights rather than intuition or guesswork.
Enhanced decision quality	Integrating AI into decision-making processes eliminates the possibility of human error and bias, resulting in more accurate and objective decisions. This capability is especially crucial for complex decisions that involve multiple variables and stakeholders.
Improved operational efficiency	AI integration can automate routine tasks, freeing up time for employees to focus on more critical decision-making activities. This streamlining of operational processes improves efficiency and productivity, ultimately contributing to the organization's bottom line.

4.1. *The importance of decision-making in businesses*

Understanding the importance of decision-making in a startup cannot be overstated. Effective decision-making can lead to better outcomes, driving growth and fostering innovation. Conversely, poor decisions can result in significant losses of time and money and missed opportunities, which could bankrupt a startup. Therefore, aligning decision-making processes with strategic objectives is critical. Leaders must ensure that decisions are made efficiently, based on accurate data, sound intuition, and a clear understanding and execution of the business model (Jorzik *et al.*, 2024). Fostering a decision-making culture that encourages creativity, agility, and informed risk-taking can significantly enhance an organization's ability to adapt to changes and seize new opportunities. This holistic approach to decision-making empowers businesses to navigate the complexities of the modern business environment confidently.

4.2. *Decision-making through the use of AI*

The adoption of AI for decision-making and acceleration can fundamentally shift a startup's culture toward innovation and efficiency. GenAI stands out as a transformative force for startups (Mishra & Tripathi, 2021; Mishra & Mishra, 2023). This technology, e.g., open.ai and perplexity.ai, characterized by its ability to generate new content and solutions from existing data, is not just a tool for innovation but also a strategic asset that can redefine competitive boundaries and help accelerate growth. As startups harness GenAI to innovate, automate, and optimize their processes, they position themselves to disrupt traditional industries, create new markets, and capture larger market share (Bahoo *et al.*, 2023; Gupta & Yang, 2024).

Integrating AI into business models has revolutionized the speed and efficiency of organizational decision-making. AI systems analyze vast datasets rapidly, uncovering insights and trends that humans might overlook or take much longer to find. This capability enables businesses to react quickly to market changes, optimize operations, and tailor customer experiences in real time. Additionally, AI-driven predictive analytics (e.g., Prophet, 2024, open-source predictive analytics software) can inform strategic planning, reducing the risk associated with decision-making by forecasting future trends and outcomes with high accuracy. Through these mechanisms, AI not only accelerates the decision-making process but also enhances its quality, driving growth and innovation in today's competitive business landscape (Kuzior *et al.*, 2023).

Implementation of GenAI in startups presents several challenges that need careful consideration to ensure successful integration and utilization. Table 2 lists 10 key challenges identified thus far.

Table 2. Challenges of implementing GenAI in startups.

Quality control and output management	One of the primary challenges is maintaining control over the quality and output of the AI-generated content. Startups must ensure that the content is accurate, relevant, and free from biases or errors that could harm the company's reputation or lead to misinformation.
Legal and intellectual property issues	Startups must navigate complex legal landscapes when using GenAI. Issues such as copyright infringement, trademark risks, and the ownership of AI-generated content can pose significant legal challenges. For instance, using AI to generate logos or branding elements could inadvertently infringe on existing trademarks, leading to legal disputes.
Overdependence on technology	There's a risk of becoming overly dependent on GenAI technologies. This overreliance can make startups vulnerable if the technology fails or if there are disruptions in the AI service. Startups must maintain a balance and ensure that they have contingency plans in place.
Cybersecurity threats	As with any technology that handles data, GenAI systems are susceptible to cybersecurity threats. Hackers can manipulate AI systems to generate harmful or misleading content, disrupt operations, or steal sensitive information. Protecting these systems requires significant investment in security measures.
Ethical and bias concerns	GenAI can perpetuate or even exacerbate existing biases if not carefully monitored. These biases can also lead to ethical concerns, especially if the AI is used in HR or customer-facing roles. Ensuring fairness and avoiding bias in AI-generated outputs is a significant challenge.
Data quality and management	GenAI's effectiveness heavily depends on the quality of the data it is trained on. If the training data are biased, outdated, or incomplete, the outputs generated by the AI will likely be flawed. Managing and continually updating the data to keep AI effective is challenging and ongoing.

(*Continued*)

Table 2. (*Continued*)

Integration and scalability	Integrating GenAI into existing systems can be technically challenging, especially for startups without in-house expertise. Additionally, as the startup grows, scaling the AI solutions to keep up with increased demands can present further challenges.
Cost of implementation	While GenAI can ultimately save costs by automating tasks and improving efficiency, the initial setup, operation, and maintenance of AI systems can be costly. These costs can be a significant barrier for startups with limited financial resources.
Managing customer and public perception	Public perception of AI can be mixed, and some customers might have reservations about interacting with AI systems. Managing these perceptions and ensuring transparent communication about how AI is used can be challenging but is essential for maintaining trust.
Keeping up with rapid technological changes	AI and its associated technologies are rapidly evolving, and keeping up with the latest developments, tools, and best practices can be overwhelming for startups. Continuous learning and adaptation are required to fully leverage the benefits of GenAI.

Source: Loureiro *et al.* (2021), Lee *et al.* (2024), and Bessen *et al.* (2022).

5. Integrating Human Intuition with AI for Enhanced Decision-Making

Integrating human intuition with AI enhances decision-making processes by combining the computational efficiency of AI with the nuanced understanding of humans. This convergence facilitates a more dynamic and flexible decision-making framework that adapts to unexpected changes and recognizes the subtleties of human emotions and social dynamics (Von Garrel & Jahn, 2023). Human intuition adds a layer of creativity and ethical consideration that AI alone cannot replicate, leading to decisions that are effective, ethically sound, and socially responsible. To achieve this integration effectively, organizations must foster an environment where human insights are valued and AI tools are seen as complementary assets rather than replacements for human decision makers. Training programs that emphasize the importance of this synergy and technologies that facilitate seamless collaboration between human intuition and AI analytics will be crucial for businesses aiming to leverage the full potential of their decision-making capabilities.

Entrepreneurs often develop "expert intuition" through years of experience and exposure to a wide range of situations. This ability to recognize patterns allows them to make quick, informed decisions. For example, seasoned startup founders or experienced CEOs may rely on their intuition to identify promising business opportunities.

"You can't connect the dots looking forward, you can only connect them looking backward. So you have to trust that the dots will somehow connect in your future. You have to trust in something — your gut, destiny, life, karma, whatever. This approach has never let me down, and it has made all the difference in my life" (Steve Jobs in his Stanford University graduation speech, 2005).

Making quick decisions is invaluable in the fast-paced startup environment. The main advantages of intuition over AI include intuition allowing entrepreneurs to make prompt decisions by synthesizing complex and incomplete information without requiring extensive data analysis. This capability is particularly crucial in the early stages of a startup, where speed and agility can determine market positioning and survival.

5.1. *Pattern recognition and opportunity identification*

Entrepreneurs often succeed by identifying patterns and opportunities that are not apparent to others. Intuitive processes enable the recognition of subtle cues and emerging trends that may be overlooked by AI systems, which require explicit programming or significant historical data to identify patterns.

5.2. *Emotional and social intelligence*

Startups require technical skills and the ability to navigate human emotions and social interactions. Intuition is closely linked to emotional intelligence, enabling entrepreneurs to understand and respond effectively to the emotional states of customers, investors, and employees. This aspect of intuition is critical in leadership, negotiation, and building customer relationships, where AI cannot fully replicate human nuanced understanding.

5.3. *Creativity and innovation*

Intuition plays a critical role in creativity and innovation, which are essential for startups aiming to disrupt markets with novel products or services. Unlike AI, which typically extends existing ideas, intuition can lead to groundbreaking innovations by making non-linear, imaginative leaps. Intuitive insights often lead to unique business ideas and creative problem-solving strategies that are not derived from existing data.

5.4. *Complementarity of intuition and AI*

While this chapter emphasizes the superiority of intuition in certain aspects of startup development, it also acknowledges the complementary role of AI. Integrating intuitive decision-making with AI-driven data analysis can provide a more holistic approach to business strategy. This integration allows startups to leverage the speed and efficiency of AI while maintaining the human touch essential for creative and ethical decision-making.

6. Conclusions

By integrating AI, intuition, and innovative business models, an entrepreneur can significantly expedite decision-making processes within their startup. AI's ability to analyze and interpret large datasets offers a foundation for making informed decisions quickly and more accurately. When combined with human intuition, which brings in elements of creativity, empathy, and ethical considerations, the decision-making process becomes more holistic. Furthermore, by continuously innovating business models, organizations can ensure that their strategies remain relevant and responsive to market demands. This synergy between technology, human insight/hindsight/foresight, and strategic innovation enables companies to make decisions more quickly and ensure that these decisions are well rounded, taking into account both quantitative data and qualitative human insights. This approach accelerates decision-making and enhances the quality of the decisions made, leading to more sustainable growth and competitive advantage in the dynamic business environment. Instead of relying on one specific approach or tool, startups must strive to strike a balance between AI and human intuition.

As technology evolves, so too will the ways in which AI and intuition contribute to decision-making within startups. We can anticipate advancements in AI that learn from vast datasets and understand the context of decisions, making integration with human intuition even more seamless. Future AI systems could potentially offer predictions and insights that are highly adapted to specific startup cultures and goals, allowing for decisions that are not just smart in the data-driven sense but also wise, with a deep understanding of human values and ethics.

Organizations will likely adopt more sophisticated AI models that can handle ambiguity and complexity similar to human intuition, thus opening up new possibilities for solving unprecedented challenges. Developing AI tools designed to enhance human creativity and ethical reasoning could further elevate the decision-making process. The ongoing convergence of AI technology with human cognitive and emotional strengths promises a future where decision-making is more efficient, innovative, and aligned with the broader objectives of humanity and society. As such, startups must continue to embrace and adapt to these advancements to stay competitive in the ever-evolving business landscape. So instead of relying on one specific approach or tool, organizations must strive to balance AI, human intuition, and organizational culture for successful decision-making. With this integration, businesses can harness the power of technology while maintaining their ethical standards and achieving long-term goals. With this approach, we can move toward a future where AI and human intuition work hand in hand, paving the way for innovative solutions to complex problems. This synergy will enhance decision-making and foster a more inclusive, ethical, and creative organizational environment.

While AI offers significant processing power and operational efficiency advantages, intuition provides a competitive edge in areas critical to startup success, including decision-making in uncertain environments, emotional intelligence, and innovative capacity. For startups navigating the complex and rapidly changing business landscape, fostering a balance between intuitive insights and AI capabilities can lead to more robust business model and sustainable and successful outcomes.

References

Adams, S. (2019). Surfing the hype cycle to infinity and beyond: Anticipating coming technology transformations means watching the waves of change to find the right wave to catch and the right time to catch it. *Research-Technology Management*, 62(3): 45+.

Bahoo, S., Cucculelli, M., & Qamar, D. (2023). Artificial intelligence and corporate innovation: A review and research agenda. *Technological Forecasting and Social Change*, 188: 122264.

Bessen, J., Impink, S., & Seamans, R. (2022). The cost of ethical AI development for AI startups. *2022 AAAI/ACM Conference on AI, Ethics, and Society*, Oxford, UK, May 19–21, pp. 92–106.

Blank, S. & Dorf, B. (2020). *The Startup Owner's Manual: The Step-by-Step Guide for Building a Great Company*. London: John Wiley & Sons and Springer Science & Business Media.

Blank, S. (2013). Why the lean start-up changes everything. *Harvard Business Review*, May: 1–9.

Brem, A., Giones, F., & Werle, M. (2021). The AI digital revolution in innovation: A conceptual framework of artificial intelligence technologies for the management of innovation. *IEEE Transactions on Engineering Management*, 70(2): 770–776.

CB Insights (2019). The top 20 reasons startups fail. Report. https://www.cbinsights.com/research/startup-failure-post-mortem/.

Chen, C. (2006). CiteSpace II: Detecting and visualizing emerging trends and transient patterns in scientific literature. *Journal of the American Society for Information Science and Technology*, 57(3): 359–377.

Dane, E., Rockmann, K., & Pratt, M. (2012). When should I trust my gut? Linking domain expertise to intuitive decision-making effectiveness. *Organizational Behavior and Human Decision Processes*, 119(2): 187–194.

De Dreu, C. K. W. (2003). Time pressure and closing of the mind in negotiation, *Organizational Behavior and Human Decision Processes*, 91(2): 280–295.

Gobet, F. & Philippe, C. (2009). Expertise and intuition: A tale of three theories. *Minds and Machines*, 19(2): 151–180.

Gore, J. & Sadler-Smith, E. (2011). Unpacking intuition: A process and outcome framework. *Review of General Psychology*, 15(4): 304–316.

Gupta, G. & Bose, I. (2022). Digital transformation in entrepreneurial firms through information exchange with operating environment. *Information & Management*, 59(3): 103243.

Gupta, V. & Yang, H. (2024). Study protocol for factors influencing the adoption of ChatGPT technology by startups: Perceptions and attitudes of entrepreneurs. *PLoS ONE*, 19(2): e0298427.

Jorzik, P., Yigit, A., Kanbach, D. K., Kraus, S., & Dabić, M. (2024). Artificial intelligence-enabled business model innovation: Competencies and roles of top management. *IEEE Transactions on Engineering Management*, 71: 7044–7056.

Julmi, C. (2019). When ration decision-making becomes irrational: A critical assessment and re-conceptualization of intuition effectiveness. *Business Research*, 12(1): 291–314.

Kakar, A. (2024). *Driving Venture Capital Funding Efficiencies Through Data Driven Models. Why Is This Important and What Are Its Implications for the Startup Ecosystem*? Doctoral Thesis, Durham University. https://etheses.dur.ac.uk/15363/.

Kuzior, A., Sira, M., & Brożek, P. (2023). Use of artificial intelligence in terms of open innovation process and management. *Sustainability*, 15(9): 7205.

Lee, B., Kim, B., & Ureta, V. I. (2024). Enhancing the competitiveness of AI technology-based startups in the digital era. *Administrative Sciences*, 14(1): 6.

Lisa, S., Ibrahim, D. Y., & Borges, G. L. (2020). The success of startups through digital transformation. *International Journal of Open Information Technologies*, 8(5): 53–56.

Loureiro, S, Guerreiro, J., & Tussyadiah, I. (2021). Artificial intelligence in business: State of the art and future research agenda. *Journal of Business Research*, 129: 911–926.

Markovitch, S. & Willmott, P. (2014). Accelerating the digitization of business processes. *McKinsey.com*.

Mishra, S. & Mishra, P. (2023). AI business models and its impact on business strategic framework. *International Journal of Financial Engineering*, 10(02): 2350001.

Mishra, S. & Tripathi, A. R. (2021). AI business model: An integrative business approach. *Journal of Innovation and Entrepreneurship*, 10(1).

Moore, G. A. (2014). *Crossing the Chasm: Marketing and Selling Disruptive Products to Mainstream Customers*, 3rd Edition. New York, NY: Harper Business.

Osterwalder, A., Pigneur, Y., Clark, T., & Smith, A. (2010). *Business Model Generation: A Handbook for Visionaries, Game Changers, and Challengers*. Hoboken, NJ: John Wiley & Sons.

Ozgur, D. & Steinert, M. (2016). The hype cycle model: A review and future directions. *Technological Forecasting and Social Change*, 108: 28–41.

Prophet Open Source Predictive and Forecasting Analytics (2023). https://pypi.org/project/prophet/ and https://facebook.github.io/prophet/.

Ries, E. (2011). *The Lean Startup: How Today's Entrepreneurs Use Continuous Innovation to Create Radically Successful Businesses*. New York, NY: Crown Currency.

Sreenivasan, A. & Suresh, M. (2023). Digital transformation in start-ups: A bibliometric analysis. *Digital Transformation and Society*, 2(3): 276–292.

Startup Genome (2019). *Global Startup Ecosystem Report*. https://startupgenome.com/reports/global-startup-ecosystem-report-2019.

Tischlinger, D. & Van Wordragen, B. (2019). *What are the Critical Success Factors of Start-Ups in the Digital Transformation*? A Multiple Case-Study, Master Thesis, 92.

Von Garrel, J. & Jahn, C. (2023). Design framework for the implementation of AI-based (service) business models for small and medium-sized manufacturing enterprises. *Journal of the Knowledge Economy*, 14(3): 3551–3569.

Weber, M., Beutter, M., Weking, J., Böhm, M., & Krcmar, H. (2022). AI startup business models. *Business & Information Systems Engineering*, 64(1): 91–109.

Wickman, G. (2012). *Traction: Get a Grip on Your Business*, Expanded Edition. BenBella Books, Dallas, Texas.

Wonder, J. & Blake, J. (1992). Creativity east and west: Intuition vs. logic? *The Journal of Creative Behavior*, 26(3): 172–185.

World Economic Forum (2021). Waves of change: Understanding the driving force of innovation cycles. https://www.weforum.org/agenda/2021/07/this-is-a-visualization-of-the-history-of-innovation-cycles/.

https://doi.org/10.1142/9789811296475_0005

Chapter 5

Human-Centric and AI-Centric Approaches in Organizational AI Implementation

Oren Eilam

Bitaon Shira, Israel

1. Introduction

Artificial intelligence (AI) is transforming industries and society at an unprecedented pace. AI can automate tasks, enhance decision-making, enable new products and services, and drive innovation and efficiency across sectors (Davenport, 2018; Daugherty & Wilson, 2018).

The rapid AI advancements have been fueled by the growth in data (Agrawal *et al.*, 2018), increasingly powerful computing resources (Langlotz *et al.*, 2019), and new AI architectures and techniques, such as deep learning and reinforcement learning (LeCun *et al.*, 2015).

As a result, AI has moved from research into the mainstream. Organizations of all sizes recognize AI's potential to transform operations, products, and services (Ransbotham *et al.*, 2019). AI is being applied across industries, including health care, finance, retail, manufacturing, transportation, agriculture, and energy (Chui *et al.*, 2018; Pallathadka *et al.*, 2023a,b).

However, AI also raises significant challenges and concerns. Organizations struggle with AI system complexity, talent scarcity, and integration difficulties (Davenport & Ronanki, 2018). There are growing concerns about AI's ethical and societal implications, such as bias, job impact (Dastin, 2022; Noble, 2018), and unintended consequences (Bostrom, 2014).

Organizations face critical choices in AI adoption between human-centric AI, prioritizing human needs and values, and AI-centric AI, focused on maximizing AI performance and efficiency (Raisch & Krakowski, 2021; Shneiderman, 2020b, 2022).

This choice has significant implications for AI success, ethics, and societal impact. Organizations must consider trade-offs between human and AI capabilities, the evolving nature of work, and the interplay of technological, organizational, and societal factors.

This chapter provides an analysis of the human-centric and AI-centric approaches to AI implementation in organizations. By examining the principles, strategies, and implications of these approaches, we aim to contribute to the growing academic literature on organizational AI implementation and help organizations make informed decisions about their AI adoption and implementation strategies.

2. Human-Centric Approach to AI Implementation

2.1. *Definition and principles of human-centric AI*

Human-centric AI is an approach that prioritizes human values, needs, and interests in the design, development, and deployment of AI systems. It aims to ensure AI technologies align with human goals, augment human capabilities, and respect human autonomy and dignity (Shneiderman, 2020b, 2022).

The key principles of human-centric AI are as follows:

1. **Human agency and oversight:** AI systems should support and enhance human decision-making, with humans retaining meaningful control (Amershi *et al.*, 2019b).
2. **Transparency and explainability:** AI systems should be transparent about their capabilities, limitations, and decision-making processes, providing clear explanations (Arrieta *et al.*, 2020).

3. **Fairness and non-discrimination:** AI systems should avoid biases and ensure fair treatment of all individuals and groups (Mehrabi *et al.*, 2021).
4. **Privacy and security:** AI systems should respect privacy rights, protect personal data, and incorporate robust security measures (Floridi & Cowls, 2019).
5. **Accountability and redress:** AI systems should have clear mechanisms for accountability and redress in the case of errors, failures, or harmful outcomes (Diakopoulos, 2016).
6. **Human values and ethical considerations:** AI systems should align with human values and ethical principles, considering broader societal and long-term implications (Jobin *et al.*, 2019).

Human-centric AI aims to create trustworthy, beneficial, and aligned AI systems through interdisciplinary collaboration (Shneiderman, 2020b, 2022). However, implementation can be challenging, requiring a balance of technical, economic, and social considerations, ongoing dialog, and adaptation. Organizations adopting human-centric AI must invest in necessary skills, processes, and governance mechanisms to ensure responsible and effective AI development and deployment (Xu *et al.*, 2023).

2.2. *Importance of human involvement in AI development and deployment*

The human-centric approach emphasizes the crucial role of human involvement throughout the AI development and deployment lifecycle to ensure AI systems align with human values, needs, and expectations. Human judgment and oversight are critical in shaping AI systems' performance and impact (Pasquale, 2020).

Human involvement is essential in defining problems and goals for AI systems. Humans must work with domain experts and stakeholders to identify the right problems, define measurable objectives, and specify ethical and societal constraints (Bryson & Winfield, 2017). Failure to involve humans can result in AI systems misaligned with human values or having unintended consequences.

Human involvement is also necessary for preparing and curating training data. Humans must ensure data quality, representativeness, and fairness and document assumptions, limitations, and potential biases (Gebru *et al.*, 2021; Miceli *et al.*, 2020).

Humans are essential in testing, validating, and monitoring AI systems. They must rigorously test AI systems, validate performance against benchmarks, monitor outputs for errors or anomalies, and establish clear processes for human oversight and intervention (Ribeiro *et al.*, 2020; Raji & Buolamwini, 2019).

Involvement of humans is critical in interpreting and communicating AI system outputs. Humans must translate outputs into actionable insights, provide explanations and context, facilitate human–AI interaction, and transparently communicate capabilities, limitations, and uncertainties (Miller, 2019; Shneiderman, 2022).

Finally, human involvement is essential in the ongoing monitoring and governance of AI systems. Humans must establish policies, procedures, and accountability mechanisms, ensure alignment with human values and legal and ethical standards, and engage in public dialog about AI's societal implications (Gasser & Almeida, 2017; Fjeld *et al.*, 2020).

By emphasizing human involvement throughout the AI lifecycle, organizations can create more transparent, accountable, and value-aligned AI systems, fostering greater trust and adoption. The success of AI depends not only on its technical capabilities but also on the human judgment, oversight, and collaboration guiding its development and use.

2.3. *Strategies for fostering human–AI collaboration*

According to the human-centric approach, organizations must foster effective human–AI collaboration to harness AI's potential and mitigate risks. This involves designing AI systems that augment human capabilities and developing practices, processes, and cultures supporting human–AI interaction and joint decision-making (Wilson & Daugherty, 2018).

Key strategies for fostering human–AI collaboration include the following:

1. Designing AI systems with human-centered interfaces and interaction modalities, which provide clear and intuitive ways for humans to input knowledge, preferences, and feedback, and interpret AI outputs (Amershi *et al.*, 2019b; Abdul *et al.*, 2018): This lowers barriers to collaboration and enables seamless integration of AI into human workflows.

2. Developing AI systems that provide explanations and justifications for their outputs using Explainable AI (XAI) techniques (Adadi & Berrada, 2018): This fosters trust and acceptance and enables humans to spot errors, biases, or limitations in AI outputs (Ribeiro *et al.*, 2016) and provide targeted feedback (Lage *et al.*, 2019).
3. Establishing clear roles and responsibilities for humans and AI systems in decision-making processes and defining tasks performed by AI and those remaining under human control (Jarrahi, 2018): This ensures AI is used appropriately and humans retain meaningful control (Shneiderman, 2020a, 2022).
4. Investing in training and education programs to help humans develop skills and knowledge to work effectively with AI systems, including technical and non-technical skills (Luo *et al.*, 2019): This fosters a culture of continuous learning and experimentation encourages employees to explore new ways of using AI (Raisch & Krakowski, 2021).
5. Involving diverse stakeholders in the design, development, and governance of AI systems, including AI experts, domain experts, end-users, policymakers, and the public (Fjeld *et al.*, 2020): This ensures AI systems align with human values and needs, and potential risks are mitigated. Participatory design and co-creation methodologies help build transparent, accountable, and societally aligned AI systems (Lee *et al.*, 2019).

By implementing these strategies and building a culture of human–AI collaboration, organizations can create AI systems that augment human capabilities while ensuring responsible and ethical AI development and use. Leveraging the strengths of both humans and AI systems unlocks new forms of value creation, innovation, and competitive advantage.

2.4. *Adaptability and future-proofing potential of human-centric approaches*

Human-centric approaches to AI development and deployment offer several advantages for future-proofing and enabling organizations to navigate the evolving AI landscape.

One key advantage is the emphasis on developing human capabilities and skills alongside AI systems. Investing in AI literacy and collaboration skills training helps foster an adaptable and resilient workforce (Wilson & Daugherty, 2018). As AI technologies evolve, employees with a strong foundation in these skills can better adapt to new tools and workflows, avoiding skill obsolescence.

Human-centric AI approaches also prioritize the development of AI systems that augment and empower human decision-making rather than replacing it entirely (Raisch & Krakowski, 2021). This collaborative approach allows organizations to leverage human expertise and judgment while benefiting from AI's data processing and pattern recognition capabilities. By striking the right balance between human and AI agency, organizations can create more resilient and adaptable decision-making processes that can withstand the uncertainties of the future (Grønsund & Aanestad, 2020).

Another advantage is the emphasis on ethical and responsible AI development practices. Embedding the principles of transparency, fairness, and accountability into AI system design and governance helps ensure alignment with human values and societal expectations over time (Leslie, 2019). Proactively addressing ethical and societal concerns helps build and maintain public trust in AI technologies.

Human-centric approaches recognize the importance of diverse perspectives and interdisciplinary collaboration in shaping AI's future (Fjeld *et al.*, 2020). Involving non-technical stakeholders in AI development and governance ensures socially and culturally appropriate AI technologies and fosters creative and innovative solutions.

Finally, human-centric approaches emphasize continuous learning and adaptation as AI technologies and societal conditions change. Establishing mechanisms for regular feedback, evaluation, and improvement of AI systems ensures AI strategies remain relevant and effective over time (Robert *et al.*, 2020a).

While human-centric approaches offer significant potential for adaptability and future-proofing, they also come with challenges, such as the time, resources, and organizational change required. Organizations must navigate trade-offs between efficiency and control and find the right balance of human and AI capabilities.

Ultimately, successful human-centric AI adoption requires embracing a mindset of continuous learning, experimentation, and adaptation, staying attuned to the evolving AI landscape and stakeholder expectations. By putting humans at the center of AI development and use, organizations can unlock AI's full potential while ensuring alignment with human values and interests over the long term.

2.5. *Case studies and examples of human-centric implementation*

Some of the following real-world case studies demonstrate how organizations have successfully leveraged human-centric principles to develop and deploy AI systems that augment human capabilities while addressing ethical and societal concerns:

1. **IBM's Watson for Oncology:** This cognitive computing system assists oncologists in making evidence-based cancer treatment decisions. It combines natural language processing, machine learning, medical literature, and patient data to provide personalized treatment recommendations. However, it is designed to support and enhance, rather than replace, the expertise and judgment of human oncologists, who review recommendations, consider patient preferences and contextual factors, and make final treatment decisions (Somashekhar *et al.*, 2017).
2. **XAI in financial services:** XAI provides clear and interpretable explanations for AI system decisions and predictions, enabling human users to understand, trust, and audit these systems (Arrieta *et al.*, 2020; Van der Velden *et al.*, 2022). FICO's Explainable Machine Learning Challenge promotes the development of XAI techniques for credit scoring decisions (Rudin & Radin, 2019), fostering trust and accountability in AI-based financial decision-making while complying with regulatory and ethical standards.
3. **Adaptive learning systems in education:** The Generalized Intelligent Framework for Tutoring (GIFT) is an open-source platform that supports the design and delivery of adaptive tutoring systems (Sottilare *et al.*, 2017). It uses machine learning to model student knowledge, skills, and affective states, providing tailored feedback and guidance. However, it also incorporates human tutors and subject matter experts to monitor student progress, adjust instructional strategies, and provide additional support, combining AI-driven personalization with human oversight and intervention.
4. **Human-centric AI in smart cities and urban planning:** Initiatives in cities like Amsterdam and Helsinki leverage AI technologies to address urban challenges while promoting public participation and civic engagement (Floridi, 2020). Residents are encouraged to

provide input and feedback on AI systems in their communities. This human-centric and participatory approach to AI governance ensures AI technologies serve citizens' needs and values, foster public trust and accountability, and promote inclusive and sustainable urban development.

These case studies illustrate the diverse applications of human-centric AI across industries, prioritizing human involvement, explainability, adaptability, and ethical alignment. As AI continues to advance, organizations and policymakers should learn from these examples and adopt human-centric principles in the design, development, and governance of AI technologies.

3. AI-Centric Approach to AI Implementation

3.1. *Definition and principles of AI-centric approach*

The AI-centric approach prioritizes the development and deployment of AI systems that can operate autonomously and optimize performance based on predefined objectives and metrics. Unlike human-centric approaches, which focus on augmenting human decision-making, AI-centric approaches aim to maximize the efficiency, accuracy, and scalability of AI systems, often with minimal human intervention (Russell & Norvig, 2021).

Key principles of the AI-centric approach include the following:

1. **Autonomy:** Developing AI systems that can operate independently, learn from data, adapt to changing environments, and optimize performance based on specified goals and constraints (Barocas *et al.*, 2023).
2. **Efficiency:** Prioritizing AI systems that can process large volumes of data quickly and accurately, leveraging advanced computing infrastructure (Gill *et al.*, 2022).
3. **Scalability:** Designing modular and reusable AI components that can be easily scaled up or down depending on the problem domain's size and complexity (Mungoli, 2023).
4. **Optimization:** Developing AI systems that continuously improve performance based on predefined objectives and metrics, using techniques such as reinforcement learning, evolutionary algorithms, and automated machine learning (He *et al.*, 2021).

5. **Specialization:** Prioritizing narrow or specialized AI systems optimized for specific tasks or domains allows for more focused and efficient development but potentially limits generalizability and adaptability (Hajikhani & Cole, 2024).

The AI-centric approach has been driven by rapid advancements in AI technologies and the increasing availability of large-scale datasets and computing resources. It has been influential in domains such as online advertising, fraud detection, and supply chain optimization, where speed, accuracy, and scale are critical (Ransbotham *et al.*, 2019).

However, the AI-centric approach has limitations and challenges. By prioritizing autonomy and efficiency, it may neglect human factors, such as transparency, accountability, and fairness. It may also be more vulnerable to biases, errors, and unexpected failures or unintended consequences (Selbst *et al.*, 2019). The focus on specialized AI systems may limit adaptability to changing circumstances or complex problems requiring holistic approaches.

To mitigate these challenges, organizations adopting AI-centric approaches may need to invest in additional safeguards and governance mechanisms, such as algorithmic auditing, explainability techniques, and human oversight (Koshiyama *et al.*, 2021). They may also need to balance the benefits of autonomy and efficiency with the need for human involvement and collaboration, particularly in high-stakes applications.

3.2. *Focus on AI capabilities and potential*

The AI-centric approach emphasizes maximizing the capabilities and potential of AI technologies by investing heavily in advanced AI algorithms, architectures, and infrastructures that push the boundaries of what is possible (Chui *et al.*, 2018).

One key focus is developing deep learning techniques that automatically learn hierarchical representations and features from large-scale datasets (Goodfellow *et al.*, 2016). Deep learning has achieved breakthrough performance in domains such as image and speech recognition, natural language processing, and game playing, often surpassing human-level performance on specific tasks (LeCun *et al.*, 2015). Leveraging deep learning and other advanced AI techniques can unlock new opportunities for automation, optimization, and innovation across industries and applications.

Another focus is developing reinforcement learning and adaptive AI systems that learn from experience and improve performance over time (Sutton & Barto, 2018). Reinforcement learning has been used to train AI agents to play complex games, control robots, and optimize system configurations, discovering novel strategies and solutions (Silver *et al.*, 2017). Developing AI systems that continuously learn and adapt to changing environments and objectives creates more resilient and dynamic applications that handle uncertainty and variability.

AI-centric approaches also prioritize developing large-scale AI infrastructures and platforms supporting the training, deployment, and management of complex AI systems (Ratner *et al.*, 2019). This includes investing in high-performance computing hardware, distributed computing frameworks, and cloud-based AI services and APIs (Ishakian *et al.*, 2018).

In addition to technical investments, AI-centric approaches focus on building organizational capabilities and cultures supporting AI innovation and experimentation, such as dedicated AI research and development teams, collaborations with academic institutions and industry partners (Ransbotham *et al.*, 2017), and agile development processes (Amershi *et al.*, 2019a).

However, the focus on AI capabilities and potential raises challenges and risks, such as the potential for AI systems to perpetuate biases and inequities (Barocas & Selbst, 2016) or have unintended consequences and negative externalities (Zuboff, 2019). Organizations adopting AI-centric approaches may need to invest in safeguards and governance mechanisms, such as algorithmic impact assessments, explainability techniques, and human oversight (Wirtz *et al.*, 2023), and engage in stakeholder engagement and communication to build trust and ensure alignment with societal values and expectations (Leslie, 2019).

Thus, while the focus on AI capabilities and potential in AI-centric approaches can enable organizations to push boundaries and create new forms of value and innovation, it is important to balance this focus with recognition of AI systems' limitations and risks and to develop responsible and ethical AI practices ensuring long-term benefits for individuals, organizations, and society.

3.3. *Strategies for optimizing AI performance and efficiency*

To fully realize the potential of AI-centric approaches, organizations should adopt strategies and practices that optimize the performance and efficiency of their AI systems. This involves technical, operational, and organizational measures that enable AI systems to learn, adapt, and improve over time while ensuring scalability, reliability, and cost-effectiveness.

Key strategies for optimizing AI performance include the following:

1. Advanced techniques for model selection, training, and tuning, such as automated machine learning (AutoML) tools and frameworks that automatically search for the best models and hyperparameters (He *et al.*, 2021): This reduces development time and effort while improving accuracy and robustness.
2. Transfer learning and pre-trained models that leverage knowledge and features learned from related tasks or domains (Pan & Yang, 2010): This reduces data and computation requirements while improving generalization and adaptation capabilities.
3. Efficient and scalable computing infrastructures, such as distributed computing frameworks (Zaharia *et al.*, 2016) and specialized hardware (Konda & Shah, 2021): This reduces the time and cost of AI development and deployment while enabling more complex and data-intensive applications.
4. Model compression and acceleration techniques, such as quantization, pruning, and knowledge distillation (Cheng *et al.*, 2017): This reduces the size and computational requirements of AI models while preserving accuracy and performance, enabling efficient deployment on resource-constrained devices.

Effective data management and governance practices, such as data pipelines and workflows (Polyzotis *et al.*, 2017) and data versioning and lineage tools (Schelter *et al.*, 2017), can also optimize AI performance and efficiency by ensuring data quality, consistency, and accessibility.

Continuous monitoring, testing, and improvement of AI systems, using monitoring and alerting tools (Breck *et al.*, 2017) and A/B testing and experimentation platforms (Tang *et al.*, 2010), can ensure that AI systems remain relevant, effective, and aligned with goals and strategies over time.

While these strategies can help optimize AI performance and efficiency, they require significant investments in skills, tools, and processes. Organizations need to develop talent and expertise in data science, machine learning, and AI engineering while fostering collaboration and knowledge sharing. They also need to establish clear governance and accountability mechanisms, ensuring responsible and ethical AI development and use while balancing innovation, agility, and compliance.

3.4. *Modularity, scalability, and adaptability of AI-centric approaches*

AI-centric approaches often prioritize developing modular, scalable, and adaptable AI systems that can be easily integrated, extended, and modified to meet changing business requirements and technological landscapes. These characteristics enable more agile, efficient, and resilient AI deployments for long-term value creation and competitive advantage.

Modularity refers to designing AI systems as loosely coupled, independently deployable components or services that can be combined and reconfigured in various ways (Baldwin & Clark, 2000; Schilling, 2000; Sun & Guyon, 2023). Modular AI architectures, such as microservices or serverless functions, allow decomposing complex systems into smaller, manageable units that can be developed, tested, and deployed separately. This enables faster, incremental development, easier maintenance, and updating of individual components without affecting the entire system. Modularity also facilitates the reuse and sharing of AI components across projects and domains, reducing duplication and increasing consistency.

Scalability refers to the ability of AI systems to handle increasing amounts of data, users, and requests without compromising performance or efficiency (Mungoli, 2023). Scalable AI architectures, such as distributed computing clusters or cloud-based platforms, allow dynamic allocation and provisioning of computing resources based on the changing workload and demand. This enables organizations to start small and scale up AI deployments as needed while optimizing resource utilization and cost. Scalability is crucial for AI applications involving real-time or near-real-time processing of large data volumes.

Adaptability refers to the ability of AI systems to learn, evolve, and improve over time based on new data, feedback, or requirements (Kadlec & Gabrys, 2009). Adaptable AI architectures, such as online learning or reinforcement learning, allow continuous updating and refinement of AI models based on the changing environment and user needs. This enables organizations to adapt more quickly and effectively to new market trends, customer preferences, or competitive landscape. Adaptability is crucial for AI applications involving dynamic or non-stationary data.

To achieve modularity, scalability, and adaptability in AI-centric approaches, organizations can adopt best practices and patterns, such as microservices architecture, containerization and orchestration, serverless computing, transfer learning and fine-tuning, and continual learning and adaptation.

While these practices can help build more modular, scalable, and adaptable AI systems, they also require significant investments in skills, tools, and processes. Organizations need expertise in cloud computing, DevOps, and AI engineering while establishing governance and security frameworks ensuring reliability, safety, and compliance. They also need to foster a culture of experimentation, collaboration, and continuous improvement.

The modularity, scalability, and adaptability of AI-centric approaches depend not only on technical choices and practices but also on organizational and human factors shaping the design, development, and operation of AI systems. As organizations navigate the complexities and uncertainties of AI, they need to balance the benefits and risks of AI-centric approaches while ensuring alignment with stakeholders' values, goals, and contexts.

3.5. *Case studies and examples of AI-centric implementation*

Some of the following real-world case studies and examples illustrate the potential and challenges of AI-centric approaches across different industries, domains, and applications:

1. DeepMind's AlphaFold system revolutionized protein structure prediction using deep learning, achieving unprecedented accuracy and speed (Jumper *et al.*, 2021). AlphaFold demonstrates the power of AI-centric approaches to tackle complex scientific challenges and has the potential to accelerate drug discovery, disease diagnosis, and biomaterials design.
2. NVIDIA's autonomous vehicle platform leverages deep learning, computer vision, and sensor fusion techniques to enable self-driving cars

(Rao & Frtunikj, 2018). By providing an end-to-end solution, NVIDIA has enabled car manufacturers and suppliers to accelerate the development and deployment of self-driving technologies while ensuring safety, reliability, and scalability.
3. Amazon has pioneered AI-centric approaches in the retail industry to optimize operations and customer experiences. Amazon's AI systems span recommendation engines (Hardesty, 2019), demand forecasting, warehouse robotics, and delivery drones, achieving significant improvements in efficiency, customer satisfaction, and revenue growth.
4. In health care, AI-centric approaches have shown promising results in improving patient outcomes, reducing costs, and accelerating medical research (Esteva *et al.*, 2019).

4. Comparative Analysis of Human-Centric and AI-Centric Approaches

4.1. *Key differences and similarities between the two approaches*

Human-centric and AI-centric approaches to AI adoption differ in their focus, priorities, and decision-making processes but share the common goal of leveraging AI for business value and innovation.

The key differences include the following:

- **Human involvement:** Human-centric approaches prioritize human oversight, collaboration, and adaptability (Rai, 2020), while AI-centric approaches prioritize automation, efficiency, and scalability, minimizing human intervention (Kaplan & Haenlein, 2020).
- **Ethical and societal considerations:** Human-centric approaches emphasize alignment with human values, fairness, and transparency (Shneiderman, 2020b, 2022), prioritizing explainable and accountable AI. AI-centric approaches may prioritize performance and efficiency over interpretability and transparency (Shin & Park, 2019).
- **Decision-making processes:** Human-centric approaches emphasize human-in-the-loop decision-making, combining AI insights with human judgment (Malone, 2018; Mosqueira-Rey *et al.*, 2023; Wu *et al.*, 2022).
- AI-centric approaches may seek to automate decision-making entirely, relying on AI algorithms (Agrawal *et al.*, 2018).

Similarities include the following:

- Both approaches recognize AI's transformative potential in improving efficiency, productivity, and decision-making across domains and industries.
- Both emphasize the importance of data quality, model performance, and continuous learning for effective and reliable AI systems.

As AI technologies advance, the boundaries between human-centric and AI-centric approaches may blur, leading to hybrid approaches that combine the strengths of both (Rai *et al.*, 2019). These hybrid approaches balance human oversight and collaboration with AI automation efficiency and scalability, adapting to specific organizational and industry needs.

4.2. *Strengths and limitations of each approach*

As AI technologies evolve and mature, the strengths and limitations of human-centric and AI-centric approaches become increasingly relevant in shaping the future of AI adoption. Each approach offers distinct advantages and challenges in the context of technological advancements.

Human-centric approaches have several strengths:

- By prioritizing human involvement, oversight, and collaboration, they ensure AI systems remain aligned with human values, goals, and interests (Robert *et al.*, 2020a).
- They provide a framework for addressing ethical and responsible AI development concerns by emphasizing transparency, accountability, and fairness (Shneiderman, 2020b, 2022).
- By fostering human–AI collaboration and leveraging complementary strengths, they enable organizations to adapt effectively to changing business needs and societal expectations (Daugherty & Wilson, 2018).

However, human-centric approaches also face limitations:

- As AI systems become more complex and autonomous, humans' ability to understand, interpret, and control their behavior may diminish (Lyytinen *et al.*, 2020), challenging transparency, accountability, and trust.

- The emphasis on human involvement and oversight may limit the speed, efficiency, and scalability of AI adoption, potentially putting organizations at a competitive disadvantage (Wirtz *et al.*, 2023).

AI-centric approaches offer strengths in efficiency, scalability, and technological capabilities:

- By prioritizing automation and optimization, they enable organizations to leverage AI's full potential in processing vast amounts of data, identifying insights, and making rapid, accurate decisions (Agrawal *et al.*, 2018).
- As AI technologies advance, AI-centric approaches help organizations stay at the forefront of innovation, continuously improving and adapting AI systems (Jordan & Mitchell, 2015).
- By minimizing the need for human intervention and oversight, they can reduce costs and complexities associated with human–AI collaboration, enabling more streamlined and agile AI deployment (Fountaine *et al.*, 2019).

However, AI-centric approaches also face limitations and risks:

- As AI systems become more autonomous and opaque, the potential for unintended consequences, biases, and errors increases (Bostrom, 2014).
- Without adequate human oversight and intervention, AI-centric approaches may lead to decisions and actions misaligned with organizational goals, societal values, and ethical principles (Gasser & Almeida, 2017).
- The focus on efficiency and automation may come at the cost of flexibility, adaptability, and resilience, leaving organizations vulnerable to technological disruptions and competitive shifts (Shukla & Mattar, 2019).

The strengths and limitations of human-centric and AI-centric approaches highlight the need for a balanced and context-specific approach to AI adoption. Hybrid approaches combining the best elements of both strategies may be beneficial (Raisch & Krakowski, 2021; Vial, 2021). By leveraging the strengths of human judgment, creativity, and adaptability alongside AI's efficiency, scalability, and technological capabilities, organizations can develop more resilient, responsible, and future-proof AI systems. This requires ongoing investment in AI governance, talent development, stakeholder engagement, and a willingness to experiment, learn, and adapt as the technology landscape evolves (Dwivedi *et al.*, 2021).

4.3. *Strategic considerations for AI investment*

Organizations navigating the complex landscape of AI adoption must consider strategic factors for investment timing and the choice of AI implementation approaches to determine the success and long-term value of AI initiatives. Key factors influencing AI investment decisions include the trade-offs between different investment strategies and the importance of balancing short-term and long-term considerations.

One primary strategic consideration is the balance between the potential benefits of early adoption and the risks of premature or misaligned investments. Early adopters may gain competitive advantages by leveraging AI's efficiency, scalability, and innovation potential before their peers (Bughin *et al.*, 2017), developing valuable expertise, data assets, and market positioning (Fountaine *et al.*, 2019). However, early AI investments also carry significant risks and uncertainties due to the rapid pace of technological change and the evolving AI landscape (Agrawal *et al.*, 2018). Premature or poorly aligned investments may result in suboptimal performance, wasted resources, or reputational damage (Davenport & Mittal, 2020).

Organizations must carefully consider the timing and scope of their AI investments based on strategic factors, such as industry dynamics, competitive landscape, market positioning, internal capabilities, resources, and risk tolerance (Lichtenthaler, 2018). The optimal approach may vary depending on the level of data intensity, automation potential, customer engagement, regulation, and social sensitivity in the organization's domain (Canhoto & Clear, 2020).

Choosing between different AI implementation approaches, such as human-centric, AI-centric, or hybrid, is a key strategic consideration. Each approach offers distinct strengths and limitations in terms of efficiency, scalability, adaptability, and ethical alignment (Rai *et al.*, 2019). Organizations must evaluate the trade-offs and complementarities between these approaches and their fit with the organization's overall strategy, culture, and values (Davenport & Ronanki, 2018).

Moreover, organizations must balance short-term and long-term considerations in their AI investment strategies. While short-term gains in efficiency, cost savings, or customer satisfaction can be attractive, organizations must also invest in the long-term foundations of successful AI adoption, such as data governance, talent development, and ethical frameworks (Davenport, 2018). A strategic and holistic view of AI investment ensures that AI initiatives are technically feasible, economically viable, socially responsible, and aligned with long-term goals and values (Merendino *et al.*, 2018).

Given the high levels of uncertainty and complexity surrounding AI technologies and their business implications, organizations are advised to prioritize flexibility and adaptability in their AI investment strategies (Reim *et al.*, 2021). This may involve adopting modular and scalable AI architectures, investing in continuous learning and experimentation, and fostering a culture of agility and resilience (Ghasemaghaei & Calic, 2020).

In conclusion, strategic considerations for AI investment timing and strategies are critical for organizations seeking to maximize value and minimize risks. Carefully evaluating the trade-offs between early and late adoption, human-centric and AI-centric approaches, and short-term and long-term priorities can help organizations develop more informed, balanced, and resilient AI investment strategies.

4.4. *The case for a hybrid approach: Balancing human and AI priorities over time*

As organizations grapple with the challenges and opportunities of AI adoption, the case for a hybrid approach that balances human and AI priorities over time becomes increasingly compelling. This section explores the key arguments for a hybrid approach, the strategies for developing a resilient and future-proof AI adoption strategy, and the role of return on investment (ROI) in shaping AI investment decisions.

As organizations grapple with AI adoption challenges and opportunities, a compelling case emerges for a hybrid approach that balances human and AI priorities over time (Raisch & Krakowski, 2021). The success of AI adoption depends not only on AI systems' technical capabilities but also on the effective integration of human and machine intelligence (Jarrahi, 2018). AI-centric approaches offer efficiency, scalability, and accuracy gains but may introduce bias, opacity, and misalignment risks with human values and goals (Tambe *et al.*, 2019). Human-centric approaches ensure greater transparency, accountability, and ethical alignment but may limit AI systems' speed, consistency, and data-driven insights (Rai *et al.*, 2019). A hybrid model combines both approaches' strengths, harnessing AI's power while preserving human judgment, creativity, and adaptability (Wilson & Daugherty, 2018).

The optimal balance between human and AI priorities may shift over time as technologies, business needs, and societal expectations evolve (Morikawa, 2017). As AI systems become more sophisticated and autonomous, humans' role may shift from direct control to higher-level supervision, governance, and value alignment (Jarrahi, 2018). Simultaneously, as AI adoption becomes more widespread and consequential, the need for human oversight, accountability, and ethical reflection may become more critical (Anderson & Anderson, 2018). A flexible, adaptable hybrid approach ensures AI strategies remain resilient and future-proof over time (Amabile, 2020).

To develop a resilient, future-proof AI adoption strategy, organizations can do the following:

- Invest in human–AI collaboration skills and practices, such as XAI, interactive machine learning, and participatory design (Robert *et al.*, 2020b), fostering transparency, trust, and shared understanding (Shneiderman, 2020b, 2022).
- Adopt a modular, adaptable AI architecture allowing easy addition, modification, or replacement of AI components as technologies and requirements change (Lyytinen *et al.*, 2020), reducing the risks of technical debt, vendor lock-in, and obsolescence (Mikkelsen & Shridharan, 2019).
- Establish robust governance frameworks and ethical guidelines ensuring responsible, accountable AI use (Gasser & Almeida, 2017), involving diverse stakeholders in AI policies, standards, and metrics development.
- Embrace continuous learning, experimentation, and adaptation, leveraging feedback loops, iterative development, and agile methodologies to respond rapidly to changing circumstances and optimize AI performance (Amabile, 2020).

ROI plays a critical role in shaping AI investment strategies and justifying and prioritizing initiatives (Fountaine *et al.*, 2019; Wirtz *et al.*, 2023).

While AI adoption benefits can be significant, costs and risks can also be substantial (Obwegeser *et al.*, 2019). Organizations must assess expected returns and payback periods, considering direct technology acquisition and development costs and indirect organizational change, process redesign, and talent upskilling costs (Balasubramanian *et al.*, 2022). They must also consider AI adoption's potential impacts on broader stakeholder value, such as customer satisfaction, employee well-being, and societal welfare, which may not be easily quantifiable in traditional ROI metrics.

To optimize AI investments' ROI, organizations can do the following:

- Prioritize AI use cases with clear, measurable links to business outcomes, such as revenue growth, cost reduction, or risk mitigation (Bughin *et al.*, 2017), generating quick wins and building momentum for broader adoption (Davenport & Ronanki, 2018).
- Adopt a staged, iterative approach, starting with small-scale pilots and proofs-of-concept before scaling to enterprise-wide deployments (Ransbotham *et al.*, 2019), reducing large-scale failure risks and optimizing strategies based on real-world feedback and performance (Amabile, 2020).
- Leverage external partnerships and ecosystems to access complementary AI skills, technologies, and best practices, reducing in-house development costs and risks, collaborating with vendors, research institutions, and industry consortia to accelerate adoption and benefit from shared knowledge and resources (Rane, 2023).
- Establish clear metrics and governance mechanisms for measuring and communicating AI investments' value, ensuring transparency, accountability, and alignment with strategic priorities (Enholm *et al.*, 2022).

In conclusion, a strong, growing case exists for a hybrid approach to AI adoption balancing human and AI priorities over time. By leveraging human and machine intelligence strengths, organizations can develop more resilient, adaptable, and socially responsible AI strategies, generating sustainable value for all stakeholders. Realizing this potential requires a strategic, holistic approach to AI investments, prioritizing human–AI collaboration, ethical governance, continuous learning, and measurable ROI. AI adoption success depends on organizations' ability to navigate the complex, evolving AI landscape while staying true to their core values and purpose.

5. Conclusions

The growing adoption of AI technologies presents significant opportunities and challenges for organizations. The choice between human-centric and AI-centric approaches to AI implementation has emerged as a critical strategic consideration with far-reaching implications for organizational performance, ethical alignment, and societal impact.

This chapter has analyzed the key principles, strategies, and trade-offs associated with human-centric and AI-centric approaches. Human-centric approaches prioritize human oversight, collaboration, and adaptability, ensuring alignment with human values and goals, while AI-centric approaches emphasize automation, efficiency, and scalability, leveraging AI's full potential for data-driven insights and decision-making.

The comparative analysis highlights the strengths and limitations of each approach in the context of rapidly evolving AI technologies and business landscapes. While human-centric approaches offer greater transparency, accountability, and ethical alignment but may face challenges in keeping pace with AI-driven innovation, AI-centric approaches enable organizations to harness AI's transformative potential fully but may introduce risks and uncertainties related to unintended consequences, biases, and misalignment with human values and goals.

In many cases, the optimal approach to AI adoption will likely be a hybrid one, balancing human and AI priorities over time based on each organization's specific context, goals, and constraints. By leveraging the complementary strengths of human judgment, creativity, and adaptability alongside AI's efficiency, scalability, and predictive power, organizations can develop more resilient, responsible, and future-proof AI strategies that generate sustainable value for all stakeholders.

To realize the full potential of this hybrid approach, organizations must adopt a strategic, holistic, and adaptive mindset toward AI adoption, continuously learning, experimenting, and refining their strategies based on real-world feedback and performance. This requires investments in AI talent, infrastructure, and governance frameworks, as well as a strong commitment to ethical principles, stakeholder engagement, and continuous improvement.

As the AI landscape continues to evolve, the insights and recommendations provided in this chapter can guide organizations seeking to navigate the complexities and uncertainties of AI adoption. By carefully considering the trade-offs and synergies between human and AI capabilities and developing strategies that prioritize transparency, accountability, and alignment with human values, organizations can position themselves to reap the transformative benefits of AI while mitigating its risks and challenges.

The success of AI adoption will depend on the technological sophistication of AI systems and the human wisdom, creativity, and collaboration that guide their development and deployment. As we move toward an increasingly AI-driven future, it is imperative to cultivate a culture of responsible and inclusive innovation, ensuring that the power of AI is harnessed for the benefit of all humanity.

References

Abdul, A., Vermeulen, J., Wang, D., Lim, B. Y., & Kankanhalli, M. (2018). Trends and trajectories for explainable, accountable and intelligible systems: An HCI research agenda. In: *Proceedings of the 2018 CHI Conference on Human Factors in Computing Systems*, pp. 1–18.

Adadi, A. & Berrada, M. (2018). Peeking inside the black-box: A survey on explainable artificial intelligence (XAI). *IEEE Access*, 6: 52138–52160.

Agrawal, A., Gans, J., & Goldfarb, A. (2018). Prediction machines: The simple economics of artificial intelligence. *Harvard Business Press*.

Amabile, T. M. (2020). Creativity, artificial intelligence, and a world of surprises. *Academy of Management Discoveries*, 6(3): 351–354.

Amershi, S., Begel, A., Bird, C., DeLine, R., Gall, H., Kamar, E., ..., & Zimmermann, T. (2019a). Software engineering for machine learning: A case study. In: *2019 IEEE/ACM 41st International Conference on Software Engineering: Software Engineering in Practice (ICSE-SEIP)*, pp. 291–300. IEEE.

Amershi, S., Weld, D., Vorvoreanu, M., Fourney, A., Nushi, B., Collisson, P., ..., & Horvitz, E. (2019b). Guidelines for human-AI interaction. In *Proceedings of the 2019 CHI Conference on Human Factors in Computing Systems*, pp. 1–13.

Anderson, M. & Anderson, S. L. (eds.) (2018). *Machine Ethics.* Cambridge University Press.

Arrieta, A. B., Díaz-Rodríguez, N., Del Ser, J., Bennetot, A., Tabik, S., Barbado, A., ..., & Herrera, F. (2020). Explainable Artificial Intelligence (XAI): Concepts, taxonomies, opportunities and challenges toward responsible AI. *Information Fusion*, 58: 82–115.

Balasubramanian, N., Ye, Y., & Xu, M. (2022). Substituting human decision-making with machine learning: Implications for organizational learning. *Academy of Management Review*, 47(3): 448–465.

Baldwin, C. Y. & Clark, K. B. (2000). *Design Rules, Volume 1: The Power of Modularity*. MIT Press.

Barocas, S., Hardt, M., & Narayanan, A. (2023). *Fairness and Machine Learning*. MIT Press.

Barocas, S. & Selbst, A. D. (2016). Big data's disparate impact. *California Law Review*, 104: 671–732.

Bostrom, N. (2014). *Superintelligence: Paths, Dangers, Strategies*. Oxford University Press.

Breck, E., Cai, S., Nielsen, E., Salib, M., & Sculley, D. (2017). The ML test score: A rubric for ML production readiness and technical debt reduction. In: *2017 IEEE International Conference on Big Data (Big Data)*, December, pp. 1123–1132. IEEE.

Brock, J. K. & Von Wangenheim, F. (2019). Demystifying AI: What digital transformation leaders can teach you about realistic artificial intelligence. *California Management Review*, 61(4): 110–134.

Bryson, J. & Winfield, A. (2017). Standardizing ethical design for artificial intelligence and autonomous systems. *Computer*, 50(5): 116–119.

Bughin, J., Hazan, E., Ramaswamy, S., Chui, M., Allas, T., Dahlström, P., ..., & Trench, M. (2017). Artificial intelligence: The next digital frontier? *McKinsey Global Institute*.

Canhoto, A. I. & Clear, F. (2020). Artificial intelligence and machine learning as business tools: A framework for diagnosing value destruction potential. *Business Horizons*, 63(2): 183–193.

Cheng, Y., Wang, D., Zhou, P., & Zhang, T. (2017). A survey of model compression and acceleration for deep neural networks. arXiv preprint, *arXiv:1710.09282*.

Chui, M., Manyika, J., Miremadi, M., Henke, N., Chung, R., Nel, P., & Malhotra, S. (2018). Notes from the AI frontier: Insights from hundreds of use cases. *McKinsey Global Institute*.

Dastin, J. (2022). Amazon scraps secret AI recruiting tool that showed bias against women. In: *Ethics of Data and Analytics*, pp. 296–299. Auerbach Publications.

Daugherty, P. R. & Wilson, H. J. (2018). Human + machine: Reimagining work in the age of AI. *Harvard Business Press*.

Davenport, T. H. (2018). *The AI Advantage: How to Put the Artificial Intelligence Revolution to Work*. MIT Press.

Davenport, T. H. & Mittal, N. (2020). How CEOs can lead a data-driven culture. *Harvard Business Review*. https://hbr.org/2020/03/how-ceos-can-lead-a-data-driven-culture.

Davenport, T. H. & Ronanki, R. (2018). Artificial intelligence for the real world. *Harvard Business Review*, 96(1): 108–116.

Diakopoulos, N. (2016). Accountability in algorithmic decision making. *Communications of the ACM*, 59(2): 56–62.

Dwivedi, Y. K., Hughes, L., Ismagilova, E., Aarts, G., Coombs, C., Crick, T., ..., & Williams, M. D. (2021). Artificial Intelligence (AI): Multidisciplinary perspectives on emerging challenges, opportunities, and agenda for research, practice and policy. *International Journal of Information Management*, 57: 101994.

Enholm, I. M., Papagiannidis, E., Mikalef, P., & Krogstie, J. (2022). Artificial intelligence and business value: A literature review. *Information Systems Frontiers*, 24(5): 1709–1734.

Esteva, A., Robicquet, A., Ramsundar, B., Kuleshov, V., DePristo, M., Chou, K., ..., & Dean, J. (2019). A guide to deep learning in healthcare. *Nature Medicine*, 25(1): 24–29.

Fjeld, J., Achten, N., Hilligoss, H., Nagy, A., & Srikumar, M. (2020). Principled artificial intelligence: Mapping consensus in ethical and rights-based approaches to principles for AI. *SSRN, Berkman Klein Center Research Publication*, January 2020.

Floridi, L. (2020). Artificial intelligence as a public service: Learning from Amsterdam and Helsinki. *Philosophy & Technology*, 33(4): 541–546.

Floridi, L. & Cowls, J. (2019). A unified framework of five principles for AI in society. *Harvard Data Science Review*, June 2019.

Fountaine, T., McCarthy, B., & Saleh, T. (2019). Building the AI-powered organization. *Harvard Business Review*, 97(4): 62–73.

Gasser, U. & Almeida, V. A. (2017). A layered model for AI governance. *IEEE Internet Computing*, 21(6): 58–62.

Gebru, T., Morgenstern, J., Vecchione, B., Vaughan, J. W., Wallach, H., Iii, H. D., & Crawford, K. (2021). Datasheets for datasets. *Communications of the ACM*, 64(12): 86–92.

Ghasemaghaei, M. & Calic, G. (2020). Assessing the impact of big data on firm innovation performance: Big data is not always better data. *Journal of Business Research*, 108: 147–162.

Gill, S. S., Xu, M., Ottaviani, C., Patros, P., Bahsoon, R., Shaghaghi, A., ..., & Uhlig, S. (2022). AI for next generation computing: Emerging trends and future directions. *Internet of Things*, 19: 100514.

Goodfellow, I., Bengio, Y., & Courville, A. (2016). *Deep Learning*. MIT Press.

Grønsund, T. & Aanestad, M. (2020). Augmenting the algorithm: Emerging human-in-the-loop work configurations. *The Journal of Strategic Information Systems*, 29(2): 101614.

Hajikhani, A. & Cole, C. (2024). A critical review of large language models: Sensitivity, bias, and the path toward specialized AI. *Quantitative Science Studies*, 1–22.

Hardesty, L. (2019). The history of Amazon's recommendation algorithm. *Amazon Science*. https://www.amazon.science/the-history-of-amazons-recommendation-algorithm.

He, X., Zhao, K., & Chu, X. (2021). AutoML: A survey of the state-of-the-art. *Knowledge-Based Systems*, 212: 106622.

Ishakian, V., Muthusamy, V., & Slominski, A. (2018, April). Serving deep learning models in a serverless platform. In: *2018 IEEE International Conference on Cloud Engineering (IC2E)*, pp. 257–262. IEEE.

Jarrahi, M. H. (2018). Artificial intelligence and the future of work: Human-AI symbiosis in organizational decision making. *Business Horizons*, 61(4): 577–586.

Jobin, A., Ienca, M., & Vayena, E. (2019). The global landscape of AI ethics guidelines. *Nature Machine Intelligence*, 1(9): 389–399.

Jordan, M. I. & Mitchell, T. M. (2015). Machine learning: Trends, perspectives, and prospects. *Science*, 349(6245): 255–260.

Jumper, J., Evans, R., Pritzel, A., Green, T., Figurnov, M., Ronneberger, O., ..., & Hassabis, D. (2021). Highly accurate protein structure prediction with AlphaFold. *Nature*, 596(7873): 583–589.

Kadlec, P. & Gabrys, B. (2009). Architecture for development of adaptive on-line prediction models. *Memetic Computing*, 1: 241–269.

Kaplan, A. & Haenlein, M. (2020). Rulers of the world, unite! The challenges and opportunities of artificial intelligence. *Business Horizons*, 63(1): 37–50.

Konda, S. R. & Shah, V. (2021). Evolving computer architectures for AI-intensive workloads: Challenges and innovations. *International Journal of Computer Science and Technology*, 5(4): 29–45.

Koshiyama, A., Kazim, E., Treleaven, P., Rai, P., Szpruch, L., Pavey, G., ..., & Lomas, E. (2021). Towards algorithm auditing: A survey on managing legal, ethical and technological risks of AI, ML and associated algorithms. *SSRN*.

Lage, I., Chen, E., He, J., Narayanan, M., Kim, B., Gershman, S. J., & Doshi-Velez, F. (2019). Human evaluation of models built for interpretability. In: *Proceedings of the AAAI Conference on Human Computation and Crowdsourcing*, Vol. 7, pp. 59–67.

Langlotz, C. P., Allen, B., Erickson, B. J., Kalpathy-Cramer, J., Bigelow, K., Cook, T. S., ..., & Kandarpa, K. (2019). A roadmap for foundational research on artificial intelligence in medical imaging: From the 2018 NIH/RSNA/ACR/The Academy Workshop. *Radiology*, 291(3): 781–791.

LeCun, Y., Bengio, Y., & Hinton, G. (2015). Deep learning. *Nature*, 521(7553): 436–444.

Lee, K. (2018). *AI Superpowers: China, Silicon Valley, and the New World Order*. Houghton Mifflin.

Lee, M. K., Kusbit, D., Kahng, A., Kim, J. T., Yuan, X., Chan, A., ..., & Procaccia, A. D. (2019). WeBuildAI: Participatory framework for algorithmic governance. In: *Proceedings of the ACM on Human-Computer Interaction, 3*(CSCW), pp. 1–35.

Leslie, D. (2019). Understanding artificial intelligence ethics and safety. arXiv preprint, *arXiv:1906.05684*.

Lichtenthaler, U. (2018). Beyond artificial intelligence: why companies need to go the extra step. *Journal of Business Strategy*, 41(1): 19–26.

Luo, X., Tong, S., Fang, Z., & Qu, Z. (2019). Frontiers: Machines vs. humans: The impact of artificial intelligence chatbot disclosure on customer purchases. *Marketing Science*, 38(6): 937–947.

Lyytinen, K., Nickerson, J. V., & King, J. L. (2020). Metahuman systems = humans + machines that learn. *Journal of Information Technology*, 36(4): 427–445.

Malone, T. W. (2018). *Superminds: The Surprising Power of People and Computers Thinking Together*. Little, Brown Spark.

Mehrabi, N., Morstatter, F., Saxena, N., Lerman, K., & Galstyan, A. (2021). A survey on bias and fairness in machine learning. *ACM Computing Surveys (CSUR)*, 54(6): 1–35.

Merendino, A., Dibb, S., Meadows, M., Quinn, L., Wilson, D., Simkin, L., & Canhoto, A. (2018). Big data, big decisions: The impact of big data on board level decision-making. *Journal of Business Research*, 93: 67–78.

Miceli, M., Schuessler, M., & Yang, T. (2020). Between subjectivity and imposition: Power dynamics in data annotation for computer vision. In: *Proceedings of the ACM on Human-Computer Interaction*, 4(CSCW2), pp. 1–25.

Mikalef, P., Fjørtoft, S. O., & Torvatn, H. Y. (2019). Artificial Intelligence in the public sector: A study of challenges and opportunities for Norwegian municipalities. In: *Digital Transformation for a Sustainable Society in the 21st Century: 18th IFIP WG 6.11 Conference on e-Business, e-Services, and e-Society, I3E 2019*, Trondheim, Norway, September 18–20, pp. 267–277. Springer International Publishing.

Mikalef, P., Pappas, I. O., Krogstie, J., & Giannakos, M. (2018). Big data analytics capabilities: A systematic literature review and research agenda. *Information Systems and e-Business Management*, 16: 547–578.

Mikkelsen, D. & Shridharan, K. (2019). Building scalable and adaptable systems: A review of emerging architectural patterns. In: *Proceedings of the 20th International Conference on Agile Software Development: Companion*, pp. 1–4.

Miller, T. (2019). Explanation in artificial intelligence: Insights from the social sciences. *Artificial Intelligence*, 267: 1–38.

Morikawa, M. (2017). *Who are Afraid of Losing Their Jobs to Artificial Intelligence and Robots?* Evidence from a Survey No. 71. GLO Discussion Paper.

Mosqueira-Rey, E., Hernández-Pereira, E., Alonso-Ríos, D., Bobes-Bascarán, J., & Fernández-Leal, Á. (2023). Human-in-the-loop machine learning: A state of the art. *Artificial Intelligence Review*, 56(4): 3005–3054.

Mungoli, N. (2023). Scalable, distributed AI frameworks: Leveraging cloud computing for enhanced deep learning performance and efficiency. arXiv preprint, *arXiv:2304.13738*.

Noble, S. U. (2018). *Algorithms of Oppression: How Search Engines Reinforce Racism*. New York, NY: New York University Press.

Obwegeser, N., Nielsen, D. T., & Spandet, N. M. (2019). Continual process improvement for ITIL service operations: A lean perspective. *Information Systems Management*, 36(2): 141–167.

Pallathadka, H., Mustafa, M., Sanchez, D. T., Sajja, G. S., Gour, S., & Naved, M. (2023). Impact of machine learning on management, healthcare and agriculture. *Materials Today: Proceedings*, 80: 2803–2806.

Pallathadka, H., Ramirez-Asís, E., Loli-Poma, T. P., Kaliyaperumal, K., Ventayen, R. J. M., & Naved, M. (2023). Applications of artificial intelligence in business management, e-commerce and finance. *Materials Today: Proceedings*, 80: 2610–2613.

Pan, S. J. & Yang, Q. (2010). A survey on transfer learning. *IEEE Transactions on Knowledge and Data Engineering*, 22(10): 1345–1359.

Parisi, G. I., Kemker, R., Part, J. L., Kanan, C., & Wermter, S. (2019). Continual lifelong learning with neural networks: A review. *Neural Networks*, 113: 54–71.

Pasquale, F. (2020). *New Laws of Robotics*. Harvard University Press.

Plastino, E. & Purdy, M. (2018). Game changing value from Artificial Intelligence: Eight strategies. *Strategy & Leadership*, 46(1): 16–22.

Polyzotis, N., Roy, S., Whang, S. E., & Zinkevich, M. (2017). Data management challenges in production machine learning. In: *Proceedings of the 2017 ACM International Conference on Management of Data*, pp. 1723–1726.

Rai, A. (2020). Explainable AI: From black box to glass box. *Journal of the Academy of Marketing Science*, 48: 137–141.

Rai, A., Constantinides, P., & Sarker, S. (2019). Next-generation digital platforms: Toward human–AI hybrids. *Management Information Systems Quarterly*, 43(1): iii–ix.

Raji, I. D. & Buolamwini, J. (2019). Actionable auditing: Investigating the impact of publicly naming biased performance results of commercial AI products. In: *Proceedings of the 2019 AAAI/ACM Conference on AI, Ethics, and Society*, pp. 429–435.

Raisch, S. & Krakowski, S. (2021). Artificial intelligence and management: The automation–augmentation paradox. *Academy of Management Review*, 46(1): 192–210.

Rane, N. L. (2023). Multidisciplinary collaboration: Key players in successful implementation of ChatGPT and similar generative artificial intelligence in manufacturing, finance, retail, transportation, and construction industry.

Ransbotham, S., Khodabandeh, S., Fehling, R., LaFountain, B., & Kiron, D. (2019). Winning with AI. *MIT Sloan Management Review*.

Ransbotham, S., Kiron, D., Gerbert, P., & Reeves, M. (2017). Reshaping business with artificial intelligence: Closing the gap between ambition and action. *MIT Sloan Management Review*, 59(1).

Rao, Q. & Frtunikj, J. (2018). Deep learning for self-driving cars: Chances and challenges. In: *Proceedings of the 1st International Workshop on Software Engineering for AI in Autonomous Systems*, pp. 35–38.

Ratner, A., Alistarh, D., Alonso, G., Bailis, P., Bird, S., Carlini, N., ..., & Zhang, C. (2019). MLSys: The new frontier of machine learning systems. arXiv preprint, *arXiv:1904.03257.*

Reim, W., Åström, J., & Eriksson, O. (2020). Implementation of artificial intelligence (AI): A roadmap for business model innovation. *AI*, 1(2): 11.

Ribeiro, M. T., Singh, S., & Guestrin, C. (2016, August). "Why should I trust you?" Explaining the predictions of any classifier. In: *Proceedings of the 22nd ACM SIGKDD International Conference on Knowledge Discovery and Data Mining*, pp. 1135–1144.

Ribeiro, M. T., Wu, T., Guestrin, C., & Singh, S. (2020). Beyond accuracy: Behavioral testing of NLP models with CheckList. arXiv preprint, *arXiv:2005.04118.*

Robert, L. P., Bansal, G., & Lütge, C. (2020). ICIS 2019 SIGHCI workshop panel report: Human-computer interaction challenges and opportunities for fair, trustworthy and ethical artificial intelligence. *AIS Transactions on Human-Computer Interaction*, 12(2): 96–108.

Robert, L. P., Pierce, C., Marquis, L., Kim, S., & Alahmad, R. (2020). Designing fair AI for managing employees in organizations: A review, critique, and design agenda. *Human–Computer Interaction*, 35(5–6): 545–575.

Rudin, C. & Radin, J. (2019). Why are we using black box models in AI when we don't need to? A lesson from an explainable AI competition. *Harvard Data Science Review*, 1(2).

Russell, S. & Norvig, P. (2021). *Artificial Intelligence: A Modern Approach*, 4th edition. Pearson.

Schelter, S., Böse, J., Kirschnick, J., Klein, T., & Seufert, S. (2017). Automatically tracking metadata and provenance of machine learning experiments. In: *Proceedings of Machine Learning Systems Workshop at NIPS 2017.*

Schilling, M. A. (2000). Toward a general modular systems theory and its application to interfirm product modularity. *Academy of Management Review*, 25(2): 312–334.

Selbst, A. D., Boyd, D., Friedler, S. A., Venkatasubramanian, S., & Vertesi, J. (2019). Fairness and abstraction in sociotechnical systems. In: *Proceedings of the Conference on Fairness, Accountability, and Transparency*, pp. 59–68.

Shin, D. & Park, Y. J. (2019). Role of fairness, accountability, and transparency in algorithmic affordance. *Computers in Human Behavior*, 98: 277–284.

Shneiderman, B. (2020). Human-centered artificial intelligence: Reliable, safe & trustworthy. *International Journal of Human–Computer Interaction*, 36(6): 495–504.

Shneiderman, B. (2020). Human-centered artificial intelligence: Three fresh ideas. *AIS Transactions on Human-Computer Interaction*, 12(3): 109–124.

Shneiderman, B. (2022). *Human-Centered AI*. Oxford University Press.

Shrestha, Y. R., Krishna, V., & von Krogh, G. (2021). Augmenting organizational decision-making with deep learning algorithms: Principles, promises, and challenges. *Journal of Business Research*, 123: 588–603.

Shukla, M. & Mattar, L. (2019). Next generation smart sustainable auditing systems using big data analytics: Understanding the interaction of critical barriers. *Computers & Industrial Engineering*, 128: 1015–1026.

Silver, D., Schrittwieser, J., Simonyan, K., Antonoglou, I., Huang, A., Guez, A., ..., & Hassabis, D. (2017). Mastering the game of go without human knowledge. *Nature*, 550(7676): 354–359.

Somashekhar, S. P., Kumarc, R., Rauthan, A., Arun, K. R., Patil, P., & Ramya, Y. E. (2017). Abstract S6-07: Double blinded validation study to assess performance of IBM artificial intelligence platform, Watson for oncology in comparison with Manipal multidisciplinary tumour board–First study of 638 breast cancer cases. *Cancer Research*, 77(4_Supplement): S6-07.

Sottilare, R. A., Brawner, K. W., Goldberg, B. S., & Holden, H. K. (2017). The generalized intelligent framework for tutoring (GIFT). In: *Fundamental Issues in Defense Training and Simulation*, pp. 223–233. CRC Press.

Sun, H. & Guyon, I. (2023). Modularity in deep learning: A survey. In: *Science and Information Conference*, pp. 561–595. Cham, Switzerland: Springer Nature.

Sutton, R. S. & Barto, A. G. (2018). *Reinforcement Learning: An Introduction*, 2nd edition. MIT Press.

Tambe, P., Cappelli, P., & Yakubovich, V. (2019). Artificial intelligence in human resources management: Challenges and a path forward. *California Management Review*, 61(4): 15–42.

Tang, D., Agarwal, A., O'Brien, D., & Meyer, M. (2010). Overlapping experiment infrastructure: More, better, faster experimentation. In: *Proceedings of the 16th ACM SIGKDD International Conference on Knowledge Discovery and Data Mining*, pp. 17–26.

Van der Velden, B. H., Kuijf, H. J., Gilhuijs, K. G., & Viergever, M. A. (2022). Explainable artificial intelligence (XAI) in deep learning-based medical image analysis. *Medical Image Analysis*, 79: 102470.

Vial, G. (2021). Understanding digital transformation: A review and a research agenda. *Journal of Strategic Information Systems*, 28(2): 118–144.

Wilson, H. J. & Daugherty, P. R. (2018). Collaborative intelligence: Humans and AI are joining forces. *Harvard Business Review*, 96(4): 114–123.

Wirtz, J., Kunz, W. H., Hartley, N., & Tarbit, J. (2023). Corporate digital responsibility in service firms and their ecosystems. *Journal of Service Research*, 26(2): 173–190.

Wu, X., Xiao, L., Sun, Y., Zhang, J., Ma, T., & He, L. (2022). A survey of human-in-the-loop for machine learning. *Future Generation Computer Systems*, 135: 364–381.

Xu, W., Dainoff, M. J., Ge, L., & Gao, Z. (2023). Transitioning to human Interaction with AI systems: New challenges and opportunities for HCI professionals to enable human-centered AI. *International Journal of Human–Computer Interaction*, 39(3): 494–518.

Zaharia, M., Xin, R. S., Wendell, P., Das, T., Armbrust, M., Dave, A., ..., & Stoica, I. (2016). Apache spark: A unified engine for big data processing. *Communications of the ACM*, 59(11): 56–65.

Zhuang, F., Qi, Z., Duan, K., Xi, D., Zhu, Y., Zhu, H., ..., & He, Q. (2020). A comprehensive survey on transfer learning. *Proceedings of the IEEE*, 109(1): 43–76.

Zuboff, S. (2019). *The Age of Surveillance Capitalism: The Fight for a Human Future at the New Frontier of Power*. PublicAffairs.

https://doi.org/10.1142/9789811296475_0006

Chapter 6

From Data to Decision: Unraveling the Impact of Analytics and AI in the Business Decision-Making Process

Tereza Raquel Merlo

University of North Texas, Denton, TX, USA

1. Introduction

Organizations have long recognized the benefits of using data and analytics to improve performance and increase revenue since the introduction of information technology in the workplace, more specifically in the late 20th century, a period marked by the introduction of information and communication technology (ICT) in the workplace, which is commonly referred to as the "digital age" or the "information age." This period is characterized by the widespread adoption of digital technologies, including computers, the Internet, mobile devices, and software applications, which have transformed the way organizations operate and conduct business. Nonetheless, challenges have become more pronounced in managing, implementing, and efficiently utilizing information systems and intricate technological infrastructures. Additionally, handling complex datasets and navigating the realm of intelligent machines that steer the ongoing digital transformation and reshape industries pose further complexities.

In the beginning of the 21st century, information has become a transformative force in the workplace, placing data at the center of every critical organizational decision. The new era of 4.0 technologies, integrating digital technologies into business processes, has become critical to sustain and ensure innovation and growth (Zong & Guan, 2024). Data analytics and the capabilities of systems introduced by artificial intelligence (AI) are transforming the learning, processing, and management of data, as well as redefining the concept and application of intelligence.

Data use, analysis, and visualization represent essential aspects of the data analytics process, along with data quality, integrity, management, and compliance. The digital transformation is consolidating a world that revolves around data and how it drives decisions and societal revolutions. From data capturing, cleaning, transfer, storage, and use, companies are facing challenges in defining and implementing the most effective data platform solutions while focusing on increasing profitability. The complexities of data governance, management, storage, security, and use rely on even more complex technological infrastructure that is costly. Schmuck and Georgescu (2024, p. 165) defend that "data governance is a promising approach to successfully maximize the value of this data and thus contribute to the company's success," and that data governance enables data value creation.

By harnessing the power of data, organizations can gain valuable insights into market trends, customer preferences, and operational efficiency. Data analytics and AI play pivotal roles in modern business decision-making processes. Through machine learning (ML) and big data analytics (BDA) tools, cloud computing, and intricate data infrastructure, the possibilities to underline framework to enable data compliance and governance are endless. Data analytics enables companies to analyze vast amounts of information quickly and accurately, identifying patterns and correlations that inform strategic decisions. The more advanced applications of data analytics leverage AI to anticipate scenarios and swiftly implement effective business strategies (Waller & Fawcett, 2013).

Additionally, AI technologies, such as machine learning and predictive analytics, allow businesses to forecast future trends and outcomes with greater precision. With the integration of data analytics and AI into their decision-making processes, organizations can enhance their competitiveness, optimize resource allocation, and drive innovation in an increasingly data-driven world. Therefore, strategic decisions in the adoption and implementation of technological apparatuses must include a well-designed business plan that will contemplate several aspects of human training, development, and retention, as well as clear guidelines to optimize decision-making and business outcomes.

In this chapter, we delve into the pivotal role of analytics and AI in facilitating digital transformation across various industries. We begin by exploring the foundational concepts of data analytics and AI, highlighting their evolution and adoption in the business landscape. Drawing on existing literature, we examine the transformative potential of these technologies in optimizing decision-making processes, enhancing operational efficiency, and driving innovation. The literature review section discusses key frameworks, models, and methodologies employed in leveraging analytics and AI for digital transformation and substantiates the conclusions.

2. Theoretical Framework and Background

The methodological approach to this study focused on a recent and seminal work reviewing the literature on data analytics, AI, and decision-making in businesses, based on the understanding that data analytics has been incredibly transformed and enhanced, assuming new layers of complexity and importance at the core of most businesses nowadays, impacting — and defining — business performance and competitiveness. Subsequently, a roadmap to leverage data in business is presented in an effort to illustrate nine critical steps to be considered in data and business strategy initiatives pursuing business process improvement and competitive outcomes in a data-driven organizational culture.

2.1. *Big data analytics in businesses*

In an era driven by massive data production and insatiable data consumption, characterized by the five Vs, Volume, Velocity, Variety, Value, and Veracity, the complexities in data scale increase rapidly, creating large datasets "that are too large for traditional software tools to handle, store, organize, and analyze are referred to as big data" (Singh *et al.*, 2024, p. 4). In the past decade (2010–2019), there has been a growing trend among web users to seek out web pages discussing topics, such as "artificial intelligence" and its associated terms, such as "big data," "business intelligence," and "machine learning" (Sestino *et al.*, 2021).

Data analytics is the foundational layer and the leader of this triad. Its main responsibility is to convert unprocessed data into useful insights. Patterns, trends, and correlations that are frequently concealed within the data are revealed through data analytics, a methodical process that involves data inspection, cleansing, modeling, and interpretation. These discoveries enable organizations to make well-informed decisions, streamline operations, and seize fresh opportunities.

Data come in various forms, each critical for comprehensive analytics: structured data (highly organized data, easily searchable in databases); unstructured data (information that does not have a predefined data model); and semi-structured data (a mix of structured and unstructured data). There are various types of data analytics in businesses: (a) **descriptive analytics:** This type focuses on understanding historical data to determine what has happened in the past; (b) **predictive analytics:** By analyzing current and historical data, predictive analytics forecasts future trends and behaviors; and (c) **prescriptive analytics:** This advanced form of analytics suggests possible outcomes and actions to achieve desired results.

The purpose of data analytics is to initiate the interaction by laying the groundwork for the ensuing data-driven initiatives. In the Foreword of the book, *Creating and Sustaining an Information Governance Program*, Merlo (2024a, p. xvii) defends, "as businesses increasingly rely on data-driven insights to inform decision-making aspects, data management, governance and quality are invaluable for organizations seeking to optimize their operations and enhance service delivery." It entails analyzing raw data to extract actionable insights that inform decision-making processes.

Businesses utilize analytics to optimize their operations, improve customer experiences, and identify new market opportunities. Sharma (2024, p. 112) investigated BDA in business processes aiming at collecting insights and assessing implications through the examination of hundreds of references in the field, identifying the trend and future of BDA in business processes, and concluding that BDA is in everything in businesses: "from planning to execution, all aspects of business process has employed big data analytics tools in one way or another." As per the authors' findings, BDA constitutes a crucial component of contemporary business operations, particularly within the context of the Internet of Things (IoT). Key technologies such as AI, deep learning, decision support systems, neural networks, predictive analysis, cloud computing, and machine learning have emerged as prevalent tools within the realm of BDA, collectively shaping the landscape of Industry 4.0.

Elgendy and Elragal (2016, p. 1072) defined that "Big data analytics is where advanced analytic techniques are applied on big data (sets). Analytics based on large data samples can help reveal and leverage business change." In a study conducted by Olaniyi *et al.* (2023, p. 70), investigating BDA and business intelligence (BI) in the decision-making process, it was concluded that "Big data analytics and business intelligence are crucial for success and innovation in business to sustain a competitive edge, and integrating big data analytics with business intelligence has revolutionized decision-making for many organizations." This concurs with the work of Elgendy and Elragal (2016) focusing on the impact of data analytics on the decision-making process, where the authors found that the integration of BDA into the decision-making process was significantly enhanced.

2.2. *The intersection of AI and businesses*

2.2.1. *What is AI and what are its impacts on business operations and strategies?*

AI is "a multidisciplinary field of knowledge with many nuanced definitions contingent on the context and perspective in which it is being applied and investigated. The consensus defining AI focuses on the development and use of specific applications like machine learning, natural language, and complex computer systems designed with the purpose of imitating human intelligence." (Merlo, 2024b, p. 3). AI pertains to the emulation of human intelligence processes by machines. These processes typically encompass learning, reasoning, and self-correction.

AI's integration into business operations is multifaceted and continuously expanding, as highlighted by the following quote:

> "[...]cognitive technologies were developed by human inventors, ranging from the invention of writing in Sumeria and Mesoamerica, to the modern interfaces of designers such as Douglas Engelbart, Alan Kay, and others. Examples such as those ... suggest that AI systems can enable the creation of new cognitive technologies." (Carter and Nielsen, 2017, pp. 60–61).

An examination of the current applications of AI algorithms in data and business management conducted by the AI Observatory at Politecnico di Milano (2018) generated a report, presenting the classification of five categories of solutions to R&D, innovation processes, and organizational learning:

- **Intelligent data processing:** This allows the management of structured and unstructured data to extract information from raw data and take action on this basis. This process leads to the establishment of a "pattern of discovery" among applications. Through this process, connections are established using the "predictive analysis."
- **Virtual assistant/chatbot:** Software agents execute commands and respond to requests through natural language interactions.
- **Recommendation:** This involves guiding user preferences based on information gathered from human activities on multiple online platforms, designed to understand and respond to the user's interest or potential interest.
- **Image processing:** This allows gathering and analyzing data from images or videos.
- **Language processing:** This allows the creation of language algorithms aiming at the creation of documents, translation of materials, etc.

Nalini *et al.* (2021, p. 3167) investigated the impact of AI on marketing and concluded "that Artificial Intelligence drives the opportunities of achieving things with a higher degree of accuracy and faster."

Marketing exemplifies how the strategic use of AI augments teams' performance by requiring fewer human nuances and allowing more tactical decisions by relying on the following: more accurate data analysis, automated decision-making, real-time increased personalization, natural language processing, minimal errors, higher cost savings, increased ROI, and faster decision-making (Nalini *et al.*, 2021, pp. 3162–3163). AI significantly benefits financial and banking industries by efficiently managing data, retrieving information, handling large volumes of computations, and improving cost-effectiveness.

Păvăloaia and Necula (2023) conducted a study examining the impact of AI as a disruptive technology across various industries, including education, healthcare, and agriculture. The results indicated a predominantly positive outlook, emphasizing the advantages of emerging technologies, such as IoT, blockchain, 5G, and 3D printing.

The rapid adoption of AI across industries is poised to revolutionize traditional business practices. AI enables businesses to achieve tasks with greater accuracy and speed, driving opportunities for innovation. In the financial and banking sectors, AI plays a crucial role in data management, information retrieval, computational tasks, and cost efficiency. Moreover, AI's predictive capabilities empower organizations to identify potential customers and anticipate purchasing behavior, thereby enhancing sales and customer satisfaction. To enable businesses to maximize the benefits of data analytics and AI, cultivating a data-driven culture is paramount. This encompasses three key elements:

1. **Commitment from leadership:** Executives must demonstrate prioritization and allocate resources toward data analytics and AI initiatives.
2. **Continuous employee training:** Implementation of ongoing educational opportunities and training initiatives ensures that employees are given the tools to develop the necessary skills to effectively utilize and share data and interpret analytics that will create smooth business operations, faster response to issues, and higher probability of preventing errors.
3. **Encouraging cross-functional collaboration:** Promotion of sharing of data and insights among different divisions fosters a collaborative approach to problem-solving and decision-making.

Cautela *et al.* (2019, p. 114) concluded that AI prompts a new approach to organizational culture and leadership that defines design thinking (DT): "[...]as an alternative way to innovative products and services respect to the classical stage-gate model mostly linked to technology-push innovative patterns." Simultaneously, a select few disruptive technologies, such as AI and machine learning, are continuing to reshape how companies handle their knowledge and catalyze innovation and design processes.

The strategic deployment of data analytics and AI involves cultivating a data-driven culture and establishing a framework for seamlessly integrating AI into the fabric of workplace digital transformation. This strategy provides comprehensive guidance on various aspects, including data management, intelligent decision-making, maintaining a pragmatic perspective, fostering integration, encouraging collaboration, embracing agility, and demonstrating effective leadership.

Organizations must invest in digital technologies such as the IoT, cloud computing, BDA, cloud computing solutions, and numerous data management tools to transform their operations, improve products and services, enhance customer experiences, attain operational efficiency, introduce new products or services, and innovate business models. According to the Gartner Survey on organizational digital business initiatives, 69% of boards of directors have advocated digital acceleration and 48% of respondents have increased investment in the digital business (Lyengar *et al.*, 2021). Digital business transformation refers to how organizations can alter their value creation and change the scope of their business in this digital age (Hess *et al.*, 2016). The ability to manage and exploit data is becoming a competitive competency in digital business transformation for organizations (Dremel *et al.*, 2017).

2.3. *Leveraging data analytics and AI in decision-making in businesses*

Cao *et al.* (2015) defend that there is a clear link between business analytics applications and the facilitation of data-driven decision-making. The authors argue that business analytics contributes to managers' knowledge and understanding by demonstrating how business analytics should be implemented to improve decision-making effectiveness (DME). Cao *et al.* (2015, p. 384) also concluded that "business analytics, through the mediation of a data-driven environment, positively influences information processing capability, which in turn has a positive effect on DME," highlighting that there is no statistical difference between DME in large- and medium-sized companies, with some differences between manufacturing and professional services industries.

Singh *et al.* (2024, p. 2) defend that "as the fundamental layer, data analytics enables us to convert unprocessed data into meaningful insights. It uncovers secrets by methodically examining and interpreting patterns, shedding light on the way ahead. It propels optimization, informs tactics, and directs us towards more intelligent decisions." In the research conducted by Ibeh *et al.* (2024), a thorough examination of the influence of business analytics on decision-making highlights a crucial observation: AI offers tools for business analysis to navigate extensive datasets and derive meaningful insights. This aids companies in moving forward with a comprehensive understanding of the factors facilitating and hindering decision-making in business.

Achieving digital transformation through analytics involves leveraging data to drive business innovation, efficiency, and competitive advantage. Step 1 involves building a data-driven culture, where leaders will "lead by example" and invest in data literacy, encouraging participation, questions, collaboration, and brainstorming. Leaders will introduce, train, and evaluate data compliance, governance, and use, promoting continuous improvement and openness to feedback and changes. Tools and technologies for data access, analysis, and visualization are provided, and emphasis is given to trust, reliability, and data quality and accuracy. In discussing digital transformation in business, Brock & von Wangenheim (2019, p. 9) found that "Integrated data management, the most pronounced difference between leaders and laggards, refers to the organizational capability of managing customer and organizational data in a holistic and integrated fashion, avoiding data silos and incompatible data formats."

In defining and communicating objectives and allocating resources in technology (Steps 2 and 3), businesses seek to develop an optimal flow of information among staff, leaders, and stakeholders, better aligning business objectives and more effective work in collaboration through an aligned perspective on the effective elimination of — or reduction of — efforts and increase in efficiency. In addition, defining lines of communication leads to consistency in the use, interpretation, and shared values and policies, allows for clear key performance indicators (KPIs), and ensures higher accountability. Furthermore, creating an organizational culture that can quickly recognize and respond to changes, whether internal or external, allows adjusting to emerging trends and meeting customer demands and satisfaction.

Steps 4–6, from data gathering to the need to adopt an agile approach to data management, involve a structured process in which data will be collected, processed, generated, and distributed from multiple sources within an organization, enabling a data processing analysis based on advanced analytics techniques and AI algorithms to extract valuable insights critical to businesses.

The optimization of business operations (Step 7) will result from the valuable insights extracted from the data generated, producing helpful analytics to be applied to mitigate risks, capitalize on opportunities, and lead business improvements (Step 8). This process should enhance customer experience, define a more competitive position in the market, and enable an environment of creativity, knowledge exchange, and innovation.

By methodically incorporating these actions (Step 9), organizations can leverage the potential of analytics to propel their journey of digital transformation, resulting in continuous innovation and growth. Various tools support data analytics, each with distinct features designed to address diverse business requirements: BI platforms such as Tableau and Power BI facilitate visualization and reporting; statistical analysis tools: Software such as R and SAS is employed for advanced statistical modeling; and big data technologies: Frameworks such as Hadoop and Spark manage substantial datasets across distributed systems.

Assessing and establishing an environment conducive to digital inclusion and productivity in the workplace demands leadership capacity to evaluate team members' skills and knowledge, assess the current technological infrastructure, and gauge the organization's preparedness for digital transformation. Subsequently, it involves delineating precise objectives and performance metrics that harmonize with the business objectives and strategies and embracing a well-defined business roadmap delineating the sequence of activities and milestones for implementation. Opportunities associated with AI are considered to be the most important technological development, with regard to their enormous potential for adding value and competitive advantage (Brock & von Wangenheim, 2019).

3. Conclusions

In conclusion, embedding analytics and AI capabilities into decision-making processes across various organizational levels is essential for fostering a data-driven culture. Providing training and support to employees for the effective utilization of analytics tools and AI technologies further reinforces this culture. Establishing mechanisms for ongoing monitoring and governance ensures the ethical and responsible use of data- and AI-driven insights.

By following the nine-step roadmap, organizations can optimize their comprehension and improve data and business operations processes as they harness the transformative potential of analytics and AI to drive digital evolution and achieve sustainable competitive advantage in today's dynamic business environment. Looking ahead, the future promises even more sophisticated AI and analytics capabilities, including edge AI, explainable AI, extended reality, and augmented analytics, and unimaginable possibilities of replicating, imitating, and even surpassing human activities and intelligence. Different industries will continue to witness the unique applications of AI and data analytics, presenting boundless opportunities for innovation and growth.

Notwithstanding the benefits, challenges such as data privacy concerns, high implementation costs, and the need for specialized skills and knowledge persist. However, by adopting a strategic, ethical, and inclusive approach, organizations can navigate these obstacles and leverage analytics and AI to drive innovation, agility, and competitive advantage more successfully. Embracing data-driven decision-making processes and investing in cutting-edge technologies enable organizations to adapt quickly and effectively to changing market dynamics, redefine industry standards, and thrive in an increasingly digital-centric business environment.

Additionally, a critical aspect for AI-equipped organizations to consider is the complex and costly nature of technology implementation. For many industries, there are significant challenges in upgrading IT infrastructure and addressing scalability, regulatory compliance, computing storage solutions, software licensing, system integration, and, importantly, staff training and professional development to ensure the necessary skills for an AI-driven environment. The fast pace in which digital transformation is impacting the workplace and society can already be noted, with some careers quickly, and inevitably, becoming obsolete, and new roles emerging, with more to be created or reinvented.

Ultimately, the ability to navigate these technological and workforce transitions will determine an organization's success in the digital era. Again, by fostering a culture of continuous learning and innovation, businesses can not only mitigate the disruptions caused by AI and advanced analytics but also harness their full potential to achieve sustained growth and competitive advantage. In this way, organizations can build a resilient and adaptable workforce, ready to tackle the challenges and seize the opportunities presented by the rapidly evolving digital landscape.

References

Albright, S. C. & Winston, W. L. (2019). *Business Analytics: Data Analysis & Decision Making*, 7th edition. Boston, MA: Cengage.

Brock, J. K.-U. & Von Wangenheim, F. (2019). Demystifying AI: What digital transformation leaders can teach you about realistic artificial intelligence. *California Management Review*, 61: 110–134.

Cao, G., Duan, Y., & Li, G. (2015). Linking business analytics to decision making effectiveness: A path model analysis. *IEEE Transactions on Engineering Management*, 62(3): 384–395.

Carter, S. & Nielsen, M. (2017). Using artificial intelligence to augment human intelligence. *Distill*. Retrieved May 20, 2024, from https://distill.pub/2017/aia/?ref=webdesignernews.com.

Cautela C., Mortati M., Dell'Era C., & Gastaldi L. (2019). The impact of artificial intelligence on design thinking practice: Insights from the ecosystem of start-ups. *Strategic Design Research Journal*, 12(1): 114–134.

Elgendy, N. & Elragal, A. (2016). Big data analytics in support of the decision-making process. *Procedia Computer Science*, 100: 1071–1084.

Hess, T., Matt, C., Benlian, A., & Wiesböck, F. (2016). Options for formulating a digital transformation strategy. *MIS Quarterly Executive*, 15(2): 123–139.

Ibeh, C. V., Asuzu, O. F., Olorunsogo, T., Elufioye, O. A., Nduubuisi, N. L., & Daraojimba, A. I. (2024). Business analytics and decision science: A review of techniques in strategic business decision making. *World Journal of Advanced Research and Reviews*, 21(02): 1761–1769.

Lyengar, P., Furlonger, D., & Lopez, J. (2021). Survey analysis: Executive leaders should align to board priorities for 2021. *Gartner Research*, pp. 1–25.

Merlo, T. R. (2024a). *AI and Data Analytics Applications in Organizational Management*. Hershey, PA: IGI Global.

Merlo, T. R. (2024b). Foreword. In: Helge, K. & Rookey, C. (eds.), *Creating and Sustaining an Information Governance Program*, pp. xvi–xviii. Hershey, PA: IGI Global.

Nalini, K., Radhakrishnan, P., Yogi, G., Santhiya, S., & Harivardhini, V. (2021). Impact of artificial intelligence (AI) on marketing. *International Journal of Aquatic Science*, 12(02): 3159.

Observatory of Artificial Intelligence Report 2018 (2018). Politecnico di Milano. Retrieved May 21, 2024, from https://www.osservatori.net/it_it/pubblicazioni?productor_name=499.

Olaniyi, O., Abalaka, A., & Olabanji, S. (2023). Utilizing big data analytics and business intelligence for improved decision-making at leading fortune company. *Journal of Scientific Research and Reports*, 29: 64–72.

Păvăloaia, V.-D. & Sabina-Cristiana, N. (2023). Artificial intelligence as a disruptive technology: A systematic literature review. *Electronics*, 12(5): 1102.

Sestino, A. & De Mauro, A. (2021). Leveraging artificial intelligence in business: Implications, applications and methods. *Technology Analysis and Strategic Management*, 34: 1–14.

Sharma, S. (2024). Big data analytics in business process: Insights and implications. In: Farhaoui, Y., Hussain, A., Saba, T., Taherdoost, H., & Verma, A. (eds.), *Artificial Intelligence, Data Science and Applications*. Lecture Notes in Networks and Systems, Volume 837. Cham, Switzerland: Springer.

Singh, P., Mishra, A., Dixit, M., & Srivastava, A. (2024). *Data Analytics and Machine Learning: Navigating the Big Data Landscape*. Singapore: Springer.

Schmuck, M. & Georgescu, M. (n.d.). Enabling data value creation with data governance: A success measurement model. In: *CS & IT Conference Proceedings,* 14(8). Retrieved from https://csitcp.net/abstract/14/148csit16.

Waller, M. A. & Fawcett, S. E. (2013). Data science, predictive analytics, and big data: A revolution that will transform supply chain design and management. *Journal of Business Logistics*, 34(2): 77–84.

Zong, Z. & Guan, Y. (2024). AI-driven intelligent data analytics and predictive analysis in industry 4.0: Transforming knowledge, innovation, and efficiency. *Journal Knowledge Economy*.

https://doi.org/10.1142/9789811296475_0007

Chapter 7

The Organizational Impacts of Digital Transformation

Ben Apple and Trisha Shields

Naval Surface Warfare Center, Carderock Division,
Bethesda, MD, USA

1. Introduction

In the rapidly evolving landscape of the 21st century, the phenomenon of digital transformation has emerged as a pivotal force reshaping the contours of organizational structures, processes, and cultures across industries. At its core, digital transformation transcends the mere adoption of digital technologies; it represents a profound reimagining of business operations, strategies, and models in response to the digital age's demands and opportunities. This chapter embarks on an analytical journey to dissect the impacts of digital transformation on organizations, aiming to unravel how this digital upheaval influences organizational dynamics from the architecture of corporate hierarchies to the ethos that drives innovation.

The impetus for digital transformation stems from the relentless pace of technological advancements, evolving consumer expectations, and the intensifying competitive landscape that compels organizations to seek efficiency, agility, and innovation. As digital technologies become increasingly integral to everyday life, organizations are prompted to reevaluate their operational models and strategic priorities. This transformation is not merely technological but is fundamentally cultural, necessitating a shift in the mindset toward continual adaptation, experimentation, and a tolerance for failure. Without this shift, any organization that tries to apply analytics to monitor performance or discover insights and seeks to leverage technologies such as artificial intelligence (AI) will ultimately fail.

The significance of understanding digital transformation's organizational impacts cannot be overstated. It offers insights into how organizations can navigate the challenges and leverage the opportunities presented by digital technologies to achieve sustainable growth, competitive advantage, and enhanced customer value. Moreover, it sheds light on the potential pitfalls and resistance encountered during this transformative journey.

This chapter explores the nuances of digital transformation's effects on organizational structure, processes, culture, and performance. It delves into the reconfiguration of organizational hierarchies, the digitization and automation of business processes, the cultivation of a digital-forward culture, and the resultant improvements in organizational performance. Additionally, it addresses the challenges and risks inherent in navigating digital transformation, offering insights into overcoming these obstacles to harness the full potential of digital innovation.

In synthesizing perspectives from a broad array of academic literature and real-world examples, this chapter aims to contribute a rich, multidimensional understanding of digital transformation's organizational impacts. By examining the strategic implications of digital technologies and the cultural shifts they precipitate within organizations, this chapter seeks to provide a comprehensive framework for scholars and practitioners alike, guiding them through the intricacies of digital transformation in the contemporary business environment.

2. Literature Review

The literature on digital transformation encompasses a wide array of perspectives, focusing on its implications for organizational structure, processes, culture, and performance. This review synthesizes key contributions to the field, drawing upon seminal works and recent studies to outline the current understanding and emerging insights into how digital transformation reshapes organizations.

2.1. *Theoretical foundations and definitions*

Digital transformation is broadly defined as the integration of digital technology into all areas of a business, fundamentally changing how it operates and delivers value to customers (Vial, 2019). It also entails a cultural change that requires organizations to continually challenge the *status quo*, experiment, and become comfortable with failure (Westerman *et al.*, 2014). These foundational definitions set the stage for a deeper exploration of digital transformation's impacts.

2.2. *Impact on organizational structure*

Scholars have extensively debated the impact of digital transformation on organizational structure. Bharadwaj *et al.* (2013) argue that digital technologies enable more flattened organizational hierarchies by promoting transparency and democratizing information access. This view is supported by empirical evidence from companies like Zappos, which have experimented with holacratic governance models to enhance agility and responsiveness (Robertson, 2015). However, the transition to such models is not without challenges, as it requires significant cultural adaptation and change management efforts.

2.3. *Impact on organizational processes*

Digital transformation significantly influences organizational processes through the automation of routine tasks and the digitization of business operations (Davenport & Westerman, 2018). The adoption of agile methodologies is a notable trend, emphasizing rapid iteration and responsiveness to change (Hess *et al.*, 2016). This shift toward digital processes necessitates a reevaluation of traditional workflow and operational procedures, often leading to enhanced efficiency and innovation.

2.4. *Impact on organizational culture*

The literature also highlights the profound impact of digital transformation on organizational culture. Kane *et al.* (2015) emphasize the importance of fostering a digital culture characterized by agility, innovation, and a willingness to experiment. Such a culture supports the organizational shifts required by digital transformation, enabling a more flexible and adaptive approach to change. However, cultivating this culture can be challenging, requiring strong leadership and a clear vision for the digital future.

2.5. *Impact on organizational performance*

Regarding organizational performance, digital transformation is posited to offer significant benefits, including improved customer experiences, operational efficiencies, and competitive advantages (Hess *et al.*, 2016). Netflix's evolution from DVD rentals to a streaming service exemplifies how digital transformation can redefine industry landscapes and drive growth (Oswald & Kleinemeier, 2017). Nonetheless, realizing these performance benefits requires a strategic approach to digital investment and an understanding of the digital technologies that align with organizational goals.

2.6. *Challenges and risks*

The literature acknowledges several challenges and risks associated with digital transformation. These include the disruption of existing business models, the significant investment required for new technologies, and the risk of cybersecurity threats (Oswald & Kleinemeier, 2017). Moreover, the cultural shift toward a digital-first mindset often encounters resistance from within the organization, highlighting the need for effective change management strategies (Kane *et al.*, 2015).

The review of the literature on digital transformation reveals a complex landscape characterized by significant opportunities and challenges for organizations. As digital technologies continue to evolve, the ability of organizations to continuously adapt and transform will be crucial for their survival and success. Future research should continue to explore the nuances of digital transformation, particularly in the context of emerging technologies and their implications for organizational dynamics. This ongoing inquiry will be vital in guiding organizations through their digital transformation journeys, ensuring that they can navigate the challenges and seize the opportunities presented by the digital age.

3. The Impact of Digital Transformation on Organizational Structure

The impact of digital transformation on organizational structure is profound and multifaceted, redefining traditional hierarchies and operational paradigms. As organizations increasingly integrate digital technologies into their core strategies and operations, the structural implications are significant, leading to shifts toward more flattened, agile, and networked forms. This section delves into how digital transformation reshapes organizational structure, the emergence of new roles and decision-making processes, and the challenges associated with these transitions.

3.1. *Flattening hierarchies*

Digital transformation often leads to a flattening of organizational hierarchies. The adoption of digital technologies enhances communication and information flow across different levels of the organization, reducing the need for multiple layers of management (Bharadwaj *et al.*, 2013). This flattening process is not merely a structural adjustment but also a strategic realignment that enhances responsiveness and agility. The holacratic approach emphasizes the role of digital tools in facilitating collaboration and empowering employees, leading to more dynamic and flexible organizational structures.

3.2. *Role of digital technologies*

Digital technologies play a pivotal role in transforming organizational structures. Tools such as enterprise social networks, cloud computing, and data analytics platforms enable greater transparency and facilitate a culture of open communication and collaboration (Davenport & Westerman, 2018). These technologies support the decentralization of decision-making, allowing teams to respond more rapidly to market changes and customer needs. Moreover, digital platforms can bridge geographical and functional silos, fostering a more integrated and cohesive organizational structure.

3.3. *Emergence of new roles and skills*

The shift toward digital-centric organizational structures necessitates the creation of new roles and competencies. Positions such as chief digital officer (CDO) and digital transformation managers have become increasingly common, underscoring the importance of leadership in guiding digital initiatives (Hess *et al.*, 2016). Additionally, there is a growing demand for skills in data, data analytics, digital marketing, software and cloud architectures, AI, and cybersecurity, reflecting the critical competencies required to navigate the digital landscape. Moreover, digital technologies enable rapid innovation and continuous process improvement methodologies, such as DevOps, which forces the integration and blurs the organizational delineation between traditional development and operations roles. These roles and skills are essential for driving innovation, executing digital strategies, and ensuring that organizations remain competitive in a rapidly evolving digital environment.

3.4. *Challenges in transitioning structures*

Transitioning to a digital-centric organizational structure is not without challenges. Resistance to change is a significant barrier, as employees and managers accustomed to traditional hierarchies may find it difficult to adapt to new ways of working (Kane *et al.*, 2015). Moreover, the successful implementation of a flattened hierarchy requires robust change management strategies, clear communication, and ongoing support to ensure that employees feel empowered and engaged in the new structure. Ensuring alignment between digital strategies and organizational goals is also crucial, as misalignment can lead to confusion and inefficiency.

The impact of digital transformation on organizational structure is a testament to the profound changes that digital technologies bring to the business landscape. By flattening hierarchies, facilitating the emergence of new roles, and leveraging digital technologies for enhanced collaboration and decision-making, organizations can become more agile, innovative, and competitive. However, navigating the transition to a digital-centric structure requires careful planning, strong leadership, and a commitment to fostering a culture that embraces change. As organizations continue to evolve in response to digital transformation, the structures that emerge will likely be characterized by their flexibility, resilience, and ability to drive sustained growth in an increasingly digital world.

4. The Impact of Digital Transformation on Processes

A discussion of the impacts of digital transformation on the processes of an organization is outside the intent of this chapter. However, as organizations incorporate digital technologies to attain benefits such as process efficiency through automation, the reevaluation of traditional processes and workflows in a digital context should consider not only the tools and technologies but also the points in the processes where human oversight or interaction is appropriate or necessary. Automation and digital formats enable shifting processes from a manual, human-based paradigm to one that significantly reduces the need for human involvement, fundamentally changes the human role or function, or eliminates it altogether.

5. The Impact of Digital Transformation on Organizational Culture

The shift to digital necessitates a cultural transformation where agility, innovation, and a willingness to experiment become core values (Kane *et al.*, 2015). Organizations must foster an environment where learning from failures is seen as a step toward innovation, not a setback. Enabling experimentation with digital tools and approaches can help the workforce gain confidence and trust in the technologies as well as their abilities to use them, which promotes the idea of digital tools and technologies being an advantage and softening the resistance to change.

6. The Impact of Digital Transformation on Organizational Performance

Digital transformation can significantly enhance organizational performance by improving customer experiences, streamlining operations, and enabling new business models (Hess *et al.*, 2016). Despite its benefits, digital transformation poses challenges, including the disruption of existing business models, the need for significant investment in new technologies, and the risk of cybersecurity threats (Oswald & Kleinemeier, 2017). Moreover, the cultural shift required can be substantial, with resistance to change being a common obstacle. Additionally, with the rapid pace of technology, and therefore product change and advancement, future research is needed to consider how organizations determine when a technology product is mature enough to adopt, as well as when to purchase commercially available products and when to develop and maintain their own.

7. Conclusion

Digital transformation significantly impacts organizational structures, processes, culture, and performance. While it offers considerable opportunities for innovation and growth, it also presents challenges that must be carefully managed. As digital technologies continue to evolve, organizations must adapt to remain competitive in an increasingly digital world.

References

Bharadwaj, A., El Sawy, O. A., Pavlou, P. A., & Venkatraman, N. (2013). Digital business strategy: Toward a next generation of insights. *Management Information Systems Quarterly*, 37(2): 471–482.

Davenport, T. H. & Westerman, G. (2018). The digital transformation imperative. *MIT Sloan Management Review*, 59(3): 1–4.

Hess, T., Matt, C., Benlian, A., & Wiesböck, F. (2016). Options for formulating a digital transformation strategy. *MIS Quarterly Executive*, 15(2): 123–139.

Kane, G. C., Palmer, D., Phillips, A. N., Kiron, D., & Buckley, N. (2015). *Strategy, not Technology, Drives Digital Transformation*. Research Report, MIT Sloan Management Review and Deloitte University Press.

Oswald, G. & Kleinemeier, M. (2017). *Shaping the Digital Enterprise: Trends and Use Cases in Digital Innovation and Transformation*. Cham, Switzerland: Springer.

Robertson, B. J. (2015). *Holacracy: The New Management System for a Rapidly Changing World*. Henry Holt and Co.

Ross, J. W., Beath, C. M., & Mocker, M. (2019). *Designed for Digital: How to Architect Your Business for Sustained Success*. Cambridge, MA: MIT Press.

Vial, G. (2019). Understanding digital transformation: A review and a research agenda. *The Journal of Strategic Information Systems*, 28(2): 118–144.

Westerman, G., Bonnet, D., & McAfee, A. (2014). *Leading Digital: Turning Technology into Business Transformation*. Harvard Business Review Press.

https://doi.org/10.1142/9789811296475_0008

Chapter 8

Management Capabilities in the Age of Generative Artificial Intelligence (GenAI): A Conceptual Framework and Future Research Directions

Tim Heubeck and Patrick Held

University of Bayreuth, Bayreuth, Germany

1. The Relevance of GenAI for Strategic Decision-Makers

Since the release of ChatGPT in November 2022, generative artificial intelligence (GenAI) has dominated discussions on AI (Gartner, 2023). The introduction of this technology-enabled tool was groundbreaking. ChatGPT reached 100 million monthly active users just two months after launch, making it the fastest-growing consumer application in history (Reuters, 2023). The expected disruption for business is significant and viewed with great interest among practitioners and researchers alike (Budhwar *et al.*, 2023; Deloitte United States, 2024; Feuerriegel *et al.*, 2024; McKinsey, 2024). A recent report by Goldman Sachs (2023) even suggests that GenAI could raise global gross domestic product by 7%.

While there is a consensus that GenAI will significantly impact the business landscape, the concrete scope, the exact effects, and the added value are still unclear. Although research on the significance of GenAI for businesses is rapidly expanding, studies on its application in the management context remain in their infancy. There are many ideas, potential use cases, and predictions about how GenAI will benefit companies, but time must tell whether and how firms can realize these potentials.

However, given the disruptive potential of GenAI, companies must recognize the added value of this technology early on to avoid being left behind by the competition. Especially in the digital age, technological capabilities are essential for a company's survival. Past studies within the information system research stream have found that organizations gain a competitive advantage by building unique and hard-to-imitate capabilities (Bharadwaj, 2000; Gupta & George, 2016; Mikalef & Gupta, 2021). This firm-level focus on capabilities has provided management researchers with a suitable lens for analyzing competitive advantage yet omits that these organizational capabilities originate from individuals (Heubeck, 2023b).

Thus, shifting the lens from more abstract organizational capabilities to tangible managerial capabilities could provide a suitable perspective on GenAI. The theory of dynamic managerial capabilities (DMCs) offers a valuable framework for analyzing the individual-level capabilities of top managers that shape organizational strategies due to their responsibility for orchestrating a firm's asset portfolio (Helfat & Martin, 2015). Adopting this DMC lens, we propose that top managers, due to their decision-making authority, are crucial for building powerful GenAI capabilities. This argument raises the question of which specific capabilities these managers need to make successful strategic decisions and lead companies in the age of GenAI. Conversely, the question of how and to which extent GenAI influences existing managerial capabilities arises.

In this chapter, we address these interrelated research questions and present an extended framework for DMCs in the age of GenAI. The remainder of this chapter is structured as follows. First, we briefly outline GenAI's fundamental principles from the user perspective. Next, we explain the basics of DMC theory and its underlying four dimensions. We then consider each of the four dimensions in the context of GenAI. We also discuss potential interrelationships between the four dimensions. After that, we combine our previous insights into our extended DMC framework in the age of GenAI. Finally, we point out directions for future research.

2. The Foundations of GenAI

ChatGPT is based on a large language model (LLM) that uses GenAI, with GenAI being an umbrella term that refers to "computational techniques that are capable of generating seemingly new, meaningful content such as text, images, or audio from training data" (Feuerriegel *et al.*, 2024). Thus, GenAI systems are different from conventional AI algorithms, as the latter are based on machine learning used mainly for analysis and pattern recognition in large datasets to derive forecasts and predictions. In other words, GenAI generates entirely new content based solely on user prompts. To provide an illustrative example, we ask ChatGPT (by writing a prompt) to generate an exemplary dialog of how it could support managers in strategic decision-making; here is the result:

> **Manager:** Hey, ChatGPT, I'm torn between expanding into smart home devices or enhancing our current offerings. Can you help me decide?
> **ChatGPT:** Of course. Let's get into the details. Can you share how our current products are performing and the opportunities you see in both directions?
> **Manager:** Our smart thermostats and security cameras are doing well, but there's a growing demand for more smart home products like lighting systems and smart appliances. On the other hand, we could improve our existing products by adding advanced features and expanding compatibility.
> **ChatGPT:** Understanding the market is key. Both options seem promising. Expanding could capture new markets while enhancing current offerings could boost loyalty and revenue. Have we looked into competitors for both?
> **Manager:** We've started, but we need more depth. For new products, we need insights into features and pricing. For existing ones, we want to see where we stand against competitors.
> **ChatGPT:** A thorough competitive analysis is crucial. We should aim to fill market gaps and offer unique value. For new products, innovation is key. For existing ones, reliability and design should be emphasized. Also, market saturation and preferences matter.

Manager: Agreed. Timing matters, too. Any suggestions on when to act?
ChatGPT: Indeed. Given the industry's pace, we need to move fast. I'd suggest a feasibility study to gauge ROI and resource needs. Gathering market feedback can minimize risks.

ChatGPT generated this completely new dialog based on our input, extensive training data, and sophisticated language model programming. This also means that someone else asking the same question will get a different answer. Thus, the revolutionary breakthrough ChatGPT and other GenAI tools realized is the perceived human-like responses in conjunction with the quality of the responses. Interaction with ChatGPT simulates a classic conversation in which the bot can answer further questions and specifications, admit errors, and describe if it does not know an answer. To stay with our example above, we could provide additional context based on the result and thus sharpen it further. We could also say that the answer is too long and not concrete enough. So we could refine the result until we are satisfied with it and it creates real added value. By increasing the description throughout the collaboration, we added more and more context to the generative AI — the more context and precise the description, the better the result.

As described above, we wanted to ensure that all readers have the same basic understanding of GenAI and that this user perspective is sufficient in the context of this article (for a deep-dive into basic mathematical principles and technical functioning of GenAI, see Feuerriegel *et al.*, 2024).

3. Theory of Dynamic Managerial Capabilities

Dynamic managerial capabilities (DMCs) is a micro-level theory that focalizes "the capabilities with which managers build, integrate, and reconfigure organizational resources and competences" (Adner & Helfat, 2003: 1020). Top managers' innate and developed dynamic capabilities have great organizational significance because they allow them to reconfigure organizational assets — comprising resources and capabilities — to realize organizational strategies as the foundation of competitive advantages and, ultimately, organizational performance. Thus, this theoretical lens highlights that the individual capabilities of top managers are critical

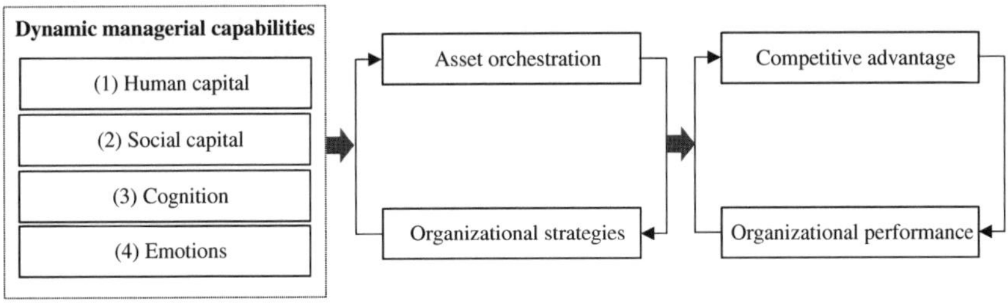

Figure 1. Dynamic managerial capabilities: Underlying components and organizational effects.

Source: Based on Adner & Helfat (2003) and Heubeck (2023a).

for organizational survival in the long run (Helfat & Martin, 2015; Heubeck & Meckl, 2022b).

Historically, the strength of DMCs was argued to be contingent on three dimensions — managerial human capital, social capital, and cognition (Adner & Helfat, 2003). Later theoretical refinements introduced a fourth dimension of DMCs: managers' emotions (Huy & Zott, 2019). Emotions seem to play an integral role in the context of GenAI, as evidenced by a recent Deloitte report (Deloitte United States, 2024). Therefore, we will adopt a four-part dimensionalization of DMCs to understand the intricacies of GenAI better. Figure 1 summarizes these elementary considerations for our research and depicts the reinforcing relationship within the causal chain of DMCs. We note that there are also critical interdependencies between the four dimensions of DMCs, which we turn to in greater detail in Section 4.5.

DMC theory provides a useful theoretical framework for studying, first, which managerial capabilities are required in the age of GenAI and, second, how GenAI can impact managerial capabilities — both positively through facilitating learning and negatively by rendering existing managerial capabilities outdated. Further, expanding the theoretical perspective of DMCs to the current age of GenAI is highly warranted, given that top management is responsible for making strategic decisions on GenAI. Therefore, the following chapter aims to assess the four dimensions of DMCs in the context of GenAI and then discuss the interactions between these dimensions to derive a framework of DMCs that applies to GenAI.

4. A Framework for Dynamic Managerial Capabilities in the Age of GenAI

4.1. *Managers' human capital in the age of GenAI*

Human capital refers to the knowledge and skills of managers to design, implement, and adopt organizational strategies, which managers develop formally (e.g., higher education) and informally (e.g., learning-by-doing or on-the-job training) (Becker, 2014). Therefore, managers possess not only different types of human capital but also vary in the level of their human capital. In other words, managers can be educated in different areas or gain experience at specific firms, while the strength of these skills is also determined by the level of education in this field or the tenure at the firm (Heubeck, 2023a; Heubeck & Meckl, 2023).

The role of managers is likely to be fundamentally reshaped by the proliferation of GenAI throughout the strategic decision-making process. In their exploratory review, Ng *et al.* (2021) propose a conceptualization of *AI literacy*, which represents a powerful human capital managerial capability composed of four interrelated dimensions that also apply to the GenAI context. First, *knowing and understanding GenAI* requires managers to acquire fundamental knowledge about GenAI's basic techniques and concepts. This component of GenAI literacy also requires managers to be confident with their skills and knowledge in using these technologies and have a positive attitude toward their application. Second, *using and applying GenAI* means that managers are aware of and can utilize the various applications of GenAI in different contexts. Third, *evaluating GenAI* can interact effectively with GenAI and critically evaluate its outcomes. Therefore, this GenAI literacy dimension concerns higher-order thinking skills (e.g., assessments, judgments, and forecasts) required to realize the synergistic potential between GenAI and human intelligence. Fourth, *GenAI ethics* relates to the ethical principles in using GenAI-generated information to make decisions and the extent to which human oversight is practiced. Thus, this component of GenAI literacy is driven by human-centered considerations, taking ethics, accountability, transparency, fairness, and safety into account (Ng *et al.*, 2021).

A high degree of GenAI literacy is crucial to finding new use cases, especially in uncharted territory. Here, leaders face a choice: build entirely new, best-fit GenAI solutions (more skill, resources, and time) or adapt existing models (potentially suboptimal, but faster and easier with current resources) (Kar *et al.*, 2021). Developing GenAI literacy within the workforce has become a critical management responsibility. Equally important is the evaluation of GenAI literacy among managers and employees. Possible ways to assess GenAI literacy include knowledge tests, project portfolio analysis, or artefact-based interviews (Ng *et al.*, 2021).

Realizing the synergistic potentials of GenAI requires that managers complement GenAI's more objective and computational skill set with the human element that GenAI lacks. Therefore, it becomes imperative that managers develop complementary (soft) skills, such as clear communication, empathy, or ethical leadership. The complementation of AI with human elements is also crucial in employee feedback, where the quality benefits of AI-generated feedback are reduced by the negative perception of AI feedback that undermines employee productivity (Tong *et al.*, 2021). As the boundaries between human intelligence and GenAI continue to blur, striking the delicate balance between humans and technology becomes more challenging. This monumental management task should become even more difficult as GenAI develops more human-like capabilities, such as creativity. Therefore, managers need to be aware of the potential shifts in the power balance between human intelligence and GenAI, especially with the increasing reliance on these technologies for making not only simple and structured but also highly complex and unstructured decisions (Berente *et al.*, 2021). Additionally, GenAI can generally be used for training purposes. For example, GenAI can create simulated scenarios that illustrate real-world managerial challenges through which top managers can practice decision-making, leadership skills, and problem-solving.

The underlying complexities for top management in making GenAI-related decisions rest on the fundamental issue that managers need to make both decisions about a new technology and with a new technology. Further, GenAI represents a moving target, which poses significant challenges for strategic decision-making as the underlying process typically requires clearly defined goals and known parameters (Berente *et al.*, 2021). Consequently, top managers must continually be aware of GenAI's current and future potentials and adopt a more open perspective on strategic decision-making processes, goals, and outcomes.

4.2. *Managers' social capital in the age of GenAI*

Managers acquire social capital through repeated formal and informal interactions within and across organizational boundaries. Social capital enhances strategic decision-making through increased knowledge and information exchange that spurs learning processes while facilitating the implementation of strategic decisions by making other actors' resources and capabilities available (Adner & Helfat, 2003; Heubeck, 2023a).

Human interaction with GenAI represents a double-edged sword. For one, GenAI could enhance formal and informal interactions of top managers with various stakeholders by providing real-time information and suggestions for interesting topics of conversation upfront. In this context, GenAI could also support creating personalized communication and tailoring messages to different stakeholders' specific interests and concerns by analyzing past interactions and preferences. This customization could improve customer relationships and, thus, the quality of interactions in the future. Furthermore, GenAI could relieve top managers by (partially) automating routine tasks such as replying to emails, summarizing texts, or providing practical support for information searches and research so that they have more time for social interactions.

GenAI could also lead to the development of new types of social capital — significantly beyond firms' boundaries. For example, GenAI could foster information exchange with suppliers or allow firms to grasp the bigger picture of all relevant stakeholders' interests. To the extent that GenAI fosters beneficial relationships and enhances the understanding of stakeholders, top management could develop more social capital with firm-external parties. Higher levels of social capital could ultimately lead top management to make more adept decisions based on more information and reinforced through reciprocal support from various stakeholders. GenAI could also use these data to make future decisions on a larger dataset.

On the other hand, engaging in conversations with GenAI could reduce the perceived necessity for real-world social interactions. Additionally, there is the risk that the content created by GenAI could lack authenticity. Particularly in the case of interactions, it could fail to capture the nuances of human communication. The language model may misinterpret context or tone, leading to unintended meanings. This could result in misunderstandings, conflicts, or damage to the manager's reputation if AI-generated content is perceived as insensitive, inappropriate, or inaccurate.

Sociotechnical capital is another form of social capital that has not yet been studied under the lens of DMCs. This concept, first introduced by Resnick (2001) as the "productive combinations of social relations and information and communication technology" (pp. 2–3), has recently been extended to the AI context (Makarius *et al.*, 2020). Like other digital technologies, GenAI can also spur social interactions that build the foundation for social capital. The interdependence between social contexts and technology applications builds the foundation for social capital-induced activities, including information routing, resource exchange, emotional support, coordination, and collective action. Especially in the context of GenAI, it becomes imperative to highlight that top management needs to make conscious and repeated efforts to build sociotechnical capital. Only then can managers reap the benefits of sociotechnical capital that accrue from removing interaction barriers, expanding interaction networks, restricting information flows, managing dependencies, and maintaining common history (Resnick, 2001).

The social capital dimension of DMCs also requires managers to establish a certain degree of trust in GenAI tools. However, establishing the required trust is not trivial, as demonstrated by a study that found that news is less believed when created by GenAI rather than humans (Longoni *et al.*, 2021). Therefore, it is essential to highlight that this type of trust significantly differs from traditional trust developed through repeated and positive human interactions because trust in GenAI is more of a one-way street. This implies that humans need to develop trust in GenAI, but the technology itself does not rely on trust to function; trust is irrelevant to the functioning of GenAI tools. Sufficient trust in GenAI from top management and the organization's members at large is necessary for the efficient integration of this technology into business operations and quintessential to avoid its negative repercussions, such as reduced productivity due to employee dissatisfaction or increased turnover. Therefore, managers should establish a culture of technological trust within the organization, making AI — and adapted to our context GenAI — an accepted and active partner in strategic decision-making and operative tasks (Makarius *et al.*, 2020). One potential way to achieve higher trust in GenAI is to make the narrative of GenAI more favorable within the organization, which can be realized by educating the workforce about the potential benefits and risks, making the operations more transparent and explainable, and implementing policies so that humans retain ultimate control and tackle potential biases in GenAI (Sartori & Theodorou, 2022). Furthermore, GenAI tools should be attractive to the workforce, i.e., the user interface should be user-friendly and easy to use. Top management should define clear ethical guidelines and ensure continuous monitoring and improvement of these tools.

4.3. *Managers' cognition in the age of GenAI*

Cognition differs from the previous two dimensions of DMCs in that it constitutes a meta-capability that imprints how managers make decisions based on which kinds of predispositions. Specifically, managerial cognition is related to cognitive processing — i.e., collecting, interpreting, ranking, and storing information — and cognitive structures — i.e., the personal worldviews that serve as a reference frame for decision-making. The intricacies of managerial cognition lie in the biases (i.e., irrational decision-making) and heuristics (i.e., simplified decision-making rules) that imprint organizational strategies (Heubeck, 2023a; Mundlos, 2024).

The management challenge in today's business environment relates to making adept yet swift decisions based on an enormous amount of data that are often complex, ambiguous, and fragmented (Keding, 2021). Faced with their inherently limited cognitive capacities for considering information in their decision-making and the increasing time constraints in rendering timely decisions (Heubeck & Meckl, 2022a), managers can resort to GenAI to handle the data overload by filtering, structuring, and condensing information. Thus, applying GenAI in the decision-making process to reduce decision-making complexity and improve its speed could significantly improve the quality of those decisions — maybe even making them more rational. Nevertheless, it is essential to point out that managers need to be aware of two critical sources of bias when using GenAI. The first bias relates to the *prompt bias* that managers introduce to their decision-making. The outcome of the human-machine interaction is highly contingent on which prompts managers use and how they formulate them. Using GenAI in decision-making could amplify the already-existing biases in managerial decision-making. Thus, managers must either try to frame their prompts unbiasedly or ask the GenAI technology to reduce potential prompt bias. The second bias related to *GenAI bias* is that GenAI itself could introduce unwanted bias into managerial decision-making because the outputs are always based on the initial training data from which the model learned. Therefore, existing biases related to greater societal issues (e.g., sexism or racism) as well as the firm's past decision-making itself (e.g., biased decisions that were made in the past continue to be reinforced through current and future decision-making) could be perpetuated using GenAI in decision-making. Therefore, managers need to be conscious of the potential sources of bias in GenAI-aided decision-making. This also raises the question of who is accountable for the results of GenAI-aided decision-making and which aspects of strategy development should or should not be outsourced to GenAI (Berente *et al.*, 2021; Keding, 2021). Managers need to develop a sensitive awareness of which decisions involve GenAI, and, above all, they should always question the results and not unquestioningly trust them.

Therefore, it becomes clear that organizations need to assess the synergy between human intelligence and GenAI to leverage their unique strengths. A possible way to assess this synergistic potential is to view human–GenAI interaction on a continuum between GenAI-only and human-intelligence-only applications. We provide details on specific use cases in Table 1.

This subchapter has shown that GenAI technologies help overcome the limitations of human cognitive processing. Therefore, we further dissect potential scenarios where human cognitive processing can be augmented or even substituted by GenAI. These potential applications of GenAI could consequently leverage managerial cognition in distinct ways, as summarized in Table 2. Specifically, the left side of the table relates to the two critical challenges of human information processing: *information processing constraints* that impose limitations on the amount of information humans can handle in their cognitive processing and *ineffective or local search routines* that relate to the limited search for new information beyond currently known applications. The application of GenAI in conjunction with human intelligence can lead to the *development* or *generation of ideas*, as depicted in the upper part of the table. This matrix results in four potential applications of GenAI that can effectively overcome managerial cognitive limitations (Haefner *et al.*, 2021).

4.4. *Managers' emotions in the age of GenAI*

Emotions constitute a crucial psychological dimension of DMCs. Strategic decision-making and change generally can elicit various positive and negative emotions that influence managers' decision-making processes

Table 1. Synergistic potential of GenAI and human intelligence.

GenAI-only	Hybrid			Human intelligence-only
	Human < GenAI	Human >/= GenAI	Human > Gen AI	
• Fully GenAI-based decision-making, mostly in automation or process improvement tasks • Veto rights are needed so that humans remain in control	• Collecting data or processing large data amounts due to superior machine abilities • Human intelligence as support to define data sources	• Group intelligence of humans is used to make strategic decisions • GenAI assists in the detailed interpretation of large data amounts, often helpful for operational decisions	• Alternative provision • Probability calculation • Computational efforts • GenAI is used to outsource computational tasks that do not necessarily require human intelligence • Human intelligence is needed to make the final decision based on GenAI-supported preparations	Human intelligence is required to uncover experiences, feelings, and other tacit knowledge, often combined with soft skills

Source: Based on Trunk *et al*. (2020).

Table 2. Potential applications of GenAI to leverage managerial cognition.

	Develop ideas	Generate ideas
Information processing constraints	(1) *Increased information processing*: GenAI can be used to identify and evaluate more information than possible by humans alone, which can be used to develop ideas.	(2) *Improved opportunity and threat recognition*: GenAI can be used to recognize more problems, opportunities, and threats that may be used to generate new ideas.
Ineffective or local search routines	(3) *Enhanced idea identification*: GenAI can be used to identify and evaluate more creative and explorative ideas.	(4) *Upgraded recognition of out-of-the-box opportunities*: GenAI can be used to recognize better or even create more creative and explorative opportunities, threats, and problems to generate new ideas.

Source: Based on Haefner *et al.* (2021).

and subsequent behaviors. In this sense, emotions are evoked in situations important to top managers — such as critical strategic decisions — and materialize in the objectives, but worries related to these situations are also evoked. Therefore, managers need strong emotion regulation capabilities to handle and direct their emotions toward achieving their goals and ensuring their well-being (Huy & Zott, 2019).

Emotions will likely play an even more integral element in managerial decision-making in the age of GenAI because these technologies will probably overtake more and more objective decision-making based on facts and figures in the long run. Managers will consequently be tasked to redirect their attention to the human element of decision-making, while communicating GenAI-based decisions to other managers, employees, or stakeholders will likely be a more central element of future management. In other words, managers will be less concerned with objective decisions, shifting their main tasks to intuitive and emotional ones. Therefore, implicit knowledge will take the edge over explicit knowledge, and managers will require greater emotional intelligence and rely more on their human judgment in making decisions or prioritizing alternatives. This shift in the day-to-day tasks of managers is likely to make management a

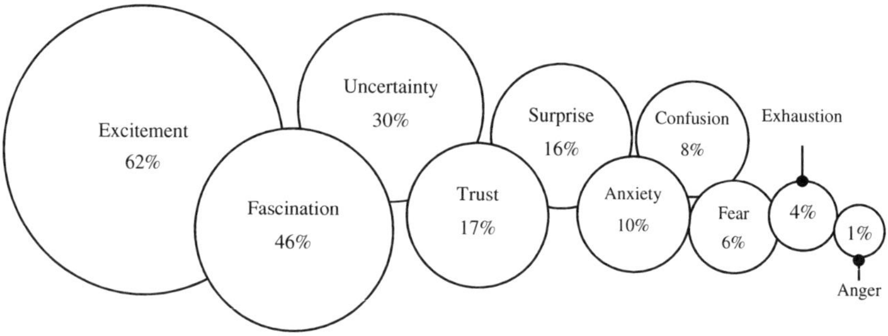

Figure 2. Deloitte Report (2024).

Note: Q: Thinking about generative AI, what emotions do you feel most about the technology (n = 2,835)?

higher-valued activity, where managers need to piece together the bigger picture of GenAI-provided information and possess more significant soft skills (Keding, 2021; Plastino & Purdy, 2018).

The proliferation of GenAI technology within the workplace will also likely lead to positive and negative emotions among managers and company employees. A recent report by Deloitte (2024) surveyed over 2,800 business and technology leaders, indicating that GenAI triggers a range of intense emotions among managers, both positive and negative (illustrated in Figure 2).

On the one hand, the results showed positive emotions like excitement or fascination. In our opinion, a reason for that could be that managers might perceive GenAI as a disruptive and new technology with great potential for real added value in their professional lives. On the other hand, the results also showed negative emotions like uncertainty and anxiety. GenAI's complexity could contribute to managers' lack of understanding, fostering uncertainty about its benefits and limitations. Furthermore, fear of job displacement might arise as managers worry about automation reducing job relevance, sparking uncertainty about their future roles. Additionally, ethical concerns regarding privacy, bias, and manipulation could leave managers uncertain about aligning GenAI use with organizational values and principles.

These negative emotions could impose significant barriers to using and implementing GenAI tools within the organizations, which could have severe negative implications for these firms in the long run. Thus, top management faces the central challenge of making GenAI a positively connotated technology by, for example, emphasizing its significant benefits for strategic decision-making. However, the emotional reaction also extends to all employees at large. Lower-level employees, especially, might fear their job security due to being replaced by GenAI technology. Therefore, top management should transparently communicate the firm's GenAI strategy, addressing concerns within the workforce and showcasing the benefits of using GenAI. Only by reducing negative emotions toward technology can company-wide cultural change occur. Thus, top management must proactively manage GenAI-induced change by reskilling its current employees. This strategy mitigates the risks from potential layoffs, such as damaged morale or company reputation, while it also allows firms to keep valuable employees with years of domain-specific knowledge and expertise. Further, this proactive approach is also valuable from an ethical and social responsibility perspective.

Finally, a reskilled workforce can also provide several opportunities because it combines existing with new knowledge, reduces the time and resources needed to onboard new personnel, and could ultimately lead to more significant innovation and competitive advantage. Outsourcing GenAI knowledge should only be the last resort for modern-day organizations that need to be equipped for future technological change, as this would infer that the valuable knowledge related to GenAI would reside nearly entirely outside of the organization. The outsourcing strategy is also improbable in mitigating negative emotions surrounding GenAI because the company effectively avoids active engagement with this critical technology.

4.5. *Interdependencies between the dimensions of dynamic managerial capabilities*

The intricate nature of DMCs stems from the interactions between their underlying dimensions. Existing research has demonstrated the significance of interactions between managers' human capital, social capital, cognition, and emotions. Therefore, DMCs influence organizational outcomes not only through the isolated effects of their underlying dimensions but also through the interdependencies between the four subcomponents that lead to additional heterogeneity in managerial capabilities (Heubeck, 2023a).

For instance, developing GenAI-related human capital might lead to more cross-function collaboration within the firm, thereby increasing social capital. Relatedly, the increased information exchange through sociotechnical capital might lead to an increase in GenAI-specific human capital. Managerial cognition is also closely related to human and social capital formation. Specifically, the potential complementarities between human intelligence and GenAI could spur human capital development. Conversely, the broader search for GenAI applications makes managers more likely to exchange ideas, collaborate with other organizational departments, or look outside the organization for potential information sources, thereby augmenting social capital. Finally, emotions toward GenAI could be heavily influenced by a manager's human, social, and cognitive capital. With more knowledge and skills related to GenAI, more social relationships that increase the salience of GenAI benefits, and a more open mindset to GenAI and its possibilities, the perception of GenAI could shift dramatically.

DMCs should, therefore, allow top managers to (1) identify productive use cases of GenAI in strategic decision-making, (2) leverage GenAI tools to make informed decisions, which involves cautiously interpreting, carefully evaluating, and taking responsibility for GenAI-generated output, (3) lead by example in dealing with GenAI applications to motivate employees using this technology, (4) foster awareness for the benefits and risks of GenAI applications within the firm, and (5) use GenAI tools in increasing the efficiency of repeatable management tasks, including data structuring, performance evaluation, or employee selection.

4.6. *Extended DMC framework*

Applying the micro-founded dynamic capabilities framework (Teece, 2007) to the individual managerial level, we argue that the strength of DMCs in today's technology-driven competitive environment affects strategic decision-making and organizational performance. In particular, GenAI, as an emergent technology with disruptive potential, could have a substantial impact, as our chapter contribution shows. In doing so, we propose a reciprocal relationship between GenAI and DMCs (illustrated in Figure 3). On the one hand, GenAI will impact a manager's existing set of DMCs. GenAI can, for example, increase a manager's human capital, influence a manager's emotions, or change social interaction with other people for managers.

On the other hand, we also suspect a strong link between DMCs and GenAI adoption. In other words, the managerial capability set of a manager determines the successful and value-creating application of the

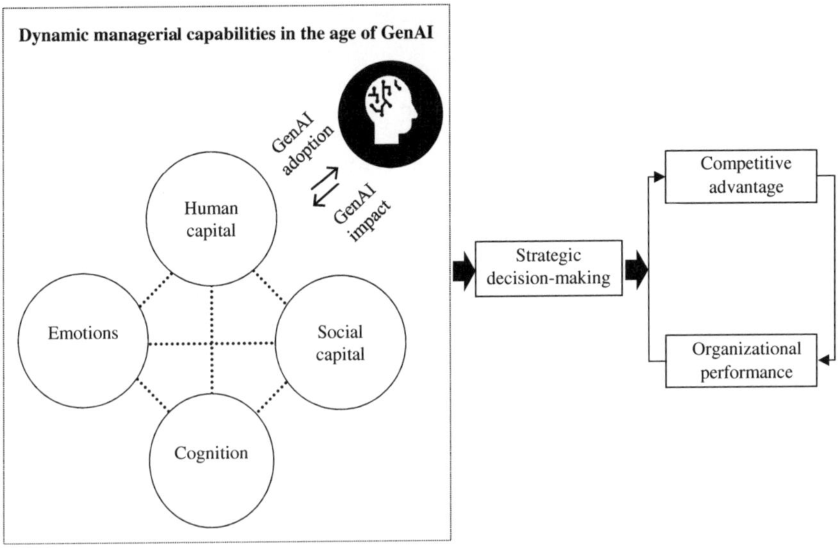

Figure 3. Extended framework for dynamic managerial capabilities in the age of GenAI.

technology, both on a personal level and thus also on an organizational level. For example, if managers have a technology-open mindset, have the skills to use the technology, and are aware of the risks of GenAI, it is more likely that they will use the technology successfully and want to use it.

Another important aspect of our framework is the interdependent nature of the four dynamic managerial capability dimensions: human capital, social capital, cognition, and emotions. As shown in the previous chapter, DMCs influence organizational outcomes not only through the isolated effects of their underlying dimensions but also through the interdependencies between the four subcomponents, which lead to additional heterogeneity in management capabilities (Heubeck, 2023a).

5. Future Research Directions for Dynamic Managerial Capabilities in the Age of GenAI

In the last chapter, we offer ideas and directions for future research on DMCs in the context of GenAI (summarized in Table 3).

In our article, we focused on the perspective of top managers and their DMCs. Although this perspective is warranted, given the focus on strategic decisions, future research could also study other hierarchical levels.

Table 3. Proposed future research directions for DMCs in the age of GenAI.

Research direction	Description
(1) Hierarchical levels	Explore perspectives beyond top managers to include middle managers' roles in facilitating digital transformation and GenAI adoption.
(2) GenAI literacy for managers	Develop concepts and guidelines to enhance managers' GenAI literacy across dimensions: knowing, understanding, using, applying, evaluating, and ethics.
(3) Ethical guidelines and trust in GenAI	Formulate clear ethical guidelines for GenAI usage within companies and investigate methods to enhance trust in technology among employees and managers.
(4) Emotional impact of GenAI on managers	Examine how managers' emotions evolve with increasing GenAI maturity and explore the influence of emotions on decision-making.
(5) Strategic value of GenAI	Investigate specific strategic choice situations where GenAI provides the most significant added value and how managers' experience influences its targeted use in decision-making.

In later developments of DMC theory, the level of analysis has also been extended to middle managers (Heubeck, 2023a), which seems particularly critical in light of middle managers' boundary-spanning role in digital transformation (Nadkarni & Prügl, 2021). Thus, middle managers could be the key to the company's technology-open and future-oriented culture. Middle managers facilitate the change by managing resistance and providing support and training to employees. They act as a bridge between the top management and the frontline employees. Hence, they are crucial to achieving an organization's overarching GenAI strategy and goals through concrete implementation initiatives within their teams.

We believe that GenAI will be a critical competitive factor in the future and is essential for the long-term survival of a company. Accordingly, building GenAI literacy is crucial for managers. Future research could develop concepts and guidelines that managers could use to increase their GenAI literacy. As we presented in Section 4.1, GenAI literacy consists of four interrelated dimensions — knowing and understanding GenAI, using and applying GenAI, evaluating GenAI, and GenAI ethics — which could be used to structure future research approaches. An earlier-mentioned example is the establishment of clear ethical guidelines for the use of GenAI within a company. Top management must take responsibility and draw up such guidelines to create a clear framework and, thus, security for employees. Future research could develop such guidelines and frameworks to ensure the responsible use of GenAI. In this context, it is also promising to investigate how trust in technology can be increased among both employees and managers.

Furthermore, it will also be interesting to examine the extent to which the increasing maturity of GenAI influences managers' emotions. While companies are currently conducting experiments and feasibility studies, over time, many actual use cases on a much larger scale will be used to increase value creation and, thereby, affect competitive advantage. As the technology is still relatively new, managers may have positive emotions like curiosity or excitement, while negative emotions such as uncertainty or fear of the new may affect their decision-making. These emotions will likely change when GenAI is no longer a novelty and managers have become accustomed to it.

Finally, future research could examine the specific strategic choice situations and decisions for which GenAI offers the most added value. Over time, managers will gain experience, which could pave the way for a more targeted use of GenAI in decision-making.

6. Chapter Take-Aways

The emergence of GenAI represents a pivotal moment in the evolution of strategic decision-making within the corporate realm. As delineated throughout this chapter, the integration of GenAI within business processes is not merely a technological upgrade but a transformative shift that necessitates a recalibration of managers' dynamic capabilities. The rapid ascent of GenAI technologies, exemplified by the meteoric rise of ChatGPT, underscores a clear message: the future and competitiveness of an organization could depend on the ability of managers to navigate GenAI landscapes.

To summarize, we have formulated a few key takeaways from this chapter:

- **Unprecedented impact and potential:** GenAI's introduction has showcased its capability to generate novel content and its potential to boost global GDP and reshape business landscapes significantly. The profound influence of GenAI on strategic decision-making and competitive advantage foregrounds its indispensable role in future business operations.

- **Reciprocal enhancement between GenAI and DMCs:** The relationship between GenAI and DMCs is inherently reciprocal. On the one hand, GenAI enriches DMCs by broadening the horizon for strategic decision-making, offering new tools for knowledge synthesis, and fostering innovative problem-solving approaches. On the other hand, robust DMCs amplify the effectiveness of GenAI deployment, as managers with sophisticated capabilities in human capital, social capital, cognition, and emotions are better positioned to harness GenAI's potential responsibly and creatively. This symbiosis underscores the need for proactive development of managerial skills that complement GenAI's capabilities, thereby ensuring that leaders adapt to and shape the evolving technological landscape, driving both organizational and technological progress forward.
- **Ethical and social implications:** The deployment of GenAI carries significant ethical and social implications, from questions of bias and trust to the impact on employment and organizational culture. Managers must navigate these challenges with a principled approach, ensuring that GenAI's integration supports both organizational goals and societal values.
- **Future research directions:** The dynamic interplay between GenAI and managerial capabilities presents rich avenues for future research. Investigations could explore the development of GenAI literacy frameworks, ethical guidelines for GenAI use, the emotional impact of GenAI on managers, and the strategic contexts where GenAI offers the most value.

In conclusion, the rise of GenAI demands a strategic, informed, and nuanced approach from today's leaders. As we stand on the precipice of this technological frontier, the ability of managers to adapt, learn, and lead in the age of GenAI will not only determine their organization's competitive edge but also shape the future of innovation and business strategy. The journey into this uncharted territory is fraught with challenges, yet it offers unprecedented opportunities for those prepared to navigate its complexities. The era of GenAI is upon us, and the time for leaders to act is now.

References

Adner, R. & Helfat, C. E. (2003). Corporate effects and dynamic managerial capabilities. *Strategic Management Journal*, 24(10): 1011–1025.

Becker, G. S. (2014). *Human Capital: A Theoretical and Empirical Analysis, with Special Reference to Education*. Chicago: University of Chicago Press.

Berente, N., Gu, B., Recker, J., & Santhanam, R. (2021). Managing artificial intelligence. *MIS Quarterly*, 45(3): 1433–1450.

Bharadwaj, A. S. (2000). A resource-based perspective on information technology capability and firm performance: An empirical investigation. *MIS Quarterly*, 24(1): 169.

Budhwar, P., Chowdhury, S., Wood, G., Aguinis, H., Bamber, G. J., Beltran, J. R., Boselie, P., Lee Cooke, F., Decker, S., DeNisi, A., Dey, P. K., Guest, D., Knoblich, A. J., Malik, A., Paauwe, J., Papagiannidis, S., Patel, C., Pereira, V., Ren, S., Rogelberg, S., Saunders, M. N. K., Tung, R. L., & Varma, A. (2023). Human resource management in the age of generative artificial intelligence: Perspectives and research directions on ChatGPT. *Human Resource Management Journal*, 33(3): 606–659.

Deloitte United States. (2024). State of Generative AI in the Enterprise 2024. February 26, 2024. https://www2.deloitte.com/us/en/pages/consulting/articles/state-of-generative-ai-in-enterprise.html.

Feuerriegel, S., Hartmann, J., Janiesch, C., & Zschech, P. (2024). Generative AI. *Business & Information Systems Engineering*, 66(1): 111–126.

Gartner. (2023). What's new in artificial intelligence from the 2023 Gartner Hype Cycle: Innovations in and around generative AI dominate and have transformative impact. March 10, 2024. https://www.gartner.com/en/articles/what-s-new-in-artificial-intelligence-from-the-2023-gartner-hype-cycle.

Goldman Sachs. (2023). Generative AI could raise global GDP by 7%. March 10, 2024. https://www.goldmansachs.com/intelligence/pages/generative-ai-could-raise-global-gdp-by-7-percent.html.

Gupta, M. & George, J. F. (2016). Toward the development of a big data analytics capability. *Information & Management*, 53(8): 1049–1064.

Haefner, N., Wincent, J., Parida, V., & Gassmann, O. (2021). Artificial intelligence and innovation management: A review, framework, and research agenda. *Technological Forecasting and Social Change*, 162: 120392.

Helfat, C. E. & Martin, J. A. (2015). Dynamic managerial capabilities. *Journal of Management*, 41(5): 1281–1312.

Heubeck, T. (2023a). Looking back to look forward: A systematic review of and research agenda for dynamic managerial capabilities. *Management Review Quarterly*: 1–45.

Heubeck, T. (2023b). Managing Innovation in a Globalized Digital Economy: An Empirical Inquiry into Managerial-, Governance-, and Firm-Level Antecedents and Contingencies. University of Bayreuth.

Heubeck, T. & Meckl, R. (2022a). Antecedents to cognitive business model evaluation: A dynamic managerial capabilities perspective. *Review of Managerial Science*, 16(8): 2441–2466.

Heubeck, T. & Meckl, R. (2022b). Dynamic managerial capabilities and R&D spending: The role of CEO founder status. *International Journal of Innovation Management*, 26(10): 1–39.

Heubeck, T. & Meckl, R. (2023). Microfoundations of innovation: A dynamic CEO capabilities perspective. *Managerial and Decision Economics*, 44(6): 3108–3126.

Huy, Q. & Zott, C. (2019). Exploring the affective underpinnings of dynamic managerial capabilities: How managers' emotion regulation behaviors mobilize resources for their firms. *Strategic Management Journal*, 40(1): 28–54.

Kar, S., Kar, A. K., & Gupta, M. P. (2021). Modeling drivers and barriers of artificial intelligence adoption: Insights from a strategic management perspective. *Intelligent Systems in Accounting, Finance and Management*, 28(4): 217–238.

Keding, C. (2021). Understanding the interplay of artificial intelligence and strategic management: Four decades of research in review. *Management Review Quarterly*, 71(1): 91–134.

Longoni, C., Fradkin, A., Cian, L., & Pennycook, G. (2021). News from artificial intelligence is believed less. *SSRN Electronic Journal* (forthcoming).

Makarius, E. E., Mukherjee, D., Fox, J. D., & Fox, A. K. (2020). Rising with the machines: A sociotechnical framework for bringing artificial intelligence into the organization. *Journal of Business Research*, 120: 262–273.

McKinsey. (2024). Economic potential of generative AI. McKinsey. February 26, 2024. https://www.mckinsey.com/capabilities/mckinsey-digital/our-insights/the-economic-potential-of-generative-ai-the-next-productivity-frontier#introduction.

Mikalef, P. & Gupta, M. (2021). Artificial intelligence capability: Conceptualization, measurement calibration, and empirical study on its impact on organizational creativity and firm performance. *Information & Management*, 58(3): 103434.

Mundlos, P. (2024). The impact of artificial intelligence on managerial attention allocation for discontinuous change: A conceptual framework. *Management Review Quarterly* (forthcoming).

Nadkarni, S. & Prügl, R. (2021). Digital transformation: A review, synthesis and opportunities for future research. *Management Review Quarterly*, 71: 233–341. https://doi.org/10.1007/s11301-020-00185-7.

Ng, D. T. K., Leung, J. K. L., Chu, S. K. W., & Qiao, M. S. (2021). Conceptualizing AI literacy: An exploratory review. *Computers and Education: Artificial Intelligence*, 2: 100041.

Plastino, E. & Purdy, M. (2018). Game changing value from artificial intelligence: Eight strategies. *Strategy & Leadership*, 46(1): 16–22.
Resnick, P. (2001). Beyond bowling together: Sociotechnical capital. *HCI in the New Millenium*, 77: 247–272.
Reuters. (2023). ChatGPT sets record for fastest-growing user base - analyst note. March 10, 2024. https://www.reuters.com/technology/chatgpt-sets-record-fastest-growing-user-base-analyst-note-2023-02-01/.
Sartori, L. & Theodorou, A. (2022). A sociotechnical perspective for the future of AI: Narratives, inequalities, and human control. *Ethics and Information Technology*, 24(1): 1–11.
Teece, D. J. (2007). Explicating dynamic capabilities: The nature and microfoundations of (sustainable) enterprise performance. *Strategic Management Journal*, 28(13): 1319–1350.
Tong, S., Jia, N., Luo, X., & Fang, Z. (2021). The Janus face of artificial intelligence feedback: Deployment versus disclosure effects on employee performance. *Strategic Management Journal*, 42(9): 1600–1631.
Trunk, A., Birkel, H., & Hartmann, E. (2020). On the current state of combining human and artificial intelligence for strategic organizational decision making. *Business Research*, 13(3): 875–919.

https://doi.org/10.1142/9789811296475_0009

Chapter 9

Insights Unleashed: Harnessing AI for Learning Analytics

Anna Lissitz

McDaniel College, Westminster, MD, USA

This chapter delves into the intersection of artificial intelligence (AI) and learning analytics to explore the transformative power they hold for education. AI is revolutionizing data collection, analysis, and utilization to elevate learning outcomes, from tailored learning journeys to predictive insights. This chapter also explores the ethical dimensions inherent in these advancements. Through real-world examples and case studies, this chapter reviews insights into AI's capacity to reimagine teaching and learning, fostering adaptability, inclusivity, and efficacy. Whether you're an educator, a researcher, a policymaker, or simply intrigued by the future of education, this chapter offers an exploration of AI and learning analytics.

After an overview of AI and learning analytics, this chapter presents examples of learning analytics tools and platforms. The role of AI in learning analytics is discussed along with examples and applications of AI in learning analytics. Some attention is given to the challenges and considerations of implementing AI with specific regard to learning analytics. Issues such as ethics, privacy, security, and biases are discussed. A list of best practices and strategies for implementation is shared. The AI field is changing at a rapid pace, and hopefully, these strategies will help stakeholders not just keep up but also advance the AI field with responsible and effective practices. Future directions and opportunities are presented before the chapter wraps up with a call to action for all stakeholders in the education industry.

1. Overview of AI and Learning Analytics

In recent years, the integration of AI and learning analytics has progressed rapidly, fueled by advancements in AI technologies and a burgeoning availability of educational data. This evolution underscores the growing recognition and significance of data-driven decision-making in education. Educational institutions increasingly adopt AI-powered learning platforms and tools, capitalizing on their potential to personalize learning experiences, offer real-time feedback, and optimize educational resources. Leveraging AI algorithms, these platforms analyze students' digital interactions to tailor adaptive learning pathways to individual needs (Sharif & Atif, 2024).

Moreover, strides in natural language processing (NLP) have extended AI's reach into many educational realms. NLP techniques are now applied to assess textual data, including student essays, forum posts, and instructor feedback (Baker, 2019). Such systems facilitate automated essay grading, sentiment analysis, and content recommendation, streamlining assessment and feedback processes.

A heightened emphasis on ethical and responsible AI usage in learning analytics has emerged. Stakeholders recognize the biases, privacy concerns, and ethical implications inherent in AI-powered educational technologies. Efforts are underway to develop guidelines, frameworks, and best practices ensuring fairness, transparency, and accountability in AI-driven educational systems (Borondo *et al.*, 2024).

Furthermore, AI technologies have infiltrated educational assessment and evaluation practices, enhancing accuracy, efficiency, and objectivity. AI-driven assessment tools analyze vast datasets to forecast student performance and glean insights into learning outcomes (Lissitz & Jiao, 2020). Additionally, AI-powered proctoring solutions monitor students during online exams, detect academic misconduct, and uphold academic integrity (Nigam *et al.*, 2021).

Beyond K-12 education, there's a growing focus on applying AI and learning analytics in higher education (Sharif & Atif, 2024), corporate training (Sabale & Gomathi, 2022), and lifelong learning contexts (Poquet & de Laat, 2021). Universities, online platforms, and corporate training providers leverage AI to personalize learning experiences, optimize curriculum design, and support continuous skill development.

Interdisciplinary collaboration has flourished in AI and learning analytics. Researchers, practitioners, and industry stakeholders from diverse fields, including computer science, education, psychology, and data science, collaborate to exchange ideas, methodologies, and best practices. Knowledge-sharing initiatives, conferences, and professional development programs facilitate this exchange.

Since 2020, AI and learning analytics have reshaped education, presenting opportunities to refine teaching and learning processes, enhance outcomes, and empower learners across diverse educational landscapes. Yet, challenges related to privacy, equity, and algorithmic bias persist, demanding ongoing attention and collaboration from all stakeholders involved in AI and education.

2. Importance of Integrating AI with Learning Analytics for Educational Improvement

The integration of AI with learning analytics stands as a pivotal endeavor in educational enhancement, poised to revolutionize teaching and learning practices, elevate student outcomes, and inform data-driven decision-making within education. This integration holds several critical facets essential for educational improvement.

Firstly, personalized learning experiences emerge as a cornerstone benefit. AI-powered learning analytics facilitates the tailoring of learning experiences to align with individual student's needs, preferences, and learning modalities. Through the analysis of student learning behaviors, performance metrics, and progress indicators, AI algorithms curate personalized recommendations, adaptive learning pathways, and targeted interventions bespoke to each learner's distinct profile (Baker, 2019). This personalized approach fosters heightened engagement, motivation, and mastery of learning objectives, culminating in improved learning outcomes.

Moreover, the synergy between AI and learning analytics promotes data-driven decision-making. By harnessing the analytical capabilities of AI, educators, administrators, and policymakers gain access to actionable insights gleaned from vast troves of educational data. AI algorithms adeptly analyze student performance trends, pinpoint areas for improvement, and forecast future outcomes, equipping stakeholders to make well-informed decisions pertaining to curriculum design, instructional methodologies, resource allocation, and student support services. This data-driven ethos optimizes educational processes, amplifies teaching efficacy, and maximizes the efficacy of educational interventions.

Furthermore, the marriage of AI with learning analytics facilitates early intervention and support mechanisms. AI-driven analytics adeptly identifies students who may be at risk of encountering academic hurdles, disengagement, or attrition, enabling timely intervention and support initiatives (Sajja *et al.*, 2023). Through the analysis of patterns in student learning behaviors, interactions, and performance metrics, AI algorithms flag potential issues, recommend pertinent interventions, and connect students with tailored support services, including tutoring, counseling, or academic advisement. This proactive stance effectively staves off academic setbacks, bolsters student retention rates, and nurtures academic triumph.

Additionally, the continuous feedback loop engendered by AI-powered learning analytics fosters perpetual improvement. These analytic results furnish educators with ongoing insights into the efficacy of educational practices, interventions, and resources. By scrutinizing data pertaining to student learning outcomes, instructional methodologies, and curriculum efficacy, AI algorithms pinpoint areas of success and avenues for refinement. This iterative process of feedback and adjustment heightens teaching efficacy, optimizes learning experiences, and engenders a culture of perpetual learning and professional development among educators.

Lastly, the integration of AI with learning analytics promotes enhanced accessibility and inclusivity within education. Through adaptive learning technologies, intelligent tutoring systems, and assistive tools, AI extends personalized support, accommodations, and alternative pathways to learners possessing diverse needs, abilities, and learning styles. This inclusive ethos ensures equitable access to high-quality education for all students, fostering an environment conducive to collective success and achievement (Sajja *et al.*, 2023).

In summation, the integration of AI with learning analytics constitutes a linchpin for educational improvement, furnishing educators, administrators, and policymakers with the tools and insights requisite for leveraging data-driven insights, personalized learning experiences, and proactive support mechanisms. Through this symbiotic relationship, educational processes are optimized, student success is championed, and a culture of continuous improvement is nurtured within the educational sphere.

3. Understanding Learning Analytics

3.1. *Definition and scope of learning analytics*

Learning analytics constitutes a comprehensive process aimed at enhancing learning and teaching practices through the gathering, analysis, and interpretation of data from various learning environments and activities. This approach employs statistical, computational, and predictive techniques to extract meaningful insights from educational data, thereby informing instructional strategies, curriculum design, and support interventions.

Within its realm, learning analytics spans a wide array of activities geared toward improving the effectiveness of teaching and learning. It encompasses the collection of diverse data types from multiple sources, including learning management systems (LMS), online platforms, and student information systems (SIS). These data, ranging from demographic information to academic performance metrics and engagement patterns, form the foundation for subsequent analysis.

Through the lens of learning analytics, educational data undergo a thorough analysis, leveraging statistical, computational, and data mining techniques. The objective is to uncover patterns, trends, and relationships that provide valuable insights into student learning trajectories and instructional effectiveness. This analytical process fosters a deeper understanding of student behaviors and performance, thus facilitating informed decision-making.

The interpretation of analytical findings is a crucial aspect of learning analytics, requiring collaboration between educators, data analysts, and stakeholders. By deriving actionable insights from the data, educators can identify areas for improvement and tailor interventions to meet individual student needs. This collaborative approach ensures that data-driven decisions align with educational goals and priorities.

Ultimately, the goal of learning analytics is to translate insights into actionable strategies that enhance teaching and learning outcomes. This may involve designing personalized learning experiences, implementing targeted interventions for at-risk students, or optimizing curriculum design based on analytical findings. Throughout this process, ethical considerations regarding privacy, data security, and responsible use of data remain paramount, ensuring that educational data are handled with integrity and respect for student rights.

3.2. *Key concepts and components* (*data collection, analysis, and visualization*)

Learning analytics draws upon data sourced from various educational environments, including LMS, SIS, online platforms, digital resources, assessments, surveys, and educational technologies. These sources yield insights into student demographics, enrollment, course engagement, academic performance, learning behaviors, and resource interactions.

Collecting relevant data from these diverse sources is a foundational step in learning analytics, essential for subsequent analysis. Data collection methods encompass automated processes, manual entries, surveys, interviews, and observational studies. Adherence to ethical guidelines, privacy protection, and data integrity maintenance are imperative throughout this phase (Martinez-Maldonado *et al.*, 2023).

Following data collection, rigorous processing and preparation are undertaken to render the data analyzable. Tasks involve cleaning to rectify errors, transforming to standardize formats, and integrating to consolidate disparate sources into a unified dataset. These steps are pivotal in ensuring data quality and reliability for subsequent analysis.

Descriptive analytics unfolds as an exploration and summarization of educational data to unveil historical trends, patterns, and relationships. Utilizing techniques such as data visualization, summary statistics, and exploratory analysis, educators gain insights into the current educational landscape and identify areas warranting further investigation.

Predictive analytics employs statistical and machine learning algorithms to forecast future outcomes based on historical data. Within learning analytics, predictive models anticipate student performance, flag at-risk students, project dropout rates, and predict learning requirements. This proactive approach empowers educators to intervene preemptively and offer targeted support.

Moving beyond prediction, prescriptive analytics recommends actions or interventions to achieve desired outcomes. By leveraging predictive insights, prescriptive models propose personalized learning paths, instructional strategies, or support interventions tailored to individual learner needs. This enables educators to make informed decisions and deliver customized interventions effectively.

Data visualization emerges as a pivotal tool in learning analytics, facilitating the presentation of complex educational data in visually comprehensible formats. Techniques such as charts, graphs, heatmaps, and dashboards enable educators to discern patterns, trends, and outliers, and effectively communicate insights to stakeholders.

Ethical considerations are paramount throughout the learning analytics process to uphold responsible data usage and safeguard student privacy rights. Key practices include obtaining informed consent, anonymizing sensitive data, ensuring data security and confidentiality, and transparently communicating data practices to stakeholders.

By understanding and leveraging these key concepts and components, educators, researchers, and policymakers can harness the power of learning analytics to improve teaching and learning outcomes, enhance student success, and foster continuous improvement in educational practice.

3.3. *Examples of learning analytics tools and platforms*

Here are some examples of learning analytics tools and platforms that have emerged or gained prominence in the last 5 years:

- **Canvas LMS with canvas analytics (Marachi & Quill, 2020):**
  - Canvas is a popular LMS used by educational institutions worldwide. Canvas Analytics is a built-in feature that provides instructors with insights into student engagement, participation, and performance within the platform. It offers data visualizations, such as course activity reports, student progress dashboards, and grade distribution charts, to help educators monitor and optimize teaching and learning activities.

- **Brightspace insights:**
  - Brightspace is an LMS developed by D2L Corporation (Huijstee, 2024). Brightspace Insights is a learning analytics tool that provides educators with actionable insights to improve student outcomes. It offers predictive analytics capabilities to identify at-risk students, personalized recommendations for interventions, and visualizations of learner progress and engagement patterns. Brightspace Insights enables instructors to adapt their teaching strategies and support students more effectively.
- **Blackboard learn ultra with blackboard data (Aljohani *et al.*, 2019):**
  - Blackboard Learn Ultra is a modern LMS offered by Blackboard Inc. Blackboard Data is an analytics platform that integrates with Blackboard Learn Ultra to provide educators with advanced analytics capabilities. It offers dashboards, reports, and predictive models to help instructors track student performance, assess course effectiveness, and identify opportunities for improvement. Blackboard Data enables data-driven decision-making and personalized support for learners.
- **Coursera insights (Shapiro *et al.*, 2017):**
  - Coursera is a popular online learning platform offering courses, certificates, and degree programs from universities and institutions worldwide. Coursera Insights is a suite of analytics tools that provides instructors and administrators with insights into learner behavior, course performance, and program outcomes. It offers dashboards, reports, and interactive visualizations to help educators understand learner needs, assess course effectiveness, and optimize curriculum design. Coursera Insights supports evidence-based decision-making and continuous improvement in online education.

These are just a few examples of learning analytics tools and platforms that have emerged or gained prominence since 2020 (Zilvinskis & Willis, 2019). There are many variations of these. As the field of learning analytics continues to evolve, educators and institutions have access to an increasing array of tools and technologies to support data-driven decision-making, personalized learning experiences, and improved educational outcomes.

4. The Role of AI in Learning Analytics

4.1. *Introduction to AI technologies relevant to learning analytics (machine learning, NLP, etc.)*

AI technologies are also revolutionizing the field of learning analytics, offering powerful tools and techniques to extract meaningful insights from educational data and inform evidence-based decision-making in education. This section explores some key AI technologies that are particularly relevant to learning analytics and their potential applications in educational settings.

Within the realm of AI, machine learning stands as a pivotal branch focused on crafting algorithms and models that enable computers to learn from data, thereby making predictions or decisions without explicit programming. This paradigm finds profound applications in learning analytics, where it delves into vast datasets to unearth patterns, trends, and relationships critical for informing instructional strategies, predicting student outcomes, and tailoring learning experiences to individual needs. Notably, machine learning techniques such as classification, regression, clustering, and recommendation systems play pivotal roles in this endeavor.

As mentioned above, NLP is another facet of AI that revolves around the interaction between computers and human languages. By equipping computers to comprehend, interpret, and generate human language in a manner that is both meaningful and contextually relevant, NLP plays a significant role in learning analytics. It enables the analysis of textual data, including student essays, forum posts, and instructor feedback, providing insights into learning behaviors, sentiment, and language proficiency. With applications ranging from automated essay grading to sentiment analysis and content recommendation, NLP enhances assessment and feedback processes in education (Tsoni *et al*., 2019).

Deep learning, a subset of machine learning, harnesses neural networks with multiple layers of interconnected nodes to decipher intricate patterns and representations from data. Renowned for its ability to autonomously extract hierarchical features from raw data, deep learning finds applications across diverse tasks, such as image recognition, speech recognition, and natural language understanding. In the domain of learning analytics, deep learning techniques scrutinize multimodal data, including text, images, and videos, to extract rich representations of learning content, interactions, and outcomes. Consequently, deep learning models enhance the accuracy and efficacy of predictive analytics, adaptive learning systems, and personalized recommendation engines in education (Doleck *et al.*, 2020).

Lastly, computer vision, a field of AI, empowers computers to comprehend and interpret visual information from the real world (Li *et al.*, 2023). By analyzing images and videos, recognizing objects, detecting patterns, and extracting meaningful insights, computer vision techniques hold significant potential in learning analytics. They enable the analysis of visual data from educational resources, instructional materials, and learning environments, shedding light on student engagement, interaction patterns, and learning behaviors. With applications ranging from automated visual feedback to monitoring student activities during online exams, computer vision augments the analysis of multimedia learning content, enriching the educational landscape.

These are just a few examples of AI technologies that are relevant to learning analytics and have the potential to transform teaching and learning processes in educational settings. By leveraging the capabilities of AI, educators, researchers, and policymakers can unlock valuable insights from educational data, personalize learning experiences, and support evidence-based decision-making to improve educational outcomes for learners.

4.2. *How AI enhances data analysis and interpretation in learning analytics*

As mentioned above, AI is revolutionizing data analysis and interpretation in learning analytics by providing advanced techniques and algorithms that can extract valuable insights from educational data. Here's an overview of how AI enhances data analysis and interpretation in learning analytics:

In the realm of automated data processing, AI technologies revolutionize the analysis of educational data by streamlining and expediting tasks. These algorithms automate processes such as preprocessing, cleaning, and standardizing raw data, ensuring their quality and consistency for subsequent analysis. By seamlessly integrating into data processing pipelines, AI significantly reduces the time and effort invested in manual data preparation tasks, enhancing efficiency and productivity across the board.

Moving beyond mere data processing, AI techniques such as machine learning and deep learning excel at uncovering patterns, trends, and relationships within intricate datasets. Within learning analytics, these algorithms delve into student performance data, learning behaviors, and interaction patterns to unearth predictive factors associated with academic success or failure. By discerning patterns in historical data, AI models forecast future outcomes, empowering educators to proactively intervene and support student achievement.

A cornerstone of AI-powered learning analytics lies in personalized learning experiences tailored to individual learner's needs, preferences, and learning styles. Through meticulous analysis of student data, including learning preferences, strengths, weaknesses, and progress, AI algorithms curate personalized recommendations, adaptive learning pathways, and targeted interventions. This tailored approach fosters heightened engagement, motivation, and learning outcomes by furnishing learners with customized support and resources aligned with their unique learning trajectories.

Furthermore, the advent of NLP techniques extends the horizons of textual data analysis in learning analytics. AI-powered NLP algorithms dissect student essays, forum posts, and instructor feedback to extract invaluable insights into learning behaviors, sentiment, and language proficiency. By offering automated essay grading, sentiment analysis, and content recommendation, NLP augments assessment and feedback processes, enriching educational experiences.

Moreover, AI facilitates the analysis of multimodal data sources, spanning text, images, videos, and sensor data, to glean deeper insights into learning experiences and outcomes. Through a fusion of techniques from computer vision, speech recognition, and NLP, AI algorithms decode diverse data types from educational resources, instructional materials, and learning environments. This holistic approach enables a comprehensive understanding of student engagement, interaction patterns, and learning behaviors, amplifying the depth and breadth of learning analytics.

Overall, AI enhances data analysis and interpretation in learning analytics by automating data processing tasks, identifying patterns and predictive factors, personalizing learning experiences, analyzing textual and multimodal data, and providing actionable insights to support evidence-based decision-making in education. By leveraging the capabilities of AI, educators, researchers, and policymakers can unlock the full potential of educational data to improve teaching and learning outcomes for learners.

4.3. *Case studies demonstrating AI-powered learning analytics solutions*

The following sections outline a few case studies of AI-powered learning analytics solutions that have been implemented in recent years.

4.3.1. *Carnegie Learning's MATHia® platform to improve math outcomes*

Carnegie Learning's MATHia® platform is an AI-powered learning analytics solution designed to improve math education outcomes. It uses machine learning algorithms to analyze students' responses to math problems, identify areas of strength and weakness, and adaptively adjust the difficulty and sequence of learning tasks to meet individual learning needs. A case study conducted by Carnegie Learning showcased how MATHia® helped a school district in Ohio improve student math proficiency scores by 17% over the course of one academic year (BusinessWire, 2024).

4.3.2. *AI-enhanced learning analytics for career decisions*

Gedrimiene *et al.* (2023) explored the advantages and challenges of an AI-enhanced LA tool for supporting career decisions from the user's perspective. A total of 106 participants interacted with the AI-enhanced LA tool and provided feedback through open-ended questionnaire responses. Data analysis was conducted using two established frameworks: the technology acceptance model (TAM) and the career decision-making model (CDM), alongside an examination of user needs. The findings revealed that the AI-enhanced LA tool offered several benefits, including the provision of career information, analysis of research findings, exploration of diverse career paths, guidance and decision support, and opportunities for self-reflection. The participants perceived the tool as particularly valuable during transitional life stages marked by uncertainty. However, they also encountered usability challenges and expressed the need for greater personalization, support for self-reflection, and additional information. Furthermore, while the AI-enhanced LA tool provided support for certain aspects of career decision-making, such as investigating options and making decisions, it fell short in providing contextual information.

4.3.3. *Ivy Tech's AI Engine for student engagement and course outcomes*

As universities transition more services online, they are inundated with vast amounts of data. Ivy Tech, a community college in Indiana with over 50,000 students, recognized the potential of their 26 terabytes of stored data to revolutionize student support. Led by Chief Technology Officer Lige Hensley, they sought to use AI-enhanced learning analytics to predict and support student success. By analyzing anonymized metadata from the LMS, they discovered patterns in online behavior that correlated with academic performance. By implementing machine-learning algorithms, they were able to predict students' final grades with 80% accuracy by the second week of the semester. In a groundbreaking pilot project, they identified at-risk students and intervened with personalized support, resulting in a significant increase in passing grades. By leveraging Google Cloud tools like TensorFlow, Ivy Tech's team continues to refine their AI engine (Google for Education, n.d.).

4.3.4. *Adaptive learning approach considering affective and cognitive factors*

Hwang *et al.* (2020) conducted a study that introduced an expert system approach that considers both the affective and cognitive aspects of individual learners. The approach is implemented through an adaptive learning system. A fifth-grade mathematics course served as the setting for an experiment comparing the learning outcomes and perceptions of students using three different learning systems: the adaptive system with affective and cognitive analysis, a cognitive-based adaptive system, and a conventional learning approach. The analysis indicated that the adaptive learning model incorporating affective and cognitive analysis outperformed the other two approaches in enhancing students' learning achievements.

4.3.5. *AI-selected interventions for "wheel-spinning" students*

In certain computerized educational systems, students may experience wheel-spinning, where they repeatedly struggle to master a skill despite their efforts. This issue is particularly worrisome in resource-limited settings. While previous research has focused on predicting and understanding the wheel-spinning behavior, there has been limited exploration into effective interventions for students experiencing this challenge. This study addresses this gap by leveraging historical student interaction data and expert inputs to automatically tailor interventions for individual students, without the need for extensive labeling of intervention datasets by experts. The method involves training a model to predict instances of wheel-spinning and utilizes Shapley values, a widely used tool in interpretable machine learning, to attribute credit to specific features of the model. This includes identifying actionable features, such as potential gaps in prerequisite knowledge. Through simulations using two different statistical student models, the approach demonstrates the ability to accurately identify appropriate interventions with over 80% accuracy before a simulated student encounters a challenging task. Moreover, the analysis of real-world data suggests that the proposed interventions align well with expert recommendations (Mu *et al.*, 2020).

These case studies demonstrate the effectiveness of AI-powered learning analytics solutions in improving student outcomes, enhancing teaching effectiveness, and promoting personalized learning experiences in diverse educational settings. By leveraging AI technologies, educators and institutions can harness the power of data to support evidence-based decision-making and optimize educational practices for the benefit of learners.

5. Applications of AI in Learning Analytics

5.1. *Personalized learning pathways and recommendations*

Personalized learning pathways and recommendations have gained significant traction in education in recent years, driven by advancements in AI and learning analytics technologies. These personalized approaches aim to tailor learning experiences to meet the individual needs, preferences, and learning styles of learners, ultimately enhancing engagement, motivation, and learning outcomes.

In recent years, AI-powered adaptive learning platforms have garnered significant attention across both K-12 and higher education realms. These platforms harness AI algorithms to meticulously analyze student performance data, learning behaviors, and interaction patterns. The result? Dynamic adjustments to the difficulty and sequence of learning tasks, all in real time. By offering personalized learning pathways tailored to individual progress, strengths, and areas for improvement, these platforms represent a transformative approach to education.

Similarly, recommendation systems have experienced a surge in popularity since 2020, particularly within online learning platforms, digital libraries, and educational apps. These systems employ AI techniques such as collaborative filtering and machine learning to sift through vast troves of learner data. Their goal is to offer tailored recommendations for educational resources — from courses and videos to articles and exercises — aligned with learners' interests and learning objectives.

Another notable advancement lies in personalized learning analytics dashboards. These dashboards serve as invaluable tools, furnishing learners with insights into their own progress, achievements, and areas for growth. By visualizing learner data in an interactive format, such as assessment scores, completion rates, and engagement metrics, these dashboards empower learners to track their development, set goals, and receive actionable feedback — all in a manner that aligns with their individual preferences and aspirations.

Intelligent tutoring systems (ITS) represent yet another frontier in AI-driven education (Lin *et al.*, 2023). These systems leverage a blend of AI techniques, including NLP and cognitive modeling, to provide personalized instruction and support. By analyzing learner interactions, responses, and performance data, ITS deliver targeted feedback, explanations, and learning activities customized to each learner's proficiency level and pace — a hallmark of effective personalized learning.

Lastly, competency-based education (CBE) platforms have gained traction as a means of tailoring learning pathways to individual mastery of specific competencies or skills. With AI and learning analytics at their core, these platforms assess learner competencies, pinpoint learning gaps, and recommend personalized learning activities. By enabling learners to progress at their own pace and focus on mastering skills aligned with their career aspirations, CBE platforms epitomize the potential of personalized education in the digital age (Abbas *et al.*, 2021).

Overall, personalized learning pathways and recommendations have emerged as key strategies for promoting learner-centered education and optimizing learning experiences in diverse educational contexts. By leveraging AI and learning analytics technologies, educators and institutions can provide learners with personalized support, resources, and feedback tailored to their individual needs, ultimately fostering a more adaptive, engaging, and effective learning environment.

5.2. *Predictive analytics for identifying at-risk students and improving retention rates*

Predictive analytics plays a crucial role in education by leveraging data-driven insights to identify students who may be at risk of academic challenges or dropout and implementing targeted interventions to support their success. In recent years, there has been a growing emphasis on predictive analytics for identifying at-risk students and improving retention rates in educational institutions.

In the realm of predictive analytics in education, the journey commences with the meticulous collection and preparation of relevant data drawn from a myriad of educational sources. These encompass LMS, SIS, and assessment tools, among others. Data acquisition spans a broad spectrum of metrics, ranging from academic performance to socio-economic indicators, all of which undergo rigorous cleaning, standardization, and preprocessing to ensure integrity and suitability for analysis.

Central to predictive analytics is the development of robust statistical and machine-learning models designed to scrutinize historical data in order to anticipate future outcomes. By leveraging techniques such as logistic regression, decision trees, and neural networks, these models delve into patterns and correlations within the data to discern factors linked with student attrition and predict those at the highest risk of dropout.

With the aid of predictive analytics, institutions can identify students exhibiting patterns or indicators associated with higher dropout risk, including academic struggles, attendance issues, and socio-economic challenges. By analyzing these markers, predictive models generate risk assessments or probability estimates, providing insights into the likelihood of a student leaving their educational journey prematurely.

Armed with this foresight, educational institutions can take proactive measures, implementing tailored interventions and support mechanisms to bolster at-risk students' chances of success. These initiatives may encompass academic tutoring, counseling services, financial aid assistance, and personalized academic guidance, among others. Predictive analytics empowers educators and advisors to allocate resources judiciously, ensuring timely and effective support for those most in need.

Furthermore, predictive analytics facilitates ongoing monitoring and evaluation of intervention strategies, enabling institutions to gauge their efficacy in improving student retention rates. By tracking the progress of at-risk students over time and assessing changes in their academic performance and engagement, institutions can refine their support strategies iteratively, fostering continuous enhancement of student success initiatives.

Overall, predictive analytics for identifying at-risk students and improving retention rates is a powerful tool for educational institutions to support student success and foster a culture of retention and persistence. By leveraging data-driven insights and targeted interventions, institutions can proactively identify and support at-risk students, ultimately improving retention rates and promoting equitable access to education for all learners.

5.3. *Adaptive learning systems powered by AI*

Adaptive learning systems powered by AI have seen significant advancements and adoption in education. These systems leverage AI algorithms to personalize learning experiences, adapt instructional content, and provide tailored support to meet the individual needs and preferences of learners.

In recent years, there has been a notable surge in the development of personalized learning pathways facilitated by adaptive learning systems. These systems meticulously analyze individual learner data, encompassing performance metrics, preferences, and learning styles. There has been a concerted effort to enhance these systems through AI-powered technologies, enabling dynamic adjustments to the difficulty, pace, and sequence of learning activities based on learners' progress and proficiency levels. By tailoring content to each learner's unique needs and learning trajectory, these personalized pathways foster deeper engagement and comprehension.

Moreover, adaptive content recommendations have gained prominence as a means of enriching the learning experience. AI algorithms scrutinize learner interactions and feedback to generate tailored recommendations for learning materials, such as videos, articles, quizzes, and exercises. The focus has been on refining recommendation systems through machine learning techniques, ensuring that suggestions align closely with learners' interests, goals, and prior knowledge. These adaptive recommendations empower learners to explore topics of interest, bridge knowledge gaps, and deepen their understanding of the subject matter.

In addition to content recommendations, adaptive learning systems offer real-time feedback and support to learners throughout their educational journey. By analyzing learner responses and identifying misconceptions, AI-powered systems provide targeted feedback, hints, or explanations in real time. There has been a concerted effort to bolster these systems with AI-driven tutoring capabilities, delivering personalized assistance and guidance to learners as they navigate challenges and strive to achieve learning objectives more effectively.

Furthermore, adaptive learning systems leverage AI to facilitate assessment and progress tracking, ensuring a comprehensive understanding of learner proficiency. By adaptively assessing knowledge and skills, identifying areas of strength and weakness, and offering feedback on performance, these systems enable educators to gauge learner progress accurately. There has been an increased emphasis on developing AI-driven assessment tools, enabling educators to personalize learning experiences based on individual learning needs.

Lastly, adaptive learning systems harness AI to provide multimodal learning experiences that cater to diverse learning preferences and styles. From virtual reality (VR) and augmented reality (AR) to immersive simulations, these AI-powered systems support interactive, multimedia-rich learning environments (Martinez-Maldonado *et al*., 2023). Efforts have focused on enhancing these systems, engaging learners through interactive exploration, hands-on experimentation, and experiential learning opportunities, thereby enhancing retention and comprehension of complex concepts.

Overall, adaptive learning systems powered by AI have emerged as innovative tools for personalized, flexible, and effective learning experiences (Baker, 2019). By leveraging AI algorithms to analyze learner data, adapt instructional content, and provide targeted support, these systems empower learners to achieve their learning goals and foster a culture of lifelong learning in diverse educational contexts.

5.4. *AI-driven assessment and feedback mechanisms*

AI-driven assessment and feedback mechanisms have transformed the landscape of educational evaluation by leveraging AI technologies to provide timely, personalized, and actionable feedback to learners. These mechanisms enhance the efficiency, effectiveness, and objectivity of assessment practices while promoting continuous improvement and personalized learning experiences.

In the realm of educational assessment, AI-driven technologies have ushered in a new era of efficiency and personalization. Automated grading and feedback mechanisms streamline the evaluation process, handling tasks such as grading multiple-choice questions, essays, and coding exercises with remarkable speed and accuracy. By leveraging NLP algorithms, these tools provide instant feedback on writing style, grammar, coherence, and content relevance, while machine learning models assess code submissions, pinpoint errors, and offer tailored suggestions for improvement. By automating these processes, educators benefit from reduced workload and faster turnaround times, while learners receive immediate feedback to support their ongoing learning journey.

Moreover, adaptive assessment systems represent a paradigm shift in assessment personalization. These AI-driven systems dynamically adjust the difficulty and sequence of questions based on learners' responses, tailoring the assessment experience to their individual proficiency levels. By analyzing learner performance in real time, adaptive algorithms identify knowledge gaps and assess mastery of specific concepts with unparalleled precision. This adaptive approach not only provides a more accurate measure of learners' knowledge and skills but also optimizes the assessment process, ensuring a more informative and insightful evaluation.

Furthermore, AI algorithms analyze assessment data to extract valuable insights into learners' performance, progress, and learning needs. Through learning analytics techniques, educators gain visibility into learners' strengths, weaknesses, and areas for improvement, enabling them to tailor instructions accordingly. Armed with data-driven insights, educators can monitor learners' progress, track trends over time, and identify opportunities for intervention or support, ultimately fostering a more responsive and effective learning environment.

In addition, AI-driven feedback mechanisms deliver personalized feedback to learners, catering to their individual performance and learning goals. These mechanisms leverage NLP algorithms to generate tailored feedback on written assignments, highlighting strengths, addressing weaknesses, and suggesting areas for improvement. By adapting the content and tone of feedback messages to match learners' preferences and needs, personalized feedback promotes a supportive learning environment, encourages self-reflection, and empowers learners to take ownership of their learning journey.

Lastly, AI-driven assessment tools support formative assessment practices by providing ongoing, real-time feedback to learners throughout the learning process. Formative assessment data inform instructional decisions, guide lesson planning, and facilitate timely interventions to address learner misconceptions or difficulties. Through the analysis of formative assessment data, AI algorithms identify struggling learners and recommend targeted interventions, such as additional practice exercises, remedial resources, or personalized tutoring sessions. By embracing formative assessment and intervention mechanisms, educators can foster continuous improvement and optimize learning outcomes for all learners.

Overall, AI-driven assessment and feedback mechanisms enhance the effectiveness, efficiency, and personalization of educational evaluation practices. By leveraging AI technologies to automate grading, provide adaptive assessments, generate data-driven insights, deliver personalized feedback, and support formative assessment and intervention, educators can create a more engaging, supportive, and effective learning environment that meets the diverse needs of learners.

6. Challenges and Considerations

6.1. *Ethical implications of AI in learning analytics*

The integration of AI into learning analytics raises various ethical considerations that need to be addressed to ensure responsible use and mitigate potential risks. Ethical implications encompass concerns related to privacy, fairness, transparency, accountability, bias, and equity in the application of AI technologies in educational settings (Borenstein & Howard, 2021).

Ethical considerations permeate the landscape of learning analytics, guiding practices related to privacy, fairness, transparency, accountability, informed consent, and educational equity. At the heart of these considerations lies the paramount importance of safeguarding student data and upholding privacy rights. As AI algorithms delve into vast pools of sensitive student information — from academic performance to personal demographics — it becomes imperative for institutions and educators to prioritize data security, obtain informed consent, and implement robust governance policies.

However, the ethical terrain of learning analytics extends beyond privacy concerns to encompass fairness and bias. AI algorithms, if not carefully monitored, risk perpetuating biases inherent in the data they analyze, potentially leading to unfair outcomes and discriminatory practices. Addressing biases requires meticulous attention to data collection, algorithm design, and decision-making processes, with efforts focused on mitigating bias through transparency, fairness-aware training, and regular audits.

Transparency and explainability are also the fundamental ethical principles in AI-driven learning analytics. Users, including learners and educators, must comprehend how AI algorithms function, their impact on decision-making processes, and their implications for educational outcomes. Transparent AI systems provide clear explanations of their predictions, recommendations, and decision-making criteria, fostering trust and accountability among users.

Moreover, ethical accountability entails delineating clear roles, obligations, and liabilities for all stakeholders involved in learning analytics initiatives. Educators, administrators, developers, and policymakers share responsibility for ethical AI practices, emphasizing the need for accountability mechanisms, oversight, and redress in the event of ethical breaches.

Respecting individuals' autonomy and right to informed consent is crucial in navigating ethical considerations surrounding data collection and usage. Learners should have agency over their data, understanding how these are collected, used, and shared, with educators facilitating transparent communication and providing opt-out mechanisms where appropriate.

Finally, ethical concerns intersect with the issues of educational equity and accessibility, highlighting the imperative to design AI-driven learning analytics systems that promote inclusivity and support learners with diverse needs. Proactive efforts to address disparities, accommodate diverse learning styles, and foster a supportive, empowering learning environment are essential to uphold ethical standards and ensure equitable access to educational opportunities for all learners.

Addressing the ethical implications of AI in learning analytics requires a multidisciplinary approach involving collaboration among educators, researchers, policymakers, technologists, and stakeholders (Holmes *et al.*, 2021). By prioritizing ethical principles, promoting transparency, accountability, and fairness, and upholding learner rights and well-being, we can harness the potential of AI technologies to advance education while mitigating potential risks and ensuring responsible use in learning analytics.

6.2. *Privacy and data security concerns*

The integration of AI into learning analytics has raised significant concerns regarding privacy and data security as advancements in technology continue to drive the collection, analysis, and utilization of vast amounts of sensitive student data.

The integration of AI into learning analytics brings with it a host of concerns, chief among them being the vulnerability of student data to breaches and unauthorized access. Educational institutions amass extensive data on students, including academic records and behavioral information, which are susceptible to cyberattacks and security breaches. Instances of data breaches in educational settings have underscored the potential harm to student privacy and security resulting from such incidents.

Another pressing issue revolves around the unauthorized sharing and commercial exploitation of student data by third-party entities. Edtech companies, in particular, have come under scrutiny for their practices of collecting, analyzing, and monetizing student data for purposes, such as targeted advertising and algorithmic profiling. Questions surrounding transparency, consent, and data ownership have been at the forefront of discussions concerning AI-driven learning analytics.

Furthermore, the inherent biases present in AI algorithms pose a significant ethical challenge, potentially leading to unfair outcomes and discrimination against marginalized student groups (Benneh Mensah, 2023). Biases ingrained in the data used to train AI models can manifest in biased predictions, recommendations, or decisions, exacerbating existing disparities in educational opportunities. Efforts to address algorithmic bias and promote fairness and accountability in AI-driven learning analytics have gained traction in recent years.

Concerns also extend to the inadequacy of data protection measures within educational institutions, leaving student privacy and confidentiality vulnerable to compromise. Weak encryption, lax authentication protocols, and insufficient security measures heighten the risk of unauthorized access, data manipulation, and theft. The need for robust data protection mechanisms to mitigate these risks and safeguard student data has become increasingly apparent.

Moreover, there is a notable lack of transparency and accountability surrounding the collection, use, and sharing of student data in AI-driven learning analytics initiatives. Educational institutions and technology vendors often fall short in adequately informing students about data practices and potential risks associated with AI technologies. Calls for greater transparency, accountability, and ethical oversight seek to address these shortcomings and ensure responsible data use in learning analytics endeavors.

Overall, privacy and data security concerns about AI in learning analytics have become increasingly prominent, highlighting the need for robust data protection measures, transparent data practices, and ethical guidelines to safeguard student privacy, security, and rights in educational settings. Addressing these concerns requires collaboration among educators, policymakers, technologists, and stakeholders to establish clear guidelines, implement effective safeguards, and promote responsible data governance practices in AI-driven learning analytics initiatives.

6.3. *Addressing biases and ensuring fairness in AI algorithms*

The issue of biases in AI algorithms and ensuring fairness in their outcomes has gained significant attention in recent years (Holmes *et al.*, 2022). Biases can arise from various sources, including biased training data, algorithmic design choices, and human biases embedded in decision-making processes. Addressing biases and ensuring fairness in AI algorithms are essential to promote equity, mitigate discrimination, and uphold ethical standards in AI-driven applications across diverse domains, including learning analytics.

Efforts have been underway to develop robust methods for detecting and assessing biases in AI algorithms. Researchers and practitioners have proposed various metrics, benchmarks, and evaluation frameworks to quantify biases, pinpoint discriminatory patterns, and gauge fairness in algorithmic outcomes. These approaches aid stakeholders in comprehending the scope of biases inherent in AI systems, enabling them to prioritize interventions aimed at mitigating their adverse effects.

In response to growing concerns, there has been a surge of interest in crafting AI algorithms that inherently embody fairness and impartiality. Researchers have devised fairness-aware machine learning algorithms that explicitly integrate fairness constraints and considerations into their optimization objectives. By doing so, these algorithms strive to counteract biases during model training and decision-making, thereby fostering equitable outcomes for individuals irrespective of their demographic attributes.

Central to the quest for fairness in AI algorithms is the imperative of transparency and explainability. Efforts have been made to develop methodologies for elucidating AI predictions, recommendations, and decision-making processes in a transparent and interpretable manner. Explainable AI techniques offer insights into the factors influencing algorithmic outputs, empowering stakeholders to assess fairness, identify biases, and tackle ethical quandaries effectively.

An essential aspect of combating biases in AI algorithms involves ensuring that training data are diverse and representative. Biases often originate from skewed or inadequately representative training datasets. To rectify this, there has been a concerted effort to gather varied and inclusive training data that accurately mirror the diversity of the target population. Techniques such as data augmentation, synthetic data generation, and algorithmic debiasing are employed to rectify biases and ensure equitable representation across all groups.

Furthermore, the formulation of ethical guidelines and regulatory frameworks has emerged as a crucial strategy for promoting fairness, transparency, and accountability in AI algorithms. These guidelines delineate principles for responsible AI development and deployment, with a focus on fairness, equity, and non-discrimination. Concurrently, regulatory endeavors seek to establish legal requirements and standards for AI systems, thereby ensuring adherence to ethical norms and safeguarding individuals' rights.

Given the multifaceted nature of the challenge, addressing biases and fostering fairness in AI algorithms necessitate collaborative efforts among diverse stakeholders. This includes researchers, developers, policymakers, educators, and impacted communities. Community engagement initiatives serve as platforms for dialog, awareness-raising, and solicitation of feedback regarding algorithmic biases and their ramifications for marginalized populations. Through stakeholder collaboration, equitable AI solutions can be co-designed to reflect the needs, values, and perspectives of all involved parties.

Overall, efforts to address biases and ensure fairness in AI algorithms since 2020 have focused on developing detection methods, designing fairness-aware algorithms, promoting transparency and explainability, improving data diversity and representation, establishing ethical guidelines and regulatory frameworks, and fostering community engagement and stakeholder collaboration. By prioritizing fairness and equity in AI development and deployment, we can mitigate biases, promote inclusive outcomes, and uphold ethical standards in AI-driven applications, including learning analytics.

6.4. *Technical challenges and limitations of AI in learning analytics*

While AI holds great promise for revolutionizing learning analytics, several technical challenges and limitations must be addressed to realize its full potential effectively. These challenges stem from the complexity of educational data, the dynamic nature of learning environments, and the inherent limitations of AI technologies.

The quality and accessibility of educational data present significant challenges in leveraging AI for learning analytics. Data often suffer from issues such as incompleteness, inconsistency, and noise, compounded by dispersion across various systems. Addressing these challenges entails employing data preprocessing techniques, cleaning algorithms, and interoperability standards to harmonize heterogeneous data sources and facilitate analysis.

Privacy and security concerns loom large in learning analytics due to the sensitive nature of student data required by AI algorithms. Compliance with regulations such as GDPR and FERPA demands robust measures for anonymizing data, implementing encryption, and securing storage and transmission against unauthorized access or breaches.

Algorithmic biases pose a threat to fairness in learning analytics, stemming from skewed training data or inherent societal biases. Detecting and mitigating biases necessitate developing detection methods, fairness-aware algorithms, and interpretability techniques to promote equity and uphold ethical standards.

The scalability and performance of AI algorithms are pivotal for handling large-scale educational datasets effectively. Optimizing algorithms requires parallel computing, distributed processing, and efficient design to manage the volume, velocity, and variety of educational data.

Interpretability and explainability are vital for AI-driven models in learning analytics to build trust and transparency. Techniques for providing transparent insights into algorithmic decisions are crucial for informed decision-making.

Adaptability and generalization are essential for AI algorithms to function across diverse learning environments and populations. Ensuring robustness and performance across different scenarios demands techniques, such as domain adaptation and transfer learning.

Human–AI collaboration is critical for effectively integrating AI into educational practices. Designing user-friendly interfaces, incorporating AI-driven insights into workflows, and providing educators with actionable recommendations facilitate seamless interaction and enhance teaching and learning practices.

Addressing these technical challenges and limitations of AI in learning analytics requires interdisciplinary collaboration, innovation, and ongoing research efforts to develop robust, scalable, and ethical AI solutions that empower educators, support learners, and promote positive educational outcomes in diverse learning environments.

7. Best Practices and Strategies

7.1. *Strategies for effective implementation of AI in learning analytics*

The implementation of AI in learning analytics requires careful planning, collaboration, and consideration of various factors to ensure successful adoption and realization of its benefits. Here's an overview of strategies for effective implementation of AI in learning analytics:

- **Define clear objectives and use cases:** Begin by defining clear objectives and use cases for AI in learning analytics. Identify specific challenges, opportunities, and goals that AI technologies can address, such as improving student outcomes, enhancing teaching effectiveness, or optimizing educational processes. Align AI initiatives with institutional priorities and strategic objectives to ensure relevance and impact.

- **Engage stakeholders and build support:** Engage stakeholders, including educators, administrators, students, parents, and IT professionals, in the planning and implementation process. Foster collaboration, communication, and buy-in from key stakeholders by soliciting their input, addressing concerns, and highlighting the potential benefits of AI in learning analytics. Build a coalition of champions and advocates to garner support and promote adoption across the organization.
- **Assess data readiness and quality:** Assess the readiness and quality of educational data available for AI-driven analytics. Evaluate the availability, completeness, accuracy, and accessibility of data sources, such as LMS, SIS, and assessment tools. Implement data governance policies, data management practices, and data quality assurance measures to ensure data readiness for AI analysis and decision-making.
- **Ensure data privacy and security:** Prioritize data privacy and security throughout the implementation process. Comply with relevant regulations, such as GDPR, FERPA, and COPPA, to protect student privacy and confidentiality. Implement robust data protection measures, encryption techniques, access controls, and audit trails to safeguard sensitive student information and prevent unauthorized access or data breaches.
- **Select appropriate AI technologies:** Select AI technologies and algorithms that align with the identified objectives and use cases for learning analytics. Choose AI models, such as machine learning, deep learning, NLP, or computer vision, based on their suitability for analyzing educational data and addressing specific challenges. Consider factors such as scalability, interpretability, and ethical considerations while selecting AI technologies.
- **Design user-centric solutions:** Design AI-driven solutions with a focus on usability, user experience, and user-centric design principles. Develop intuitive interfaces, dashboards, and visualization tools that empower educators to access, understand, and act on AI-driven insights effectively. Incorporate feedback from end-users throughout the design process to iteratively improve the usability and functionality of AI applications in learning analytics.
- **Provide training and support:** Provide comprehensive training and support to educators, administrators, and IT staff involved in using AI technologies for learning analytics. Offer professional development programs, workshops, and tutorials to build their capacity in AI concepts, tools, and methodologies. Provide ongoing technical support,

troubleshooting assistance, and knowledge-sharing opportunities to help users navigate AI-driven analytics effectively.

- **Monitor performance and evaluate impact:** Continuously monitor the performance of AI-driven analytics solutions and evaluate their impact on educational outcomes. Track key performance indicators, such as student engagement, academic achievement, retention rates, and educator satisfaction, to assess the effectiveness and ROI of AI implementations. Use data-driven insights to refine algorithms, adjust strategies, and optimize the use of AI in learning analytics over time.
- **Promote ethical use and responsible AI practices:** Promote ethical use and responsible AI practices throughout the organization. Establish guidelines, policies, and codes of conduct for ethical AI development, deployment, and usage. Foster a culture of transparency, accountability, and fairness in AI-driven analytics initiatives, emphasizing the importance of privacy, equity, and social responsibility in educational settings.

By following these strategies for the effective implementation of AI in learning analytics, educational institutions can harness the power of AI technologies to drive innovation, improve educational outcomes, and enhance the teaching and learning experience for all stakeholders.

7.2. *Collaborative approaches for integrating AI into educational environments*

The integration of AI into education environments requires collaborative efforts among various stakeholders, including educators, researchers, policymakers, technology developers, and learners. Collaborative approaches facilitate the design, development, implementation, and evaluation of AI-driven solutions that address the diverse needs and challenges of educational settings (U.S. Department of Education, 2023). Here's an overview of collaborative approaches for integrating AI into educational environments:

- **Interdisciplinary collaboration:** Interdisciplinary collaboration brings together experts from diverse fields, such as education, computer science, psychology, and data science, to collaborate on AI projects in education. By leveraging the collective expertise and perspectives of multidisciplinary teams, collaborative approaches foster innovation, creativity, and cross-pollination of ideas. Interdisciplinary collaboration ensures that AI solutions are informed by pedagogical principles, grounded in educational theory, and tailored to meet the specific needs of learners and educators (Miao *et al.*, 2021).

- **Partnerships between academia and industry:** Partnerships between academia and industry facilitate knowledge exchange, technology transfer, and joint research initiatives to advance AI in education. Academic institutions collaborate with industry partners, edtech companies, and startups to co-develop AI-driven solutions, conduct research studies, and pilot innovative technologies in real-world educational settings. These partnerships bridge the gap between theory and practice, accelerate innovation, and promote the adoption of cutting-edge AI technologies in education (Dogan & Medvidović, 2023).
- **Community engagement and stakeholder participation:** Community engagement initiatives involve educators, administrators, students, parents, and other stakeholders in the co-design, implementation, and evaluation of AI initiatives in education. Stakeholder participation ensures that AI solutions reflect the needs, preferences, and priorities of end-users, fostering user acceptance and ownership of technology-driven innovations. Community engagement promotes transparency, inclusivity, and democratic decision-making in the integration of AI into educational environments (Delgado *et al.*, 2021).
- **Collaborative research consortia:** Collaborative research consortia bring together multiple institutions, organizations, and researchers to collaborate on large-scale AI research projects in education. The consortia facilitate collaboration, resource-sharing, and collective action to address complex research challenges, such as developing AI algorithms, designing educational interventions, and evaluating their impact on teaching and learning outcomes. They foster knowledge exchange, capacity-building, and dissemination of best practices in AI-driven educational research (Amini *et al.*, 2020).
- **Professional learning communities (PLCs):** PLCs provide educators with opportunities to collaborate, share expertise, and learn from one another about integrating AI into their teaching practices. They foster peer-to-peer support, collaboration, and reflective practice among educators as they explore innovative pedagogical approaches, experiment with AI tools, and exchange insights about their experiences (Stoll & Louis, 2007). PLCs also promote continuous professional

development, teacher empowerment, and collective learning in AI-enabled educational environments.
- **Open educational resource (OER) communities:** OER communities facilitate the sharing, co-creation, and adaptation of AI-enabled educational resources and tools. Educators, content creators, and technologists collaborate within OER communities to develop and curate high-quality, openly licensed resources that leverage AI technologies to enhance teaching and learning experiences. OER communities promote collaboration, resource-sharing, and innovation in AI-driven education by democratizing access to educational content and technology (Bozkurt, 2023).
- **Policy dialog and advocacy efforts:** Policy dialog and advocacy efforts engage policymakers, government agencies, advocacy groups, and educational organizations in discussions about the ethical, legal, and regulatory implications of integrating AI into education environments. Collaborative approaches to policy development foster consensus-building, stakeholder engagement, and informed decision-making about AI governance, privacy protections, and data security in educational settings. Policy dialog and advocacy efforts promote responsible AI adoption, equity, and social inclusion in education (Miao *et al.*, 2021).

By embracing collaborative approaches for integrating AI into education environments, stakeholders can harness the collective expertise, resources, and perspectives of diverse stakeholders to develop, implement, and evaluate AI-driven solutions that enhance teaching and learning outcomes, promote equity, and foster innovation in education.

7.3. *Guidelines for responsible use of AI in learning analytics*

In the rapidly evolving landscape of learning analytics, prioritizing ethical considerations stands as a foundational pillar guiding the development and deployment of AI solutions. Upholding principles such as fairness, transparency, accountability, and privacy is paramount to safeguarding learner rights, promoting equity, and mitigating potential risks. As educational institutions increasingly harness the power of AI to enhance teaching and learning experiences, it becomes imperative to ensure that these AI-driven initiatives adhere to ethical guidelines and standards (Borondo *et al.*, 2024). By embedding ethical principles into the fabric of AI in learning analytics, we can foster a culture of responsibility, trust, and integrity, ultimately advancing the collective goal of harnessing technology for the betterment of education. Here's an overview of guidelines for the responsible use of AI in learning analytics:

- **Prioritize ethical considerations:** Uphold ethical principles, such as fairness, transparency, accountability, and privacy, throughout the development and deployment of AI in learning analytics initiatives. Ensure that AI-driven solutions adhere to ethical guidelines and standards to protect learner rights, promote equity, and mitigate potential risks.
- **Ensure data privacy and security:** Protect student privacy and ensure data security by implementing robust data protection measures, encryption techniques, and access controls. Comply with relevant regulations, such as GDPR, FERPA, and COPPA, to safeguard sensitive student information and prevent unauthorized access or data breaches.
- **Address bias and ensure fairness:** Mitigate biases in AI algorithms and ensure fairness in their outcomes by conducting bias assessments, fairness audits, and algorithmic transparency reviews. Implement fairness-aware AI techniques, such as bias detection methods, fairness constraints, and model interpretability techniques, to promote equitable outcomes for all learners.
- **Promote transparency and explainability:** Foster transparency and explainability in AI-driven analytics solutions by providing clear explanations of algorithmic predictions, recommendations, and decision-making processes. Enhance algorithmic transparency through interpretable AI methods, user-friendly interfaces, and accessible documentation to enable stakeholders to understand and interpret AI outputs effectively.
- **Empower informed decision-making:** Empower educators, administrators, and policymakers with the knowledge and tools needed to make informed decisions about AI in learning analytics. Provide comprehensive training, professional development, and educational resources to build capacity in AI concepts, ethics, and best practices for responsible AI adoption.
- **Engage stakeholders and foster collaboration:** Engage stakeholders, including educators, students, parents, policymakers, and technology developers, in collaborative efforts to design, develop, implement, and evaluate AI-driven solutions. Foster a culture of collaboration,

inclusivity, and co-creation to ensure that AI initiatives reflect the diverse needs, perspectives, and priorities of all stakeholders.

- **Promote equity and inclusion:** Promote educational equity and inclusion by addressing disparities, biases, and barriers to access in AI-driven learning analytics initiatives. Ensure that AI technologies are accessible, adaptable, and responsive to the diverse needs of learners, including those from underrepresented and marginalized communities.
- **Monitor and evaluate impact:** Continuously monitor the impact of AI in learning analytics on educational outcomes, student experiences, and institutional effectiveness. Track key performance indicators, evaluate AI interventions, and solicit feedback from stakeholders to assess the effectiveness, equity, and ethical implications of AI-driven initiatives.
- **Adopt a human-centered approach:** Adopt a human-centered approach to AI in learning analytics that prioritizes the well-being, agency, and autonomy of learners and educators. Design AI solutions that augment human capabilities, enhance teaching and learning experiences, and empower individuals to make informed decisions about their education.
- **Commit to continuous improvement:** Commit to continuous improvement and learning by embracing feedback, iterating on AI solutions, and adapting to evolving ethical, technological, and educational landscapes. Foster a culture of continuous improvement, innovation, and responsible AI adoption to ensure that AI in learning analytics continues to advance educational equity, excellence, and social good.

By adhering to these guidelines for the responsible use of AI in learning analytics, stakeholders can promote ethical AI adoption, protect learner rights, and maximize the benefits of AI technologies in enhancing teaching and learning outcomes while minimizing potential risks and unintended consequences.

8. Future Directions and Opportunities

8.1. *Emerging trends in AI and learning analytics*

In the realm of AI-driven learning analytics, ethical considerations and responsible data use have emerged as critical focal points. There is a notable shift toward developing AI models and algorithms that prioritize interpretability and transparency, offering stakeholders clear insights into decision-making processes.

Concurrently, personalized learning pathways are gaining traction, leveraging AI to tailor instruction and resources to individual learner needs. Predictive analytics plays a pivotal role in identifying at-risk students and facilitating timely interventions to support their success. NLP technologies are revolutionizing educational content analysis and feedback provision, while augmented analytics tools empower educators with actionable insights for instructional improvement.

Collaborative AI approaches are reshaping learning environments by facilitating co-creation and co-learning experiences among educators and learners. Moreover, federated learning and privacy-preserving AI techniques are being adopted to address privacy concerns associated with centralized data processing. AI-powered learning analytics platforms offer comprehensive insights into teaching and learning processes, empowering educators with data-driven decision-making capabilities.

Lastly, the importance of lifelong learning and continuous professional development in the AI era underscores the need for adaptive learning platforms and personalized professional development pathways for educators. These emerging trends collectively aim to foster ethical AI adoption, enhance educational outcomes, and promote continuous learning in the ever-evolving landscape of learning analytics.

These emerging trends in AI and learning analytics reflect the ongoing evolution and innovation in educational technology, highlighting the transformative potential of AI to enhance teaching and learning experiences, improve educational outcomes, and foster innovation in education.

8.2. *Potential innovations and advancements on the horizon*

In the realm of AI-powered educational advancements, a cohesive vision emerges for the future of learning analytics. Advanced adaptive learning systems, driven by AI, will redefine personalized learning experiences by dynamically tailoring content and instruction to individual learner needs, preferences, and progress. These systems will integrate sophisticated AI algorithms to analyze real-time learner data, predict learning trajectories, and recommend personalized pathways and interventions. Simultaneously, there will be a concerted effort to develop explainable AI models and decision support systems, providing transparent insights into AI-driven recommendations and decisions.

By employing interpretable AI techniques, educators will gain the ability to make informed decisions and take appropriate actions based on AI-generated insights. AR and VR technologies will revolutionize learning experiences, offering immersive and interactive educational environments (Al-Ansi *et al.*, 2023). AI-driven AR/VR applications will provide realistic simulations, virtual laboratories, and experiential learning opportunities, enabling learners to explore complex concepts and engage in hands-on activities in virtual settings.

Emotion-aware AI technologies will support social and emotional learning (SEL) by detecting and responding to learners' emotional states and needs. These systems will use affective computing techniques to recognize emotions, provide empathetic feedback, and offer tailored support, fostering emotional intelligence and well-being. Additionally, AI will significantly impact the creation, curation, and personalization of educational content, automating content generation and tailoring learning experiences to individual learner preferences (Sharif *et al.*, 2024).

Collaborative learning environments will be enhanced with AI-driven features to facilitate collaborative problem-solving, peer learning, and knowledge co-construction. AI-assisted assessment and feedback mechanisms will revolutionize grading and feedback processes, providing personalized feedback and assessing higher-order thinking skills efficiently. Blockchain technology will ensure secure and transparent credentialing, enhancing the credibility and portability of educational credentials (Sousa *et al.*, 2022).

Moreover, neuroadaptive learning systems will integrate brain–computer interface (BCI) technologies with AI to monitor and adapt to learners' cognitive states in real time, optimizing learning experiences and supporting neurodiverse learners (Grubov *et al.*, 2024). Finally, the focus on developing AI governance frameworks and regulatory guidelines will ensure responsible AI adoption, promote transparency, accountability, and fairness, and safeguard learner rights and well-being. These potential innovations underscore the transformative potential of AI technologies to revolutionize teaching and learning practices, improve educational outcomes, and foster innovation in education.

8.3. *Implications for the future of education and lifelong learning*

The implications for the future of education and lifelong learning from AI and analytics are profound and far-reaching, influencing various aspects of teaching, learning, and professional development.

AI and analytics enable the delivery of personalized learning experiences tailored to individual learner needs, preferences, and abilities. This shift toward personalized learning empowers learners to pursue their unique interests, learn at their own pace, and receive targeted support and feedback, enhancing engagement and motivation.

AI-driven analytics provides educators, administrators, and policymakers with actionable insights and evidence-based strategies to inform decision-making processes. By analyzing vast amounts of educational data, AI can identify patterns, predict trends, and optimize instructional practices, curriculum design, and resource allocation, leading to more effective and efficient educational interventions.

Lifelong learning is facilitated through AI-powered professional development platforms and adaptive learning systems that offer personalized learning pathways for educators. AI-driven analytics provide educators with opportunities for continuous skill development, knowledge acquisition, and pedagogical innovation, enabling them to stay abreast of emerging trends, refine their teaching practices, and adapt to evolving educational needs.

AI technologies can address barriers to access and promote inclusivity in education by providing personalized accommodations and support for diverse learners. AI-driven adaptive learning systems, assistive technologies, and language translation tools enhance accessibility for learners with disabilities, language barriers, or diverse learning needs, ensuring equitable access to educational opportunities.

AI and analytics optimize resource allocation and operational efficiency in educational institutions by automating administrative tasks, streamlining workflows, and improving resource utilization. AI-driven scheduling systems, predictive maintenance tools, and resource optimization algorithms enable schools and universities to allocate resources effectively, reduce costs, and enhance productivity.

AI and analytics empower educators and learners with tools, resources, and insights to take control of their learning journey. Educators can leverage AI-driven analytics to assess student progress, identify learning gaps, and tailor instructions to meet individual needs. Learners can use AI-powered adaptive learning platforms, intelligent tutoring systems, and self-assessment tools to take ownership of their learning, set learning goals, and track their progress over time.

The widespread adoption of AI in education necessitates ethical considerations, responsible practices, and regulatory frameworks to safeguard learner rights, privacy, and well-being. Ethical AI adoption in education requires transparency, accountability, and fairness in algorithmic decision-making, as well as adherence to data protection regulations and ethical guidelines to mitigate biases, protect privacy, and ensure equitable access to educational opportunities.

In summary, the future of education and lifelong learning from AI and analytics is characterized by personalized learning experiences, data-driven decision-making, continuous professional development, enhanced accessibility and inclusivity, optimized resource allocation and efficiency, empowerment of educators and learners, and ethical and responsible AI adoption. By embracing AI and analytics, educational institutions can harness the transformative potential of technology to advance teaching and learning practices, improve educational outcomes, and foster innovation in education.

9. Conclusions

9.1. *Reflection on the transformative potential of AI in learning analytics*

AI holds immense transformative potential in learning analytics, revolutionizing how educational data are collected, analyzed, and utilized to enhance teaching and learning experiences.

- **Personalized learning experiences:** AI enables personalized learning experiences tailored to individual learner needs, preferences, and abilities. By analyzing vast amounts of learner data, AI algorithms can adapt instruction, recommend resources, and provide targeted support, fostering greater engagement, motivation, and achievement among learners.
- **Data-driven decision-making:** AI-driven analytics provides educators, administrators, and policymakers with actionable insights and

evidence-based strategies to inform decision-making processes. By analyzing educational data in real time, AI algorithms can identify patterns, predict trends, and optimize instructional practices, curriculum design, and resource allocation, leading to more effective and efficient educational interventions.

- **Early intervention and student support:** AI-powered predictive analytics enables early identification of at-risk students and intervention strategies to improve retention rates and academic outcomes. By analyzing student data, AI algorithms can identify warning signs, such as low engagement or performance indicators, and alert educators to provide timely support and interventions to prevent academic challenges and promote student success.
- **Enhanced teaching effectiveness:** AI technologies augment teaching effectiveness by providing educators with tools and insights to personalize instruction, assess student progress, and tailor interventions. AI-driven adaptive learning systems, intelligent tutoring systems, and automated grading tools streamline administrative tasks, enabling educators to focus on instructional delivery, feedback, and interaction with students, ultimately improving teaching quality and student learning outcomes.
- **Innovative pedagogical approaches:** AI opens up new possibilities for innovative pedagogical approaches that leverage technology to enhance learning experiences. VR, AR, gamification, and simulation technologies powered by AI enable immersive and interactive learning environments, allowing learners to explore complex concepts, practice skills, and engage in hands-on activities in virtual settings, fostering deeper understanding and retention of content.
- **Continuous improvement and innovation:** AI facilitates continuous improvement and innovation in education by providing educators with insights into student learning patterns, instructional effectiveness, and areas for improvement. By analyzing feedback, evaluating interventions, and iteratively refining practices, AI-driven analytics supports a culture of continuous improvement, innovation, and evidence-based decision-making in educational institutions.
- **Increased efficiency and resource optimization:** AI streamlines administrative processes, optimizes resource allocation, and enhances operational efficiency in educational institutions. AI-powered scheduling systems, predictive maintenance tools, and resource optimization algorithms enable schools and universities to allocate resources

effectively, reduce costs, and enhance productivity, freeing up resources to invest in instructional quality and student support services.

- **Empowerment of learners:** AI empowers learners with tools and resources to take control of their learning journey, set learning goals, and track their progress. AI-driven adaptive learning platforms, intelligent tutoring systems, and self-assessment tools provide learners with personalized learning pathways, real-time feedback, and opportunities for self-directed learning, fostering autonomy, agency, and lifelong learning skills.

In summary, the transformative potential of AI in learning analytics lies in its ability to personalize learning experiences, inform data-driven decision-making, support early intervention and student support, enhance teaching effectiveness, foster innovative pedagogical approaches, promote continuous improvement and innovation, optimize resource allocation and efficiency, and empower learners to achieve their full potential in education.

9.2. *Call to action for educators, researchers, and policymakers to embrace AI-driven approaches for educational enhancement*

Educators, researchers, and policymakers are called upon to embrace AI-driven approaches for educational enhancement, recognizing the transformative potential of AI technologies to revolutionize teaching and learning experiences. Here's an overview of the call to action:

- **Foster innovation and experimentation:** Encourage educators and researchers to explore innovative pedagogical approaches and experiment with AI-driven technologies to enhance teaching and learning outcomes. Create a supportive environment that fosters creativity, risk-taking, and experimentation, enabling educators to leverage AI tools and methodologies to address diverse learning needs and challenges.
- **Invest in professional development:** Invest in professional development programs and training initiatives to build educators' capacity in AI concepts, tools, and pedagogical strategies. Provide educators with opportunities to develop digital literacy skills, learn about AI applications in education, and explore best practices for integrating AI-driven

approaches into teaching practice, curriculum design, and assessment strategies.

- **Promote collaboration and knowledge-sharing:** Foster collaboration and knowledge-sharing among educators, researchers, and policymakers to exchange insights, share best practices, and co-create innovative solutions that leverage AI technologies to enhance educational outcomes. Facilitate interdisciplinary collaborations, community-building initiatives, and networking opportunities to promote cross-pollination of ideas and collective problem-solving.
- **Support research and development:** Allocate resources and funding to support research and development initiatives that advance AI technologies and their applications in education. Invest in research projects, pilot programs, and longitudinal studies to investigate the effectiveness, scalability, and impact of AI-driven approaches on teaching and learning outcomes. Foster partnerships between academia, industry, and government agencies to facilitate knowledge transfer and technology transfer in AI-driven educational research.
- **Promote ethical AI adoption and responsible practices:** Promote ethical AI adoption and responsible practices in education by establishing guidelines, policies, and frameworks to govern the development, deployment, and usage of AI technologies. Prioritize ethical considerations, such as fairness, transparency, accountability, and privacy protection, in AI-driven educational initiatives. Raise awareness about the ethical implications of AI in education and empower stakeholders to make informed decisions about AI adoption and implementation.
- **Address equity and inclusion:** Ensure that AI-driven approaches in education promote equity, diversity, and inclusion by addressing disparities, biases, and barriers to access. Prioritize the needs of underserved and marginalized populations, including students with disabilities, English language learners, and learners from diverse socioeconomic backgrounds. Design AI interventions that are accessible, culturally responsive, and inclusive, ensuring that all learners have equitable access to high-quality educational opportunities.
- **Advocate for policy support and investment:** Advocate for policy support and investment in AI-driven approaches for educational enhancement at the local, regional, and national levels. Collaborate with policymakers, educational leaders, and advocacy groups to develop policies, initiatives, and funding mechanisms that support the integration of AI technologies into educational settings. Advocate for equitable

access to AI tools, resources, and infrastructure to ensure that all learners and educators can benefit from AI-driven innovations in education.

By embracing this call to action, educators, researchers, and policymakers can harness the transformative potential of AI technologies to enhance teaching and learning experiences, improve educational outcomes, and foster innovation in education. Together, they can create a future where AI-driven approaches empower learners to succeed in an increasingly complex and interconnected world.

References

Abbas, A., Hosseini, S., Núñez, J. L. M., & Sastre-Merino, S. (2021). Emerging technologies in education for innovative pedagogies and competency development. *Australasian Journal of Educational Technology*, 37(5): 1–5.

Al-Ansi, A. M., Jaboob, M., Garad, A., & Al-Ansi, A. (2023). Analyzing augmented reality (AR) and virtual reality (VR) recent development in education. *Social Sciences & Humanities Open*, 8(1): 100532.

Aljohani, N. R., Daud, A., Abbasi, R. A., Alowibdi, J. S., Basheri, M., & Aslam, M. A. (2019). An integrated framework for course adapted student learning analytics dashboard. *Computers in Human Behavior*, 92: 679–690.

Amini, L., Chen, C. H., Cox, D., Oliva, A., & Torralba, A. (2020). Experiences and insights for collaborative industry-academic research in artificial intelligence. *AI Magazine*, 41(1): 70–81.

Baker, R. S. (2019). Educational data mining: An advance for intelligent systems in education. *Wiley Interdisciplinary Reviews: Data Mining and Knowledge Discovery*, 9(2): e1309.

Benneh Mensah, George. (2023). Artificial intelligence and ethics: A comprehensive review of bias mitigation, transparency, and accountability in AI systems. 10.13140/RG.2.2.23381.19685/1. Retrieved from: https://www.researchgate.net/publication/375744287_Artificial_Intelligence_and_Ethics_A_Comprehensive_Review_of_Bias_Mitigation_Transparency_and_Accountability_in_AI_Systems

Borenstein, J. & Howard, A. (2021). Emerging challenges in AI and the need for AI ethics education. *AI and Ethics*, 1, 61–65.

Bozkurt, A. (2023). Generative AI, synthetic contents, open educational resources (OER), and open educational practices (OEP): A new front in the openness landscape. *Open Praxis*, 15(3): 178–184.

Carnegie Learning (2024). Carnegie learning and Ohio's Tremont School District Partner to provide personalized math instruction to students. *Business Wire*. Retrieved March 19, from https://www.businesswire.com/news/home/20240319860334/en/.

Delgado, F., Yang, S., Madaio, M., & Yang, Q. (2021). Stakeholder participation in AI: Beyond 'Add Diverse Stakeholders and Stir'. arXiv preprint, arXiv:2111.01122.

Dogan, I. D. & Medvidović, L. (2023). Generative AI in education: Strategic forecasting and recommendations. In *11th Higher Education Institutions Conference*, September, Volume 21.

Doleck, T., Lemay, D. J., Basnet, R. B., *et al.* (2020). Predictive analytics in education: A comparison of deep learning frameworks. *Educational Technology Research and Development*, 68(4): 1951–1963.

Gedrimiene, E., Celik, I., Kaasila, A., *et al.* (2024). Artificial Intelligence (AI)-enhanced learning analytics (LA) for supporting career decisions: Advantages and challenges from user perspective. *Educational Information Technology*, 29, 297–322.

Google for Education (n.d.). Ivy Tech develops machine learning algorithm to identify at-risk students and provide early intervention. Retrieved from https://edu.google.com/why-google/customer-stories/ivytech-gcp/.

Grubov, V. V., *et al.* (2024). Open-loop neuroadaptive system for enhancing student's cognitive abilities in learning. *IEEE Access*, 12, 49034–49049.

Holmes, W., Porayska-Pomsta, K., Holstein, K., Sutherland, E., Baker, T., Shum, S. B., ..., & Koedinger, K. R. (2022). Ethics of AI in education: Towards a community-wide framework. *International Journal of Artificial Intelligence in Education*, 1–23.

Huijstee, M. (2024). Enhancing learning management systems: A novel approach to improve usability through learning analytics. TScIT, 40, February 2, Enschede, The Netherlands.

Jiao, H. & Lissitz, R. (eds.) (2020). *Application of Artificial Intelligence to Assessment*. Charlotte, NC: Information Age Publishing.

Li, X., Yan, L., Zhao, L., Martinez-Maldonado, R., & Gašević, D. (2023). CVPE: A computer vision approach for scalable and privacy-preserving socio-spatial, multimodal learning analytics. In *LAK23: 13th International Learning Analytics and Knowledge Conference (LAK 2023)*, Arlington, TX, USA, March 13–17. ACM.

Lin, C. C., Huang, A. Y., & Lu, O. H. (2023). Artificial intelligence in intelligent tutoring systems toward sustainable education: A systematic review. *Smart Learning Environments*, 10(1): 41.

Marachi, R. & Quill, L. (2020). The case of Canvas: Longitudinal datafication through learning management systems. *Teaching in Higher Education*, 25(4): 418–434.

Martinez-Maldonado, R., Echeverria, V., Fernandez-Nieto, G., Yan, L., Zhao, L., Alfredo, R., ..., & Wotherspoon, R. (2023). Lessons learnt from a multimodal learning analytics deployment in-the-wild. *ACM Transactions on Computer-Human Interaction*, 31(1): 1.

Miao, F., Holmes, W., Huang, R., & Zhang, H. (2021). AI and education: A guidance for policymakers. UNESCO Publishing.

Mu, T., Jetten, A., & Brunskill, E. (2020). Towards suggesting actionable interventions for wheel spinning students. In: Rafferty, A. N., Whitehill, J., Cavalli-Sforza, V., & Romero, C. (eds.), *Proceedings of The 13th International Conference on Educational Data Mining (EDM 2020)*, pp. 183–193.

Nigam, A., Pasricha, R., Singh, T., *et al.* (2021). A systematic review on AI-based proctoring systems: Past, present and future. *Education and Information Technologies*, 26, 6421–6445.

Pelegrín Borondo, J., Olarte Pascual, C., Blanco Pascual, L., & García Milon, A. (2024). Smart ethics in the digital world: Proceedings of the ETHICOMP 2024. In: Oliva, M. A., Pelegrín Borondo, J., Murata, K., Lara Palma, A. M., & Ollé Sesé, M. (eds.), *21st International Conference on the Ethical and Social Impacts of ICT*, pp. 26–30.

Poquet, O. & De Laat, M. (2021). Developing capabilities: Lifelong learning in the age of AI. *British Journal of Educational Technology*, 52(4): 1695–1708.

Sabale, A. & Gomathi, S. (2022). Role of artificial intelligence in corporate training and development — A conceptual paper. *International Journal of Intelligent Systems and Applications in Engineering*, 10(4): 590–595.

Sajja, R., Sermet, Y., Cwiertny, D., & Demir, I. (2023). Integrating AI and learning analytics for data-driven pedagogical decisions and personalized interventions in education. arXiv preprint, arXiv:2312.09548.

Shapiro, H. B., Lee, C. H., Roth, N. E. W., Li, K., Çetinkaya-Rundel, M., & Canelas, D. A. (2017). Understanding the massive open online course (MOOC) student experience: An examination of attitudes motivations and barriers. *Computers & Education*, 110, 35–50.

Sharif, H., and Atif, A. (2024). The evolving classroom: How learning analytics is shaping the future of education and feedback mechanisms. *Education Sciences*, 14(2): 176.

Sousa, M. J., Dal Mas, F., Gonçalves, S. P., & Calandra, D. (2022). AI and blockchain as new triggers in the education arena. *European Journal of Investigation in Health, Psychology and Education*, 12(4): 445–447.

Stoll, L. & Louis, K. S. (2007). *Professional Learning Communities*. UK: McGraw-Hill Education.

Tsoni, R., Stavropoulos, E. C., & Verykios, V. S. (2019). Leveraging learning analytics with the power of words. *The Envisioning Report for Empowering Universities*, 24(10): 24–26.

U.S. Department of Education, Office of Educational Technology (2023). *Artificial Intelligence and Future of Teaching and Learning: Insights and Recommendations*. Washington, DC.

Zilvinskis, J. & Willis III, J. E. (2019). Learning Analytics in Higher Education: A Reflection. *InSight: A Journal of Scholarly Teaching*, 14, 43–54.

https://doi.org/10.1142/9789811296475_0010

Chapter 10

Knowledge Management in the Artificial Intelligence Era: The Knowledge Universe Transformer (KUT) Topology

Noam Koriat and Roy Gelbard

Bar-Ilan University, Ramat Gan, Israel

1. Introduction

At the turn of the millennium, four key technological trends such as Social, Mobile, Analytics, and Cloud (SMAC) converged and marked the genesis of the 4th Industrial Revolution (4IR) (Schwertner, 2017). Utilization of SMAC in unison empowered organizations to achieve digital transformation, thus rewriting their business story into a new "digital language" adapted to the Y, Z, and Alpha generations, who are digital natives.

In November 2022, OpenAI introduced ChatGPT, a generative artificial intelligence (GenAI) application. Within 2 months, ChatGPT reached 100 million users (Visual Capitalist, 2023), providing the capability to utilize high-performance artificial intelligence (AI) technology through natural language. This event significantly empowered SMAC's analytics pillar and positioned AI at the forefront of the revolution, giving rise to a continuous 5th Industrial Revolution (5IR): the AI Revolution.

Initially, processing substantial volumes of unstructured data, which constitute 80% of an organization's explicit knowledge (Harbert, 2021), became feasible through the utilization of natural language as a communication medium. Hence, organizations can avoid a scenario of inability to see the big explicit knowledge picture, akin to the idiom, "can't see the forest for the trees." On the contrary, organizations can face a new reality where they can seamlessly integrate, sense, process, and analyze each explicit knowledge resource, thus preventing situations where explicit resources exist, but are not accessible, akin to the idiom, "If a tree falls in a forest and no one is around to hear it, does it make a sound?" (Berkeley, 1710).

Thus, the 5IR presents a unique opportunity to reshape knowledge management (KM) practices, and in particular, explicit knowledge practices. Exploiting these opportunities is expected to provide organizations with improved competencies to adapt and keep their competitive edge in "turbulent times" (Drucker, 2012).

This chapter, theoretically and practically, explores the opportunities that 5IR technologies, particularly GenAI, are providing for KM. In addition, a new practical approach expected to shape KM in the AI era, the Knowledge Universe Transformer (KUT) topology, is proposed.

2. Background

2.1. *The 4th and 5th Industrial Revolutions, SMAC, and digital transformation*

SMAC stands as an acronym for four key technologies:

- **Social:** This covers applications and platforms that enable users to connect, collaborate, and engage in transactions.
- **Mobile:** This encompasses mobile devices technology, such as smartphones and smartwatches. These devices enable users to remain constantly connected and active, as they are portable and always connected to the Internet (Schwertner, 2017). Mobile devices serve as key data sources for analytics and AI models (The Council of Economic Advisers, 2024).
- **Analytics:** This comprises platforms that facilitate the processing, analysis, and generation of insights from large datasets, such as data generated by the usage of mobile devices (Schwertner, 2017).

- **Cloud:** This refers to cloud computing technology, which provides scalable computer infrastructure and software over the Internet, based on "pay as you go" or subscription-based business models. Cloud computing has lowered the entry barriers for entrepreneurs to access the advanced technology necessary to build innovative products and services (Vaquero *et al.*, 2008; Schwertner, 2017).

These four technologies converged together at the beginning of the millennium, enabling organizations to engage in digital transformation.

Digital transformation is a business approach for organizations to change their business models by utilizing digital skills and technology (Whelen, 2014), such as SMAC. In other words, digital transformation is rewriting the organization's business story in a new language — the language of digital natives — Y, Z, and Alpha generations.

The digital transformation revolution is known as the 4th Industrial Revolution (4IR). To illustrate how SMAC technologies are utilized in digital transformation, Waze (acquired by Google) will be examined. Waze utilizes data (Analytics) gathered from users' (Social) mobile devices (Mobile) to construct maps, routes, and road alerts, and serves as a navigation mobile application (Mobile and Cloud). Hence, the convergence of all four key technologies facilitates the digital transformation of navigation.

SMAC's analytics pillar was boosted recently, driven by the explosion of AI technologies, such as GenAI, which enable natural language interaction with computing devices, to generate diverse outputs, such as text, audio, and video. This revolution is commonly referred to as the 5th Industrial Revolution, also known as the AI Revolution.

2.2. *Intelligent organization and digital business agility*

Both 4IR and 5IR are characterized by a turbulent, high-paced business environment, necessitating continuous changes in business models and ecosystems. This era is referred to as "turbulent times" (Drucker, 2012).

To address this challenge, organizations are trying to apply organizational intelligence, characterized by the ability to tolerate change, transform, and actively impact the business environment (Pinchot & Pinchot, 1994). Intelligent organizations are flexible and conduct digital business agility. They conduct a highly collaborative culture and engage in collaborative behaviors, such as team communication and coordination (Pinchot & Pinchot, 1994; Hoegl & Gemuenden, 2001).

Intelligent organizations champion KM and invest in facilitating high availability and accessibility of knowledge assets, including organizational and social capital (Pinchot & Pinchot, 1994). Knowledge assets can be utilized to leverage the benefits of human capital (Pinchot & Pinchot, 1994; Reed *et al.*, 2006). Intelligent organizations are client-centric and keep all stakeholders, such as employees and vendors, in the knowledge flow (Pinchot & Pinchot, 1994).

Digital business agility relies on three fundamental elements (Wade & Tarling, 2016; Wade *et al.*, 2017):

1. **Hyperawareness:** This is an organizational competency for sensing changes within a turbulent business ecosystem.
2. **Informed decision-making:** This is the capacity to make informed data- and knowledge-driven decisions, upon sensing a change. Decisions driven by data and knowledge can be realized using analytics technology, particularly GenAI.
3. **Fast execution:** This is a guarantee that decisions are undertaken promptly, efficiently, and effectively.

Through the adoption of digital business agility, organizations cultivate a flux mindset that tolerates change as a continuous aspect of the business and establishes adequate organizational setup for digital transformation and innovation to thrive (Wade & Tarling, 2016; Wade *et al.*, 2017).

2.3. *Data, information, and knowledge*

Data are defined as symbols, such as letters, numbers, and images that represent an object (Ackoff, 1989; Zins, 2007). Information is processed data, commonly represented as tables with fields and values. Information is more functional and answers questions such as who, where, what, how many, and when, and thus information is meaningful data (Ackoff, 1989; Zins, 2007). Knowledge is contextual information, insights based on experience, and answers how-to questions. When integrated, knowledge serves as a foundation to facilitate new knowledge, ideas, and experiences (Ackoff, 1989; Davenport & Prusak, 2000; Zins, 2007).

Explicit knowledge can be formulated verbally and as data, and is objective, context-free, and relatively simple to imitate, duplicate, and transfer (Polyani, 1966). Dummett (1991) proposed that explicit knowledge can be elicited from an individual with an adequate prompt or inquiry. Structured explicit knowledge or structured data are stored in databases, tables, or other structured formats such as code, facilitating large-scale automated processing and analysis.

Unstructured explicit knowledge or unstructured data are stored in formats, such as documents, presentations, images, audios, and videos. The processing of unstructured explicit knowledge is complex and often requires human resources.

Implicit (tacit) knowledge is subjective, contextual, and difficult to detect, replicate, and transfer. It is difficult to formulate verbally or represent as data and often resides within the mind of the knower (Polyani, 1966; Dummett, 1991). Implicit knowledge can span a spectrum of tacitness, from a low degree of tacitness, such as skills that are easily communicated and codified, through skills that can be formulated if the right how-to question is asked, to a high degree of tacitness, such as deep embedded skills, which are not fully accessible by the knower (Ambrosini & Bowman, 2001).

Thus, we propose that large-scale unstructured explicit knowledge can be considered as low-degree tacit knowledge, since when integrated, it can express skills and knowledge that can be communicated and codified, easily by asking the right inquiry or prompt.

2.4. *Generative artificial intelligence*

Intelligence is defined as the competency to engage in abstract reasoning, comprehend and analyze unstructured data, and complex concepts, and learn from experience (Kok *et al.*, 2009). Computers were primarily designed to codify explicit tasks and efficiently perform structured data analysis. Computers face challenges in processing unstructured data, such as documents, presentations, audios, or videos, which demand human-like abilities and thinking, relying on tacit knowledge (Brynjolfsson & Raymond, 2023).

AI focuses on creating computers that can manifest human-like intelligent thinking (Kok *et al.*, 2009). AI models such as machine learning (ML) are trained in a supervised or unsupervised method, resulting in outputs that infer from existing data only. GenAI models utilize statistical algorithms to generate new content such as text, images, sound, and videos, originating from both structured and unstructured data used to train the model (Agrawal *et al.*, 2018; Brynjolfsson & Raymond, 2023).

GenAI models encompass unique challenges:

- **Inexplicability:** GenAI models use prompts as input to generate new content based on statistical algorithms. They are generally not able to explain their responses, and this limits the ability of users to validate the model's responses (Cantens, 2024).
- **Hallucination:** GenAI models may provide answers with errors, due to insufficient relevant data or reference to non-relevant data originating from the statistic domain defined by the prompt (Cantens, 2024).
- **Bias:** Given that GenAI models are trained on data generated by humans, they are prone to biases originating from the data they are trained on (The Council of Economic Advisers, 2024). This phenomenon applies to biases such as ethics or discrimination, as well as impacting issues, such as language, business, or theory.

2.5. *Knowledge management*

KM is defined as a structured process of identifying and leveraging the collective organizational explicit and implicit knowledge, enhancing the organization's competitive edge (Von Krogh, 1998). High KM competency has a positive impact on the organization's performance (Chen & Fong, 2015).

The KM culture consists of three main processes:

1. **Knowledge creation (KC):** KC, also referred to as knowledge accumulation or generation, involves the capturing and encoding of existing knowledge, combining knowledge and development, and creation of new ideas. KC is mostly facilitated by human resources integrating existing explicit and implicit knowledge (Intezari *et al.*, 2017).
2. **Knowledge sharing (KS):** KS involves making the knowledge accessible and easily retrievable (Intezari *et al.*, 2017).
3. **Knowledge implementation (KI):** KI, also referred to as knowledge conversion, application, and utilization, involves ensuring the effective application of knowledge for organizational purposes, such as new products or services (Intezari *et al.*, 2017).

3. Knowledge Universe Transformer (KUT) Topology

Given that unstructured data comprise 80% of an organization's explicit data (Harbert, 2021), and the large scale of data that organizations generate, it is imperative to develop automated methods for its large-scale processing. Without such automated capabilities, organizations depend on human resources, which are less efficient in terms of both time and cost, to process unstructured data. In addition, human resources can only process unstructured data in a limited perspective and scale, thereby restricting the ability to fully harness the knowledge benefits associated with integrating all the organizational unstructured data.

By integrating unstructured data with structured data, the organization gains the ability to see the big explicit knowledge picture and mitigate the risk of encountering the phenomenon of a hidden box, thus "what the organization does not know it knows" (Weiss & Wright, 2006).

Given that GenAI technology can efficiently and effectively process and integrate both structured and unstructured data and provides the ability to ask the right questions via prompting, we propose organizations to establish the KUT topology, as illustrated in Figure 1.

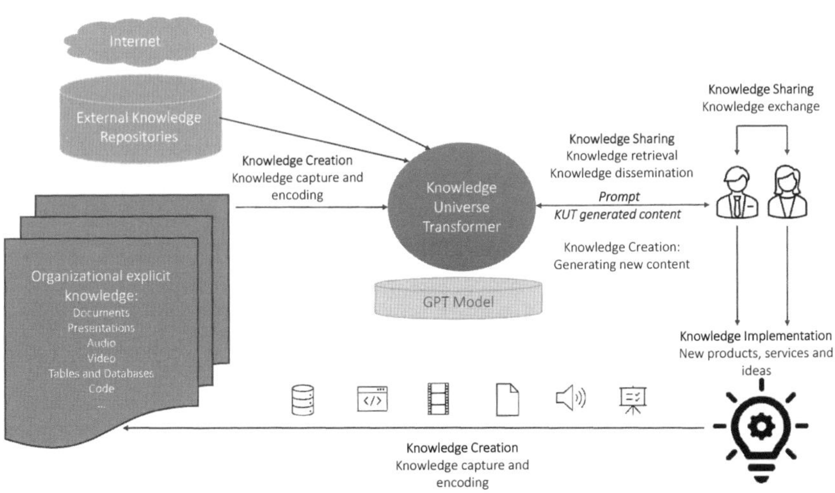

Figure 1. Proposed KUT topology.

KUT is an organizational GenAI platform that captures all the organizational data repositories, such as code, databases, documents, presentations, images, audios, and videos. By doing so, organizations can unlock the complete potential of explicit knowledge, aligning with Dummett's (1991) notion that explicit knowledge can be elicited through appropriate prompts or inquiries. Thus, any member of the organization will have the capability to query the KUT via prompts and receive integrated generated content, based on the organization's knowledge universe.

As previously proposed, large-scale integrated unstructured explicit knowledge can be viewed as low-degree tacit knowledge. KUT facilitates the codification of skills and knowledge based on the integrated organizational knowledge universe, along with the utilization of prompts. Thus, using KUT, users will be capable of retrieving wide organizational low-degree tacit knowledge as well.

Therefore, through the utilization of KUT, organizations can manifest three out of six KM applications that cover the KM spectrum: analytical KM; asset management; and process KM (Binney, 2001). Consequently, organizations can effectively promote all three fundamental KM processes.

3.1. *Knowledge creation with KUT*

KUT facilitates a single organizational platform to capture, encode, and integrate all organizational explicit data, structured and unstructured. Since low-degree tacit knowledge is often stored in organizational content such as documents, presentations, procedures, recorded sessions, and code, KUT will also encompass a segment of the organizational low-degree tacit knowledge.

As such, KUT enables users to easily generate new content, leveraging the organizational knowledge universe, using prompts. If KUT is connected to the Internet or external knowledge repositories, it facilitates integration with a broader knowledge universe. This enables KUT to generate even more creative and interesting outputs and ideas.

3.2. *Knowledge sharing with KUT*

KUT serves as a one-stop-shop for retrieving all organizational explicit and low-degree tacit knowledge. As customary in advanced generative pre-trained transformer (GPT) tools, KUT displays the sources of generated content and links to them. In addition, KUT will enable the collaboration of prompts and content among users.

3.3. *Knowledge implementation with KUT*

KUT stands as a powerful tool for the members of an organization to combine and retrieve knowledge, generate ideas, and potentially promote efficiency. It acts as an organizational hyper-sensor, providing a comprehensive 360-degree perspective of all organizational explicit and low-degree tacit knowledge. It also serves as a tool for integrating knowledge into processed content, supporting informed decision-making processes. As proposed in recent research (Noy & Zhang, 2023), GPT tools such as ChatGPT boost productivity and efficiency, facilitating augmented intelligence. Additional research (Dell'Acqua *et al.*, 2023) proposes that when utilized properly, AI serves as a quality and productivity booster. Therefore, utilizing KUT is akin to collaborating with an expert consistently, and it is expected to boost quality, productivity, and efficiency while facilitating fast execution. Consequently, it is expected to foster business digital agility, promoting innovation and applying new products, services, and ideas (Wade & Tarling, 2016; Wade *et al.*, 2017).

Through the process of creating new products, services, and ideas, KUT's outputs are expected to facilitate the generation of new organizational content, such as databases, code, documents, and presentations. These will serve as an input enriching the content of the organizational knowledge universe, on which KUT is trained, enabling KUT to continuously develop and increase its added value and fostering an iterative KC and development cycle.

4. Challenges Encountered While Implementing KUT

Organizations integrating KUT are expected to face a range of challenges inherent in GenAI, which are described in the following sections.

4.1. *Data quality barrier*

GenAI models' performance is a function of the data quality on which they are trained. Hence, the principle of "garbage in, garbage out" applies, and the quality of a model's responses is only as good as the quality of the input data and may affect a phenomenon, such as hallucination (The Council of Economic Advisers, 2024).

Therefore, organizations implementing KUT must attend to strengthen employees' proficiency in skills relevant to the content the model is trained on, such as document editing, code programming, or database administration. In addition, it is important to utilize file formats appropriately. For instance, PDF documents and presentations that are Web Content Accessibility Guidelines (WCAG)-compliant will be processed more effectively than documents that are not. In a future perspective, as content-processing technology advances, the significance of this issue is likely to diminish.

4.2. *Hallucination*

Organizational GPT models can mitigate the risk of hallucination by controlling which datasets are processed to respond. By granting users to define dataset boundaries, internal and external, such as Internet and external knowledge repositories, KUT can produce more targeted responses. Moreover, setting statistical thresholds below which the model refrains from generating responses can further mitigate the risk of hallucination.

Recent studies elucidate the mechanism underlying hallucinations proposing strategies and practices to mitigate them (Lee, 2023; Sovrano *et al.*, 2023; Liebowitz, 2025). Consequently, ongoing research in this domain is expected to reduce the hallucination phenomenon overall.

4.3. *Confidentiality and compartmentalization of knowledge*

Since GenAI models generate new content using statistical algorithms, their responses can be unpredictable and inexplicable. Training these models on sensitive, private, or confidential data may lead to sensitive data being reflected in the model's responses without any means of control.

In addition to granting users to define dataset boundaries, it is advised to grant KUT administrators the ability to establish role-based dataset boundaries. Exercising this control will ensure that the model's responses will use only data that the user is authorized to access and mitigate that risk.

4.4. *Technology acceptance*

Substantial shifts in the work environment may exhibit resistance to change among employees, which stems from the perceived repercussions of altering the *status quo* (Ford *et al.*, 2002). For instance, monitoring technologies such as employee electronic performance monitoring (EPM) may raise concerns, which can induce stress, negative feelings, and false interpretations among employees, thereby affecting long-term performance (Tziner & Rabenu, 2018). Technology acceptance models (TAMs) incorporate these factors along with various others (Marangunić & Granić, 2015). A recent study focused on the acceptance of AI technology and proposed that during the initial adoption phase, ChatGPT increases stress levels among employees, for instance, due to repercussions related to job security (Khanthavit & Khanthavit, 2023).

GenAI platforms such as KUT feature a capability to integrate and process all organizational outputs, including usage logs and patterns, and may be interpreted as a form of monitoring activity, similar to EPM. In addition, GenAI can be perceived as a technology that poses a threat to job security by replacing existing roles and creating jobs that require skills not currently possessed by employees (World Economic Forum, 2023). Moreover, it may also be perceived as a technology that could compromise employees' privacy, by capturing their usage patterns, such as chat sessions and prompts.

Hence, it is advised that organizations integrating GenAI adopt transparent principles and guidelines for employee privacy, for instance, in alignment with recommendations from labor unions such as The Future World of Work organization and UNI Global Union (Union, 2017). In addition, organizations utilizing GenAI should engage in comprehensive human resources planning, which encompasses reskilling and talent management initiatives. By employing these strategies, organizations can mitigate false perceptions and foster the acceptance of GenAI technologies.

5. Conclusions

The 5IR offers a unique opportunity and challenge for organizations to rethink KM practices as a means to cope with a high-paced turbulent business ecosystem that is disrupted by digital transformation. Due to the unique features of GenAI technology, we propose the KUT topology as a new approach to promote organizational KM, supported by GPT.

Through the adoption of KUT, organizations will initially gain a comprehensive 360-degree perspective of their integrated explicit knowledge, providing their employees with a single unified tool to facilitate all three key fundamental KM processes: knowledge creation, sharing, and implementation.

KUT is expected to promote digital business agility and assist organizations in their evolution to become intelligent organizations. This is essential for enabling organizations to foster digital transformation and innovation as a means to maintain their competitive edge and cope with the fast-paced turbulent business landscape.

KUT features the ability to process large-scale unstructured explicit knowledge, enabling the articulation of skills and knowledge that can be communicated and codified, easily by using the right prompt. Therefore, we propose that large-scale unstructured explicit knowledge could be regarded as low-degree tacit knowledge.

To conclude, GenAI technology marks the beginning of forthcoming changes in the fields of KM practices. This chapter provides insights into the potential digital transformation that the KM field can undergo, highlighting KUT topology as a potential framework in this context.

References

Ackoff, R. L. (1989). From data to wisdom. *Journal of Applied Systems Analysis*, 16(1): 3–9.

Agrawal, A., Gans, J., & Goldfarb, A. (2018). *Prediction Machines: The Simple Economics of Artificial Intelligence*. Brighton, MA: Harvard Business Review Press.

Ambrosini, V. & Bowman, C. (2001). Tacit knowledge: Some suggestions for operationalization. *Journal of Management Studies*, 38(6): 811–829.

Berkeley, G. (1710). *Treatise Concerning the Principles of Human Knowledge*. Ireland: Aaron Rhames for Jeremy Pepyat, Bookfellar in Skinner-Row.

Binney, D. (2001). The knowledge management spectrum–understanding the KM landscape. *Journal of Knowledge Management*, 5(1): 33–42.

Brynjolfsson, E., Li, D., & Raymond, L. R. (2023). *Generative AI at Work*. National Bureau of Economic Research No. w31161.

Cantens, T. (2024). How will the state think with ChatGPT? The challenges of generative artificial intelligence for public administrations. *AI & Society*, 1–12.

Chen, L. & Fong, P. S. (2015). Evaluation of knowledge management performance: An organic approach. *Information & Management*, 52(4): 431–453.

Davenport, T. H. & Prusak, L. (2000). *Working Knowledge: How Organizations Manage What They Know*. Boston, MA: Harvard Business Press.

Dell'Acqua, F., McFowland, E., Mollick, E. R., Lifshitz-Assaf, H., Kellogg, K., Rajendran, S., ..., & Lakhani, K. R. (2023). *Navigating the Jagged Technological Frontier: Field Experimental Evidence of the Effects of AI on Knowledge Worker Productivity and Quality*. Harvard Business School Technology & Operations Mgt. Unit Working Paper 24-013.

Drucker, P. (2012). *Managing in Turbulent Times*. London: Routledge.

Dummett, M. (1991). *The Logical Basis of Metaphysics*. Cambridge, MA: Harvard University Press.

Ford, J. D., Ford, L. W., & McNamara, R. T. (2002). Resistance and the background conversations of change. *Journal of Organizational Change Management*, 15(2): 105–121.

Harbert, T. (2021). Tapping the power of unstructured data. *MIT Sloan*, February 1 and 3.

Hoegl, M. & Gemuenden, H. G. (2001). Teamwork quality and the success of innovative projects: A theoretical concept and empirical evidence. *Organization Science*, 12(4): 435–449.

Intezari, A., Taskin, N., & Pauleen, D. J. (2017). Looking beyond knowledge sharing: An integrative approach to knowledge management culture. *Journal of Knowledge Management*, 21(2): 492–515.

Khanthavit, A. & Khanthavit, S. (2023). Chatgpt and stress. *ABAC Journal*, 43(3): 213–224.

Kok, J. N., Boers, E. J., Kosters, W. A., Van der Putten, P., & Poel, M. (2009). Artificial intelligence: Definition, trends, techniques, and cases. *Artificial Intelligence*, 1: 270–299.

Lee, M. (2023). A mathematical investigation of hallucination and creativity in GPT models. *Mathematics*, 11(10): 2320.

Liebowitz, J. (ed.) (2024). *Regulating Hate Speech Created by Generative AI*. New York, NY: Taylor & Francis.

Marangunić, N. & Granić, A. (2015). Technology acceptance model: A literature review from 1986 to 2013. *Universal Access in the Information Society*, 14: 81–95.

Noy, S. & Zhang, W. (2023). *Experimental Evidence on the Productivity Effects of Generative Artificial Intelligence*. MIT, Working Paper.

Pinchot, G. & Pinchot, E. (1994). *The End of Bureaucracy & The Rise of the Intelligent Organization*. San Francisco, CA: Berrett-Koehler Publishers Inc.

Polyani, M. (1966). *The Tacit Dimension*. New York, NY: Doubleday.

Reed, K. K., Lubatkin, M., & Srinivasan, N. (2006). Proposing and testing an intellectual capital-based view of the firm. *Journal of Management Studies*, 43(4): 867–893.

Schwertner, K. (2017). Digital transformation of business. *Trakia Journal of Sciences*, 15(1): 388–393.

Schwaninger, M. (2000). Managing complexity — the path toward intelligent organizations. *Systemic Practice and Action Research*, 13: 207–241.

Sovrano, F., Ahley, K., & Bacchelli, A. (2023). Toward eliminating hallucinations: GPT-based explanatory ai for intelligent textbooks and documentation. In: *CEUR Workshop Proceedings No. 3444*, pp. 54–65. CEUR-WS.

The Council of Economic Advisers (2024). *Economic Report of the President – Chapter 7: An Economic Framework for Understanding Artificial Intelligence*. The White House.

Tziner, A. & Rabenu, E. (2018). *Improving Performance Appraisal at Work: Evolution and Change*. Edward Elgar Publishing.

Union, U. G. (2017). Top 10 principles for workers' data privacy and protection. *The Future World of Work*. http://www.thefutureworldofwork.org/media/35421/uni_workers_data_protection.pdf.

Vaquero, L. M., Rodero-Merino, L., Caceres, J., & Lindner, M. (2008). A break in the clouds: Towards a cloud definition. *ACM Sigcomm Computer Communication Review*, 39(1): 50–55.

Visual Capitalist (2023). How long it took for popular apps to reach 100 million users. Retrieved from https://www.visualcapitalist.com/threads-100-million-users/.

Von Krogh, G. (1998). Care in knowledge creation. *California Management Review*, 40(3): 133.

Wade, M., Noronha, A., Macaulay, J., & Barbier, J. (2017). *Orchestrating Digital Business Transformation: Working in Concert to Achieve Digital Excellence*. Lausanne, Switzerland: International Institute for Management Development (IMD).

Wade, M. & Tarling, A. (2016). *The Digital Business Agility Imperative: How Companies Can Fight Digital Disruption*. Lausanne, Switzerland: International Institute for Management Development.

Weiss, A. & Wright, S. (2006). Dealing with the unknown: A holistic approach to marketing and competitive intelligence. *De Montfort University*.

Whalen, M. (2014). A digital transformation maturity model and your digital roadmap. *IDC*.

World Economic Forum (2023). The future of jobs report 2023.

Zins, C. (2007). Conceptual approaches for defining data, information, and knowledge. *Journal of the American Society for Information Science and Technology*, 58(4): 479–493.

https://doi.org/10.1142/9789811296475_0011

Chapter 11

Leveraging AutoML and Explainable AI for Digital Transformation

Marc Schmitt

Siemens AG, Munich, Bavaria, Germany

1. Introduction

The roles of automated machine learning (AutoML) and explainable artificial intelligence (XAI) are essential in shaping the future of business analytics (BA). This chapter explores how these technologies are transforming the landscape of human–AI collaboration, making advanced analytics accessible to a broader range of users, and enhancing the transparency necessary for trust and accountability. Such advancements are pivotal for driving digital transformation across multiple sectors.

Data have emerged as invaluable assets for organizations, fundamentally transforming the landscape of business operations and competitive strategy (Constantiou & Kallinikos, 2015; Veldkamp, 2023). To harness the potential of these vast data reserves, businesses increasingly rely on business intelligence (BI) and BA (Chen *et al.*, 2012). These disciplines are critical in extracting actionable insights from raw data, enabling organizations to make informed decisions, optimize processes, and innovate. By systematically analyzing data through various analytics techniques, companies can improve efficiency, tailor customer experiences, predict market trends, and enhance profitability, effectively turning information into a cornerstone of organizational value. Thus, the digital transformation of BA-based enterprise information systems (Sun *et al.*, 2017) is an essential transformation journey to transform organizations into a digital version of themselves that can compete in a data-driven world (Henke *et al.*, 2016).

The analytics and AI landscape is undergoing a significant transformation, largely catalyzed by the advent of generative AI (GenAI) technologies, or large language models (LLMs) such as ChatGPT (Kocoń *et al.*, 2023; Vaswani *et al.*, 2017). GenAI's ability to understand, generate, and interact using natural language has opened up new possibilities for enhancing decision-making processes, automating complex tasks, and providing deeper insights across industries. As organizations adopt these technologies, they are not only optimizing their existing operations but also discovering new opportunities for growth and innovation. This shift is expected to drive profound changes in how businesses operate, interact with customers, and leverage data, setting the stage for a dramatically transformed digital ecosystem (Cennamo & Santaló, 2019). Thus, integrating advanced AI and analytics capabilities into the foundation of modern organizations is essential to take part in the promising wave of substantial digital progress in the coming years (Suleyman, 2023).

There are three distinct types of analytics: descriptive, which explains what has happened; predictive, which forecasts future outcomes; prescriptive, which suggests actions based on predictions (Schmitt, 2023b).

- Descriptive analytics processes historical data to interpret the past through data aggregation, mining, and basic statistics. It identifies patterns, clarifies trends, and presents findings via dashboards and visualizations, aiding businesses in understanding strengths and weaknesses for informed decision-making. This analytics type is foundational in BI, preparing the ground for advanced predictive and prescriptive analyses.
- Predictive analytics extends beyond the descriptive approach to not only look at past data but also forecast future outcomes. It employs various statistical and machine-learning (ML) techniques to analyze current and historical data to make predictions about future trends and behaviors. The use case examples presented in this chapter spanning the domains of marketing, finance, cybersecurity, and health care belong to this analytics category.

- Prescriptive analytics, the most advanced analytics form, uses insights from descriptive and predictive analytics along with complex algorithms and computational models to recommend optimal decisions (Bertsimas & Kallus, 2019). By employing techniques such as simulation, optimization, and decision analysis, it guides actions to influence future outcomes, answering "what should we do?" While the examples are largely reflecting predictive analytics, prescriptive analytics is a natural extension of ML-based predictions.

ML and artificial intelligence (AI) are essential in predictive and prescriptive analytics. In predictive analytics, ML algorithms are extensively used to process large datasets and identify patterns or trends that can forecast future events. These algorithms adapt and improve their predictions over time as they are exposed to more data, enhancing their accuracy and reliability. This is especially important in domains such as marketing, finance, cybersecurity, and health care (see Sections 3 and 4), where predicting future trends or behaviors can significantly impact decision-making and/or strategic planning. Prescriptive analytics takes a step further by not just predicting outcomes but also suggesting decision options and assessing their potential impacts. Advanced AI techniques, including deep learning and reinforcement learning, are employed to simulate different scenarios and optimize decisions. This involves complex problem-solving that can account for a multitude of variables and changing conditions, aiming to provide the best course of action.

AI-driven analytics in the context of digital transformation has become a strategic imperative for organizations across the public and private sectors (Selten & Klievink, 2024). It represents a fundamental shift in how organizations leverage technology to innovate, streamline operations, and deliver enhanced customer experiences. AI and analytics stand at the core of digital transformation, offering powerful tools for data-driven decision-making and automation. These technologies not only help businesses optimize their operations but also provide insights that can lead to new products, services, and business models. Thus, this makes adopting those technologies an essential building block for competing in the age of AI (Iansiti & Lakhani, 2020). However, the complexity of AI systems and the expertise required to develop and manage them can be significant barriers. This is where automated machine learning (AutoML) and XAI come into play, simplifying the deployment of

AI solutions and making their outcomes more understandable and trustable.

AutoML and XAI are transformative technologies that can democratize AI usage and enhance transparency, respectively. AutoML automates many aspects of building AI models, which enables more stakeholders to engage with AI without needing deep technical expertise. Meanwhile, XAI focuses on making AI decisions transparent and comprehensible, which is critical for trust and accountability. By leveraging these technologies, organizations can accelerate their digital transformation initiatives, making them more efficient, scalable, and aligned with ethical standards. This chapter explores how AutoML and XAI can be harnessed effectively to drive digital transformation, ensuring that AI contributes positively to organizational goals and societal norms. Let us now explore the importance of human–AI collaboration and the partially competing narratives of automation and augmentation before we dive into the specifics of AutoML and XAI and the integration of both.

2. Toward Trustworthy Human–AI Collaboration

Algorithms have arrived at work (Kellogg *et al.*, 2020) and are increasingly competing with human labor. This is not a recent phenomenon but has been ongoing for decades. Initially impacting primarily blue-collar jobs and now increasingly affecting white-collar roles as well. Today, data-driven decisions based on AI analytics are an essential building block of modern digital enterprises (Fountaine *et al.*, 2019; Schmitt, 2023a). This shift raises questions about the balance of power between humans and AI in determining what is relevant in various contexts. For example, Faggioli *et al.* (2024) ask the following compelling question: Who "determines what is relevant? Humans or AI? Why not both?" This dilemma is often framed as the automation versus augmentation issue, which reflects the tension between machines taking over tasks against the idea of machines enhancing human capabilities. Research indicates that digital technologies are replacing human roles across both blue-collar and white-collar sectors, leading to new forms of collaboration between digital systems and human workers within organizations (Baptista *et al.*, 2020; Coombs *et al.*, 2020). In contrast to previous technological advancements (other general-purpose technologies, such as the steam engine, electricity, or the Internet) that straightforwardly increased productivity and created new jobs, ML presents a more complex scenario (Goldfarb *et al.*, 2023). As a meta-technology capable of making autonomous decisions, ML not only complicates predictions about job creation and loss but also accelerates scientific breakthroughs and innovations across multiple fields (Suleyman, 2023).

This makes the synergistic integration of machine and human capabilities essential for the successful utilization of AI/ML technologies in the context of digital transformation. The successful integration of AI into digital organizations is largely based on the trustworthiness of these systems. For AI to be considered trustworthy, it must be reliable and transparent, thereby fostering a positive environment for human–AI collaboration.

- **Reliability:** Reliability in AI systems is achieved through rigorous testing and validation to ensure that they perform as expected under diverse conditions. This includes stress testing AI models against unusual or unexpected inputs to evaluate their resilience and response accuracy. Ensuring AI systems are reliable and behave predictably builds user confidence and trust.
- **Explainability:** Transparency in AI involves the ability of the system to provide understandable explanations and justifications for its decisions and actions. By leveraging XAI techniques, such as SHAP or LIME, organizations can illuminate the reasoning behind AI-driven decisions. This transparency is crucial not only for compliance with regulatory standards but also for gaining user trust and acceptance.
- **Ethical AI:** To ensure that AI systems uphold ethical standards, organizations must develop ethical frameworks that govern the design, development, and deployment of AI technologies. These frameworks should address issues such as fairness, non-discrimination, privacy, and accountability. By embedding ethical considerations into AI systems, organizations can prevent biases and promote fairness, further enhancing trust.
- **Communication:** Engaging stakeholders through regular communication about how AI systems work, their benefits, and their limitations is vital for building trust. Educating stakeholders about AI, providing transparency about its deployment, and openly discussing its ethical implications can demystify AI technologies and foster a collaborative environment.

Trust is the cornerstone of effective human–AI collaboration. By focusing on reliability, explainability, ethical AI, and stakeholder engagement (communication), organizations can create AI systems that are not only technologically advanced but also trustworthy and beneficial to all. This emphasis on trust will enable the integration of AI into core business processes, which is essential for effective digital transformations.

3. Automated Machine Learning

3.1. *AutoML: What it is and how it works*

Automated machine learning, commonly referred to as AutoML, represents a pivotal advancement in the field of AI that aims to automate the end-to-end process of applying ML to real-world problems (Schmitt, 2023a). This technology is designed to make ML more accessible to non-experts and to enhance the efficiency of ML workflows, thus democratizing the benefits of AI innovations. At its core, AutoML focuses on simplifying the most complex aspects of ML systems. Traditionally, developing an ML model involves several stages: preprocessing data, selecting features, choosing a model family, optimizing model parameters, and validating the model's performance. Each of these steps requires specialized knowledge that can be a barrier to entry for those without a background in data science. In addition, AutoML systems improve the lives of data scientists, and they can be used for fast prototyping and testing.

AutoML usually automates the following steps of an ML pipeline:

- **Data preprocessing:** AutoML tools automatically clean the input data, handle missing values, and encode non-numerical data into a machine-readable format. This simplification allows users to focus more on the analysis rather than the preparation of data.
- **Feature engineering:** One of the most time-consuming processes in ML, feature engineering, is streamlined by AutoML platforms. These systems can automatically detect and create meaningful features from raw data, which significantly impacts a model's effectiveness and accuracy.
- **Model selection:** AutoML evaluates multiple ML models to determine which performs best for a specific task. It runs numerous algorithms — from linear regressions to more complex ensembles — and identifies the model that most suitably addresses the problem.

- **Hyperparameter tuning:** Selecting the optimal settings for each model is crucial for achieving the best performance. AutoML uses techniques such as grid search, random search, or Bayesian optimization to automatically find the best hyperparameters, thus fine-tuning the models without human intervention.
- **Model validation:** Finally, AutoML platforms automatically split the data into training and test sets, use the training set to learn the models, and evaluate them on the test set. This process includes cross-validation techniques to ensure that the model generalizes well to new, unseen data.

The goal of AutoML — especially in the context of a full ML pipeline — is not just to automate the process of building and deploying ML models but also to provide robust, scalable, and efficient solutions that can adapt over time (Schmitt, 2020). By reducing the barrier to entry and allowing more users to leverage ML tools, AutoML facilitates a broader adoption of AI technologies across various sectors. This broadening of access and simplification of processes is critical for businesses looking to integrate AI into their operations to drive innovation and efficiency. As such, AutoML is a core enabler of digital transformation in modern enterprises.

3.2. *Examples of AutoML applications in organizations*

ML and the automated version thereof have found several applications in various domains. They help companies leverage the power of AI and its potential to transform key business operations through automation and enhanced decision-making capabilities. This section contains four examples where ML has become essential: marketing, finance, cybersecurity, and healthcare.

3.2.1. *Marketing*

ML significantly enhances marketing efforts through advanced predictive analytics and recommender systems. It enables precise predictions of customer behaviors and trends, helping marketers tailor their strategies effectively. Additionally, it powers recommender systems, which ensure that customers receive personalized product suggestions based on real-time data. These applications not only improve customer engagement but also boost conversion rates by delivering more targeted, relevant content swiftly and efficiently.

3.2.2. *Finance*

In the financial services industry, assessing credit risk is important for determining the likelihood of loan or credit card repayments, or more generally, the default risk of a counterparty. Predictive ML models evaluate creditworthiness more accurately than traditional methods. Financial institutions use AutoML to process large datasets containing applicants' financial behaviors and demographic information. Additionally, ML applications in finance extend to fraud detection, algorithmic trading, portfolio management, and customer segmentation (see Section 3.2.1).

3.2.3. *Cybersecurity*

In the realm of cybersecurity, intrusion detection systems (IDS) are essential for safeguarding against threats, such as unauthorized access or breaches. AutoML plays a pivotal role in enhancing IDS by facilitating continuous learning and adaptation to evolving security challenges without constant human oversight. Cybersecurity teams utilize AutoML to process network traffic, user activities, and known threat patterns, enabling the automated identification of anomalies and the development of models to detect intrusions. This continuous refinement of algorithms ensures that detection models stay effective against emerging threats, boosting the security posture of organizations while freeing up security professionals to focus on more strategic tasks.

3.2.4. *Healthcare*

ML algorithms help in early disease detection, such as identifying patterns in imaging data that are difficult to spot, aiding in the early diagnosis of cancers and other conditions. In treatment personalization, ML models analyze vast amounts of patient data to predict which treatments are most likely to be effective for specific individuals, thus tailoring healthcare to individual needs. Another example is epidemic prediction, where ML is used for analyzing trends and data to forecast disease spread, which helps in planning and resource allocation (COVID-19).

3.3. *The role of AutoML in achieving digital transformation*

AutoML is a key component in the digital transformation strategies of various industries, acting as a catalyst for making advanced data analytics accessible to a broader range of users. It significantly reduces the barrier to entry for organizations looking to harness the power of AI. AutoML, thus, helps democratize advanced data-driven decision-making. It allows companies to rapidly iterate on solutions, optimize operations, and enhance customer experiences without the need for deep expertise in data science. As such, AutoML can be regarded as a foundational technology that accelerates the adoption of AI across sectors and therefore enables businesses to compete in the digital economy more effectively.

4. Explainable AI

4.1. *The rationale for XAI: Transparency and trust*

The rationale for XAI centers primarily around the concepts of transparency and trust. As AI technologies increasingly influence the critical aspects of daily life and businesses, it is imperative to understand those systems. Transparency in AI enables stakeholders to see inside the "black box" of AI decision-making processes (Rudin, 2019). This information is important for building trust between AI systems and their users. Trust in AI is fostered when users feel confident that the AI's operations are fair, justifiable, and ethical. XAI serves as a bridge that connects complex AI algorithms with human understanding, making these systems more usable in a way that fosters collaborative intelligence (humans and machines working together). This trust is essential for the wide-scale adoption and effective integration of AI technologies in sensitive areas, such as healthcare, finance, and law.

4.2. *Different XAI techniques*

4.2.1. *SHAP*

SHapley Additive exPlanations (SHAP) is a powerful tool for interpreting predictions made by ML models, and it plays a critical role in the domain of XAI (Chen *et al.*, 2023). Derived from game theory, particularly the Shapley values concept, SHAP provides a way to measure the contribution of each feature in a prediction by considering all possible combinations of features.

SHAP is based on the concept of Shapley values, which were developed by Lloyd Shapley in 1953. In the context of cooperative game theory, Shapley values are used to fairly distribute the payout among players depending on their contribution to the total game. Translated into the realm of ML, each feature of a dataset is treated as a "player," and the "payout" is the prediction output by the model. SHAP values quantify the impact of each feature on the prediction, considering the interaction with other features.

The process of calculating SHAP values involves assessing the change in prediction when a feature is included in a model versus when it is excluded. This is done across all possible combinations of features, providing a comprehensive view of the interactions and contributions of features:

- **Coalitions:** Features are grouped into various combinations, known as coalitions.
- **Marginal contribution:** For each coalition, the model's prediction with and without a particular feature is computed. The difference between these predictions gives the marginal contribution of that feature.
- **Averaging:** The average of these marginal contributions across all possible coalitions results in the SHAP value for each feature.

4.2.2. *LIME*

LIME, which stands for "Local Interpretable Model-agnostic Explanations" works by approximating a complex or black-box ML model (e.g., gradient boosting or deep learning) with a simpler, more interpretable model for individual predictions. Here's how this works:

- **Selection of instance:** LIME starts by selecting the specific instance for which an explanation is desired.
- **Perturbation of data:** It generates a new dataset consisting of perturbed samples around the selected instance. These perturbations involve slight modifications to the feature values of the instance, creating a pool of similar, but slightly varied, new data points.

- **Prediction by original model:** The original complex model makes predictions on this new set of perturbed data.
- **Weight assignment:** Each perturbed instance is weighted according to its proximity to the original instance. This weighting is crucial because predictions for data points closer to the original instance are more relevant for the explanation.
- **Training the interpretable model:** A simple, interpretable model (like linear regression or decision tree) is then trained on this weighted, perturbed dataset. The target outcomes for this training are the predictions made by the complex model.
- **Explanation generation:** The interpretable model, which now approximates how the original model behaves near the selected instance, is used to explain the prediction. It highlights which features were most influential in the decision-making process and how changes to those features could alter the prediction.

The result is a local explanation, meaning it applies specifically to the instance at hand and may not be generalizable across the entire dataset or other contexts. LIME is model-agnostic, which means that it can be used with any ML model, adding a layer of flexibility and utility in diverse applications where understanding model reasoning is crucial.

4.3. *Examples of XAI applications in organizations*

XAI is essential in sectors where understanding the rationale behind AI decisions is as important as the decisions themselves. By providing explanations of AI outputs, XAI helps improve decision-making processes, ensures compliance with regulations, and facilitates greater adoption of AI technologies. The following sections describe how XAI is applied in the contexts of marketing, finance, cybersecurity, and healthcare.

4.3.1. *Marketing*

The importance of XAI varies across sectors such as marketing, healthcare, and law due to differing stakes. In marketing, the main goal is to optimize strategies to maximize ROI, prioritizing accurate predictions of consumer behavior. While XAI can improve strategy refinement, the lack of explainability is less critical if the outcomes are effective. AI has been particularly successful in advertising and retail because it excels at processing large volumes of consumer data to deliver personalized experiences and targeted ads, significantly enhancing engagement and conversion rates. Moreover, this sector benefits from relatively fewer regulatory constraints, allowing for more flexible and innovative uses of AI compared to regulated fields, where strict compliance and transparency are mandatory.

4.3.2. *Finance*

The importance of XAI in the context of finance is domain-specific. For instance, while hedge funds may operate with minimal restrictions, pension funds are subject to stringent regulations. Risk management is also regulated. For example, when AI models assess creditworthiness, XAI clarifies how factors such as payment history, debt levels, or geographic location influence risk assessments. This transparency benefits internal decision makers, ensuring that models comply with varying regulatory standards, and helps customers understand credit decisions so they can improve their credit scores. XAI has the potential to facilitate regulatory compliance and ensure ethical AI practices across the diverse landscape of financial services.

4.3.3. *Cybersecurity*

In cybersecurity, where IDS must rapidly evolve to counter sophisticated threats, XAI increases their effectiveness by making their operations transparent. Traditional AI models detect threats but often fail to explain why certain behaviors are flagged as malicious. XAI enables IDS to articulate the reasons behind alerts, aiding in distinguishing false positives from real threats. This is crucial during breach investigations to understand the nature of an attack effectively. For example, if an AI model flags an anomaly in network traffic, XAI can detail factors such as unusual login times or atypical data access patterns, helping security teams assess and respond to threats swiftly, reducing downtime and potential damage. Furthermore, XAI builds trust in automated systems by providing transparency and accountability, ensuring that decisions are informed and stakeholders are confident in the system's integrity and effectiveness.

4.3.4. *Healthcare*

XAI plays a vital role in healthcare by enhancing the transparency and trustworthiness of ML applications (Yang *et al.,* 2022). As AI models are used to make critical healthcare decisions — from diagnosing diseases to recommending treatments — XAI allows medical professionals to understand the reasoning behind AI-generated insights and decisions. For instance, when a model identifies a particular pattern in medical imaging as indicative of a disease, XAI can elucidate which features of the image were significant and why, enabling doctors to verify and trust the AI's assessment. This is particularly important in treatment personalization, where understanding the basis for a recommended treatment can facilitate informed discussions between patients and healthcare providers. Furthermore, XAI contributes to public health by providing clear explanations of AI predictions in epidemic forecasting, aiding policymakers and health officials in making data-driven decisions that are crucial for effective intervention and resource management.

4.4. *The role of XAI in achieving digital transformation*

XAI is a key enabler for digital transformation by helping organizations leverage AI technologies responsibly. By making AI systems more transparent, XAI ensures that these technologies are integrated in a manner that aligns with organizational values and societal norms. When AI systems are transparent and their actions are explainable, organizations are better equipped to manage risks, comply with regulatory requirements, and engage constructively with customers and regulators about AI implementations. Also, XAI not only enhances the usability and approachability of AI technologies but also assures their integrity and effectiveness, laying a solid foundation for digital transformation across sensitive sectors, such as healthcare, finance, and law enforcement. This trust and accountability are indispensable for the successful integration and wide-scale adoption of AI in the digital age.

5. Transforming Organizations with AI and Analytics

AI and analytics are dramatically reshaping the strategy of modern organizations. As companies transition from traditional operational models to more dynamic, data-driven concepts, the role of AI and analytics becomes increasingly critical in facilitating this transformation. In the shift from automation to augmentation, AI technologies are not just replacing tasks previously done by humans but also enhancing human capabilities and creating new opportunities for innovation and decision-making. Automation through AI helps in handling repetitive and predictable tasks, while augmentation focuses on providing humans with the tools and insights needed for more complex decision-making and creative problem-solving. This blend of human expertise and AI support is crucial for organizations aiming to leverage the full spectrum of AI benefits.

Internal disagreement is a common occurrence within the context of disruptive technologies, as these innovations often challenge established norms and processes (Gans, 2024). To optimize outcomes, it is important for organizations to embrace data literacy and foster a culture that addresses and manages these disagreements constructively. The transition to a data-driven culture requires more than just the adoption of advanced technologies; it demands a comprehensive strategy to ensure that employees at all levels are equipped to understand and effectively utilize these technologies. Implementing this cultural shift is key to maximizing the benefits of AI and analytics throughout the organization. By investing in data literacy and promoting a culture that values data-driven decision-making, organizations not only enhance their operational capabilities but also build a resilient workforce capable of navigating the complexities of the digital age.

To navigate the complexities of integrating AI into core business processes, many organizations are considering the appointment of a Chief AI Officer (CAIO). This role is designed to bridge the gap between the technological potential of AI and strategic business objectives. The CAIO is responsible for overseeing the ethical deployment of AI technologies, ensuring that AI strategies align with broader business goals, and fostering an organizational culture that supports ongoing digital transformation (Schmitt, 2024). AI leadership, ideally under the role of a CAIO, should encompass the following responsibilities:

- **Strategic leadership:** The CAIO provides strategic direction for deploying AI technologies across different departments. This role involves understanding the broader business objectives and determining how AI can add value in achieving these goals. The CAIO ensures that AI initiatives are prioritized based on their potential impact and alignment with organizational strategies.

- **Data literacy:** A key responsibility of the CAIO is to promote an organizational culture that values data literacy, as outlined in the previous section. The CAIO works to implement training programs and foster an environment where data-driven decision-making is the norm. This includes developing clear policies and ensuring that all staff have the knowledge and tools they need to leverage AI effectively.
- **Ethics and regulations:** The CAIO also plays a key role in ensuring that AI applications within the company adhere to ethical guidelines and regulatory requirements. This includes setting up frameworks for AI governance, addressing issues of bias and fairness, and maintaining transparency in AI-driven processes, which make XAI essential (see Section 4).
- **Collaboration:** By facilitating collaboration across various teams, the CAIO helps break down silos and encourages a cohesive approach to AI and analytics. This role acts as a bridge between technical teams and business units, ensuring that AI solutions are developed with a clear understanding of business needs and potential impacts.
- **Innovation and adaptation:** Lastly, the CAIO is instrumental in keeping the organization at the forefront of technological advancements. This involves staying updated with AI trends and fostering innovation to maintain a competitive advantage.

By effectively managing these responsibilities, the CAIO ensures that AI technologies are implemented efficiently and beneficial for the organization's long-term growth and adaptation in the digital landscape. Finally, ethical considerations and regulatory compliance are paramount in the deployment of AI technologies. Organizations must adhere to established ethical guidelines and regulatory standards to ensure that their AI implementations do not inadvertently propagate biases or violate privacy laws. This involves embedding ethical considerations into the AI lifecycle, from development to deployment and monitoring, ensuring transparency, accountability, and fairness in AI-driven decisions. A very good example of the difficulties in this context is how the initial launch of Google Gemini, which was strongly biased, caused a strong public backlash, and had to be taken down.

6. Future Trends and Challenges

- **Technological advancements:** Technological advancements in AI are expected to push the boundaries of autonomy, with the development of more sophisticated systems capable of complex decision-making and operations without human oversight (Slumbers *et al.*, 2023). Additionally, the integration of AI with edge computing will accelerate real-time data processing at the source, enhancing responsiveness and efficiency. Further advances in key technologies and digital ecosystems will keep digital transformation on the organizational agenda for many years to come. Examples are quantum computing, which is set to redefine AI's capabilities, promising significant breakthroughs in processing speed and algorithm complexity (Castelvecchi, 2024). Others are AI-powered extended reality ecosystems that offer new forms of engagement and collaboration across national boundaries (Soliman *et al.*, 2024).
- **Integration and security challenges:** The integration of advanced AI technologies will face significant hurdles, including interoperability issues among diverse systems, which could limit functionality and scalability. Data privacy and security will be increasingly at risk as reliance on AI expands, necessitating robust protection measures (Schmitt, 2023c). Moreover, as AI systems take on more decision-making roles, mitigating biases and ensuring ethical operations will be critical to maintaining fairness and trust.
- **Economic and social implications:** The economic and social landscapes are poised to shift dramatically as AI and automation advance (Agrawal *et al.*, 2019). Job displacement in certain sectors may lead to economic challenges, while the creation of new roles in technology-driven areas could offer fresh opportunities. Organizations must strategize for workforce transitions, including re-skilling initiatives. Additionally, regulatory frameworks will need to evolve to keep pace with technological changes, ensuring that AI deployments remain safe.
- **Preparing for the future:** To navigate the upcoming changes, organizations should prioritize building a culture of continuous learning and innovation. This includes investing in education and training to keep the workforce adept with new technologies, engaging in policy discussions to shape future AI governance. By preparing proactively, companies can leverage AI advancements while mitigating associated risks. The establishment of dedicated AI leadership roles, such as a CAIO,

merits serious consideration. Such positions could play a pivotal role in orchestrating an organization's AI strategy, ensuring alignment with broader business objectives while navigating the technical and ethical complexities inherent to AI integration (Schmitt, 2024).

7. Conclusion

Integrating AutoML with XAI is an essential part in the context of AI deployments in digital transformation efforts. AutoML simplifies the creation of ML models by automating the intricate tasks of model selection, tuning, and validation, thus making advanced analytics accessible to non-experts and accelerating the work of experts. XAI complements this by providing transparency, explaining AutoML-generated models in terms understandable to humans, which enhances trust and manageability. This synergy not only aids in meeting regulatory and ethical standards by making AI decisions transparent but also increases user confidence and adoption by making the decision-making process clear. Together, AutoML and XAI improve AI implementation by providing speed and transparency, which makes them essential for organizations aiming to fully leverage AI in their digital transformation.

References

Agrawal, A., Gans, J., & Goldfarb, A. (eds.). (2019). *The Economics of Artificial Intelligence: An Agenda*. Chicago, IL: The University of Chicago Press.

Baptista, J., Stein, M.-K., Klein, S., Watson-Manheim, M. B., & Lee, J. (2020). Digital work and organisational transformation: Emergent Digital/Human work configurations in modern organisations. *The Journal of Strategic Information Systems*, 29(2): 101618.

Bertsimas, D. & Kallus, N. (2019). From predictive to prescriptive analytics. *Management Science*, 66(3): 3253.

Castelvecchi, D. (2024). The AI–quantum computing mash-up: Will it revolutionize science? *Nature*.

Cennamo, C. & Santaló, J. (2019). Generativity tension and value creation in platform ecosystems. *Organization Science*, 30(3): 617–641.

Chen, H., Chiang, R. H. L., & Storey, V. C. (2012). Business intelligence and analytics: From big data to big impact. *MIS Quarterly: Management Information Systems*, 36(4): 1165–1188.

Chen, H., Covert, I. C., Lundberg, S. M., & Lee, S.-I. (2023). Algorithms to estimate Shapley value feature attributions. *Nature Machine Intelligence*, 5(6): 590–601.

Constantiou, I. D. & Kallinikos, J. (2015). New games, new rules: Big data and the changing context of strategy. *Journal of Information Technology*, 30(1), 44–57.

Coombs, C., Hislop, D., Taneva, S. K., & Barnard, S. (2020). The strategic impacts of Intelligent Automation for knowledge and service work: An interdisciplinary review. *The Journal of Strategic Information Systems*, 29(4): 101600.

Faggioli, G., Dietz, L., Clarke, C. L. A., Demartini, G., Hagen, M., Hauff, C., Kando, N., Kanoulas, E., Potthast, M., Stein, B., & Wachsmuth, H. (2024). Who determines what is relevant? Humans or ai? Why not both? *Communications of the ACM*, 67(4): 31–34.

Fountaine, T., McCarthy, B., & Saleh, T. (2019). Building the ai-powered organization. *Harvard Business Review*. https://hbr.org/2019/07/building-the-ai-powered-organization.

Gans, J. S. (2024). Internal disagreement and disruptive technologies. *Strategy Science*, 0156.

Goldfarb, A., Taska, B., & Teodoridis, F. (2023). Could machine learning be a general purpose technology? A comparison of emerging technologies using data from online job postings. *Research Policy*, 52(1): 104653.

Henke, N., Bughin, J., Chui, M., Manyika, J., Saleh, T., Wiseman, B., & Sethupathy, G. (2016). The age of analytics: Competing in a data-driven world. *mckinsey.com*, December. https://www.mckinsey.com/business-functions/mckinsey-analytics/our-insights/the-age-of-analytics-competing-in-a-data-driven-world.

Iansiti, M. & Lakhani, K. R. (2020). Competing in the age of AI: Strategy and leadership when algorithms and networks run the world. *Harvard Business Press*.

Kellogg, K. C., Valentine, M. A., & Christin, A. (2020). Algorithms at work: The new contested terrain of control. *Academy of Management Annals*, 14(1): 366–410.

Kocoń, J., Cichecki, I., Kaszyca, O., Kochanek, M., Szydło, D., Baran, J., Bielaniewicz, J., Gruza, M., Janz, A., Kanclerz, K., Kocoń, A., Koptyra, B., Mieleszczenko-Kowszewicz, W., Miłkowski, P., Oleksy, M., Piasecki, M., Radliński, Ł., Wojtasik, K., Woźniak, S., & Kazienko, P. (2023). ChatGPT: Jack of all trades, master of none. *Information Fusion*, 99: 101861.

Rudin, C. (2019). Stop explaining black box machine learning models for high stakes decisions and use interpretable models instead. *Nature Machine Intelligence*, 1(5): 206–215.

Schmitt, M. (2020). *Artificial Intelligence in Business Analytics: Capturing Value with Machine Learning Applications in Financial Services*, Doctoral Thesis, University of Strathclyde. https://doi.org/10.48730/5s00-jd45.

Schmitt, M. (2023a). Automated machine learning: AI-driven decision making in business analytics. *Intelligent Systems with Applications*, 18: 200188.

Schmitt, M. (2023b). Deep learning in business analytics: A clash of expectations and reality. *International Journal of Information Management Data Insights*, 3(1): 100146.

Schmitt, M. (2023c). Securing the digital world: Protecting smart infrastructures and digital industries with artificial intelligence (AI)-enabled malware and intrusion detection. *Journal of Industrial Information Integration*, 36: 100520.

Schmitt, M. (2024). Strategic integration of artificial intelligence in the C-Suite: The role of the Chief AI Officer. *SSRN Electronic Journal*. https://doi.org/10.2139/ssrn.4812654.

Selten, F. & Klievink, B. (2024). Organizing public sector AI adoption: Navigating between separation and integration. *Government Information Quarterly*, 41(1): 101885.

Slumbers, O., Mguni, D. H., Blumberg, S. B., McAleer, S., Yang, Y., & Wang, J. (2023). A game-theoretic framework for managing risk in multi-agent systems. In: *Proceedings of the 40th International Conference on Machine Learning*.

Soliman, M. M., Ahmed, E., Darwish, A., & Hassanien, A. E. (2024). Artificial intelligence powered Metaverse: Analysis, challenges and future perspectives. *Artificial Intelligence Review*, 57(2): 36.

Suleyman, M. (2023). *The Coming Wave: Technology, Power, and the Twenty-First Century's Greatest Dilemma*. New York, NY: Crown.

Sun, Z., Strang, K., & Firmin, S. (2017). Business analytics-based enterprise information systems. *Journal of Computer Information Systems*, 57(2): 169–178.

Vaswani, A., Shazeer, N., Parmar, N., Uszkoreit, J., Jones, L., Gomez, A. N., Kaiser, L., & Polosukhin, I. (2017). Attention is all you need. In: *31st Conference on Neural Information Processing Systems (NIPS 2017)*, Long Beach, CA, USA.

Veldkamp, L. (2023). Valuing data as an asset. *Review of Finance*, 27(5): 1545–1562.

Yang, G., Ye, Q., & Xia, J. (2022). Unbox the black-box for the medical explainable AI via multi-modal and multi-centre data fusion: A mini-review, two showcases and beyond. *Information Fusion*, 77, 29–52.

https://doi.org/10.1142/9789811296475_0012

Chapter 12

Digital Transformation of Accounting through AI and Analytics: Enhancing Business Intelligence in the Modern Era

Musammat Tahmina Khanom

University of the Cumberlands, Williamsburg, KY, USA

1. Introduction

Digital technologies have become ubiquitous across various facets of contemporary society, spanning industries, educational institutions, and political arenas. Originating in the late 1990s, digital technologies gained prominence within the business sector, facilitating the digitization of numerous processes, including customer management, marketing strategies, online commerce, and customer engagement. Their pervasive influence highlights their transformative impact on modern business practices and customer interactions (Lombardi & Secundo, 2021, p. 1198).

The digital transformation of accounting represents a profound shift in how financial information is collected, processed, and analyzed. This chapter sheds light on the transformative impact of artificial intelligence (AI) and analytics on the accounting profession, emphasizing integrating these technologies within the broader context of business analytics. By leveraging the latest data and trends, the chapter explores the mechanisms through which AI and analytics enhance accuracy, efficiency, and strategic decision-making in accounting.

2. The Evolution of Accounting in the Digital Age

The evolution of accounting has been marked by several technological milestones from the advent of computerized accounting systems in the 20th century to the recent adoption of cloud-based solutions. Companies are increasingly digitizing their finance and accounting systems, leveraging modern technologies to tackle more complex tasks in these areas. While the board of directors and management typically dictate the technological architecture of finance and accounting in most companies, adopting technology in accounting is becoming more commonplace rather than progressive. This trend reflects a growing recognition of the benefits of technological advancements in enhancing efficiency and effectiveness within finance and accounting departments across various industries (Fülöp *et al.*, 2023, p. 998). However, the integration of AI and analytics represents a new frontier. These technologies not only automate routine tasks but also provide deeper insights through advanced data analysis, thereby transforming the role of accountants from mere recordkeepers to strategic advisors.

3. Literature Review

The integration of AI and analytics in accounting has garnered significant attention in both academic and professional literature. According to Bican and Brem (2020), digitization and digitalization, though often used interchangeably, represent distinct concepts in the realm of digital terminology. Digitization primarily involves the technical process of integrating digital technologies into various aspects of daily life. This entails converting analog information into a digital format, such as rendering physical objects programmable or communicable through coding and programming techniques. This section reviews key studies and publications highlighting the advancements, challenges, and implications of these technologies in accounting.

3.1. *Analytics and digital transformation in accounting*

AI's potential to transform accounting practices has been explored extensively. Rikhardsson *et al.* (2022, p. 323) discussed the automation of audit processes through AI, suggesting that AI can enhance the accuracy and efficiency of audits by identifying anomalies and patterns that traditional methods might overlook. Similarly, Lehner *et al.* (2022, p. 109) emphasized AI's role in real-time financial reporting and continuous auditing, proposing that AI systems can provide timely insights and reduce the latency associated with periodic audits.

Davenport and Kirby (2016) examined the broader impact of intelligent machines, including AI, on professional services, such as accounting. They argued that AI could handle complex data analysis tasks, allowing accountants to focus on strategic decision-making and advisory roles. Their work underscored the importance of developing new skill sets among accountants to leverage AI technologies effectively.

Baltzan (2021, p. 13) described business analytics as the systematic method of converting data into insights to facilitate improved decision-making. Analytics is employed for making decisions based on data and facts, assisting managers in making successful choices. Another research by MIT's Sloan School of Management and the University of Pennsylvania found that data-driven decision-making companies experience greater productivity, market value, and enhanced output and profitability.

3.2. *Predictive analytics and big data*

The advent of advanced technological innovations such as big data, AI, the Internet of Things (IoT), and predictive analytics marks the beginning of a transformative era for accountants. These high-performance tools enable accountants to guide organizations' digital transformation effectively. With a global strategic perspective, accountants can contribute significantly to the sustainable development of businesses and society (Tavares *et al.*, 2023, p. 2).

Again, the Fourth Industrial Revolution has heightened the necessity for seamless collaboration between humans and machines. This synergy is crucial for enhancing the speed and quality of decision-making processes, allowing organizations to respond more swiftly and accurately to the dynamic demands of the modern business landscape

(Varzaru, 2022, p. 2265). Here, the term "revolution" suggests a profound and sudden transformation. Historically, numerous revolutions have transpired, each bringing about the adoption of novel technologies that precipitated significant social and economic shifts. These periods of upheaval have consistently driven substantial progress, reshaping societies and economies by introducing innovative tools and methods that redefine how we live and work (Siekmann, 2023, p. 29).

In a book chapter, Arief (2024, p. 29) described how digital transformations in accounting profoundly alter business operations by lowering the costs associated with producing accounting information, providing real-time data access, and enabling the processing of vast amounts of information.

The role of predictive analytics in accounting has been a focal point of research in recent years. Raguseo (2018, p. 198) conducted an empirical investigation into the adoption of big data technologies, including predictive analytics, in various industries. The study found that companies adopting these technologies experienced significant benefits, such as improved decision-making, enhanced customer insights, and operational efficiencies. In accounting, predictive analytics can forecast financial trends, manage risks, and optimize resource allocation.

Implementing AI solutions in managerial accounting provides managers with numerous opportunities for innovation and streamlining processes. AI enhances the utilization of accounting information, making it more efficient and actionable. Additionally, the high degree of automation and customization offered by AI solutions makes them user-friendly, allowing managers to quickly adapt these technologies to their specific needs and significantly improve their decision-making processes (Varzaru, 2022, p. 2256). The research also emphasized the importance of integrating structured and unstructured data to gain comprehensive insights. The research suggested that predictive analytics could revolutionize financial planning and analysis by providing accurate forecasts and identifying potential risks.

3.3. *Ethical considerations*

While the benefits of AI and analytics are well documented, several studies have also highlighted the challenges and ethical considerations associated with their adoption. Brynjolfsson and McAfee (2014) discussed the potential job displacement due to automation and the need to reskill the workforce. In accounting, this translates to a shift in the required skill set, with a greater emphasis on data analysis and technology management.

Binns (2018) addressed the ethical implications of AI in decision-making processes. In accounting, ensuring transparency and fairness in AI-driven financial decisions is critical. The study called for robust governance frameworks to manage the ethical risks associated with AI, such as bias in algorithms and data privacy concerns.

4. AI in Accounting: Capabilities and Applications

AI's capabilities in accounting are extensive, encompassing automation, data analysis, and predictive modeling. Key applications include the following:

- **Automated data entry and reconciliation:** AI-powered systems can automatically capture and categorize financial data from various sources, significantly reducing manual data entry errors and improving efficiency. For instance, AI algorithms can match transactions with corresponding receipts and invoices, ensuring accuracy in financial records.
- **Fraud detection and risk management:** AI can analyze vast amounts of transaction data to identify patterns indicative of fraudulent activities. Machine learning models can continuously improve their detection capabilities by learning from new data, thus enhancing the robustness of fraud prevention measures.
- **Predictive analytics and forecasting:** AI-driven predictive analytics enables accountants to forecast financial trends and outcomes with greater accuracy. By analyzing historical data and identifying patterns, AI models can predict future revenue streams, cash flow, and financial risks, assisting businesses in strategic planning.
- **Natural language processing (NLP):** NLP technology allows AI systems to interpret and generate human language, facilitating more intuitive interactions with accounting software. This capability is handy for generating financial reports, answering queries, and providing insights in a user-friendly format.

5. The Role of Digital Transformation in Modern Accounting

In a study, Abdullah *et al.* (2024, p. 53) described that the advent of digital transformation has sparked notable transformations across various global industries, ushering in electronically driven enterprises such as e-government, e-banking, e-marketing, e-tourism, and, more recently, e-health. These digitally enabled sectors have amalgamated information systems across diverse domains, showcasing the expansive reach and impact of digitalization. The integration of information technology has not only revolutionized traditional industries but also paved the way for innovative business models and enhanced connectivity within and between sectors.

The most commonly acknowledged benefit of big data transformation is its capacity to expand a company's capabilities. When a company invests in new technologies, it must develop new skills and hire personnel proficient in managing these technologies. Big data allows businesses to rapidly collect and integrate structured and unstructured data from various sources, significantly enhancing their operational capabilities and decision-making processes (Raguseo, 2018, p. 198). Another study by Abdullah *et al.* (2024) stated that digital transformation yields substantial positive effects on sustainable business performance, encompassing social, environmental, and economic dimensions. Companies that adeptly embrace digital transformation and leverage their potential stand poised to attain robust returns and maintain enduring business success. By capitalizing on digital tools and strategies, organizations can enhance their competitive edge and contribute to sustainable growth across diverse spheres (p. 61).

In this transformation, analytics plays a crucial role in transforming raw financial data into actionable insights. The following sections highlight the intersection of business analytics and accounting:

- **Descriptive analytics:** Descriptive analytics involves summarizing historical data to understand what has happened in the past. In accounting, this can mean generating detailed financial statements, visualizing cash flows, and identifying trends in revenue and expenses. Tools such as dashboards and business intelligence platforms provide real-time insights into financial performance.
- **Diagnostic analytics:** This form of analytics seeks to explain why certain events occurred. In the context of accounting, diagnostic analytics can help identify the causes of financial discrepancies, variances in

budgets, and unexpected changes in financial metrics. By drilling into the data, accountants can uncover the underlying issues and take corrective actions.

- **Predictive analytics:** Building on the capabilities of AI, predictive analytics uses statistical models and machine learning algorithms to forecast future financial outcomes. This proactive approach enables businesses to anticipate market trends, manage risks, and allocate resources more effectively.
- **Prescriptive analytics:** Prescriptive analytics goes a step further by providing recommendations for future actions. In accounting, this can translate to optimizing budget allocations, suggesting investment opportunities, and advising on cost-saving measures. By integrating AI-driven insights, prescriptive analytics helps businesses make informed decisions that align with their strategic goals.

Furthermore, Feroz *et al.* (2021, p. 1530) found that digital transformation, fueled by digital technologies, initiates disruptions within organizations, profoundly influencing their value creation, strategy, and structure mechanisms. This shift has catalyzed the emergence of novel business models and induced disruptions across global markets and industries. Traditional businesses have felt the reverberations of digital transformation, often finding themselves outpaced by digitally adept firms entering the market. It is also explored by them that significant digital transformation disruptions are evident in waste management, pollution control, sustainable production, and urban sustainability sectors. These areas witness substantial changes propelled by digital innovation and technology integration (Feroz *et al.*, 2021, p. 1544).

6. Embracing the Future: Accounting in the Digital Age

The rapid pace of technological innovation has reshaped the accounting profession, challenging professionals to adapt to new tools, methodologies, and paradigms. This chapter examines accounting professionals' resilience and adaptive capacities in response to technological changes, aiming to understand how they navigate and thrive in the digital era. Malkawi and Khayrullina (2021, p. 64) described digitalization as a means of fostering economic expansion and advancing business development. However, it also poses challenges, particularly in demanding new skill sets from the workforce. As organizations strive for digital transformation, they often redefine their value creation and customer service approaches, necessitating the acquisition or development of novel digital resources and capabilities.

7. The Digital Transformation of Accounting

The accounting landscape is undergoing a significant transformation driven by rapid technological advancements. The integration of AI, blockchain, and data analytics into accounting practices not only streamlines operations but also presents new challenges and opportunities. This transition demands that accounting professionals develop a deep understanding of these innovations and adapt their skills accordingly, ensuring that they remain competitive and effective in their roles.

Emerging digital technologies positively impact managerial accounting, enhancing the roles of managerial accountants in driving sustainable organizational growth. These advancements allow accountants to leverage sophisticated tools for more accurate and comprehensive financial analysis. Consequently, managerial accountants can contribute more effectively to strategic decision-making processes, fostering long-term sustainability within their organizations (Varzaru *et al.*, 2023, p. 12).

Analyzing the impacts of AI implementation at the business unit or process level unveils numerous benefits, including performance enhancements, improved decision-making processes, cost efficiencies, customization capabilities, risk evaluations, insights into change management, competitive advantages, strategic alignments, and the establishment of new performance metrics. This comprehensive approach offers a detailed understanding of AI's transformative potential within an organization, enabling it to leverage AI effectively and capitalize on its myriad benefits (Fadi *et al.*, 2023, p. 132).

8. Adaptive Strategies for Professionals

Accounting professionals are now expected to possess a blend of technical and soft skills, ranging from data analysis and cybersecurity to critical thinking and effective communication. Adapting to technological changes is crucial for thriving in the digital era. This adaptation involves a commitment to continuous learning and staying abreast of technological trends that impact the accounting sector. Davenport and Kirby (2016) described in *MIT Sloan Management Review* (Volume 57, Issue 3, p. 25) that smart machines are rapidly progressing in tasks they excel at, outpacing human capabilities. This shift necessitates that workers develop and nurture new skill sets beyond those traditionally relied upon. However, human potential remains vast, with countless opportunities for individuals to make significant contributions for the foreseeable future.

9. Overcoming Challenges with Innovation

The shift toward digital accounting brings its own set of challenges, including the need for upskilling, potential job displacement, and ethical concerns related to data privacy. However, it also opens up opportunities for innovation, career advancement, and the creation of new value within the profession. Embracing these changes requires a proactive approach and a mindset geared toward exploration and experimentation. Fadi *et al.* (2023, p. 132) explored that adopting AI within an organization requires considering factors such as company culture, corporate governance, leadership style, ownership structure, risk tolerance, and change management practices. These elements significantly influence how the organization perceives and integrates AI into its operations, affecting decision-making processes. By examining these dimensions, organizations can make well-informed decisions that resonate with their unique characteristics and aspirations, facilitating smoother AI adoption and implementation processes.

10. Fostering Resilience through Support and Collaboration

Organizations play a crucial role in supporting their accounting workforce during this transition. By offering training programs, mentorship, and fostering a culture of innovation, companies can help their employees navigate the complexities of digital transformation. Case studies of successful adaptation underscore the importance of collaboration between accounting professionals and technology experts, highlighting how strategic partnerships can lead to enhanced resilience and organizational growth in the digital age. Kroon *et al.* (2021, p. 181) suggested that augmented intelligence offers significant prospects for accountants to enhance their expertise collaboratively, enabling them to engage in more value-added activities for their organizations.

Another study stated that it is crucial to scrutinize business models concerning their preparedness for the future and their potential impact on sustainability, considering the intertwined nature of economic and environmental sustainability. Addressing these sustainability challenges requires a holistic approach that acknowledges the interconnectedness of economic and environmental factors within business operations. Therefore, businesses must not only assess their economic viability but also evaluate their environmental footprint to ensure long-term sustainability (Bican & Brem, 2020, p. 5250).

Organizations should allocate resources to enhance various aspects of intellectual capital, including employee training, stakeholder relationships, and applied technologies. This investment aims to bolster organizational resilience in response to the challenges posed by the ongoing digital transformation today (Potrich *et al*., 2022, p. 59).

Therefore, accounting professionals must cultivate adaptive capacities to survive and thrive in the digital era. By embracing technological change, developing relevant competencies, and adopting a growth mindset, accounting professionals can position themselves as valuable assets in their organizations' digital transformation journey. Through continuous learning, collaboration, and innovation, accounting professionals can navigate technological disruption and contribute to advancing organizational intelligence in the digital age.

11. Challenges and Future Directions

In a study by Fülöp *et al*. (2023), it was discovered that the slow adoption of digital technology in the accounting profession is attributed to its highly regulated nature and the expectation of quick adaptation by clients. Transitioning from traditional to digitized activities poses challenges due to the importance of professional reasoning alongside digital technologies. Accountants must provide high-quality data while navigating additional data generated by digital processes, requiring evaluations of information reliability and ethical dilemmas. This underscores the need for accountants to possess digital competence and play a vital role in developing technological applications.

Gonçalves *et al.* (2022, p. 19) found that the primary obstacles to digital transformation in accounting appear to be resistance to change, organizational culture, and cost. Resistance to change involves the reluctance of individuals to adopt new technologies and processes, which can hinder progress. Additionally, entrenched organizational cultures may not be conducive to rapid technological adoption, and the high costs associated with implementing advanced digital tools can be a significant deterrent for many firms.

While the benefits of AI and analytics in accounting are substantial, several challenges must be addressed to realize their potential fully. Ensuring high-quality data and seamless integration across various systems remains a critical challenge. Only accurate or complete data can ensure the effectiveness of AI models and analytics. Furthermore, the increasing use of AI in accounting raises questions about regulatory compliance and ethical considerations. Organizations must navigate complex regulatory environments and ensure that AI-driven processes adhere to legal and ethical standards.

Additionally, adopting AI and analytics requires accountants to develop new data analysis, machine learning, and technology management skills. Continuous education and training equip accounting professionals with the necessary expertise. As accounting systems become more digitized, they are also more vulnerable to cyberattacks. Robust cybersecurity measures are essential to protect sensitive financial data and maintain trust in AI-driven accounting systems.

The accounting sector is presently undergoing a transformative transition toward a forward-thinking landscape. Kutnjak *et al.* (2023, p. 2519) explored that there is an anticipation of heightened collaboration between human expertise and automated systems in the foreseeable future, which may challenge conventional operation and service delivery methods within accounting. This evolving dynamic suggests a significant departure from traditional practices and implies potential disruptions in how accounting services are traditionally rendered.

12. Recommendations

As the transformation of the entrepreneurial mindset is influenced by a wide array of internal and external factors, the full recognition of technology's benefits within the accounting system may require a significant amount of time. Every stakeholder involved in the accounting system is responsible for embracing the elements of Industry 4.0, beginning with acknowledging the opportunities they present and subsequently leveraging them to their fullest potential (Kutnjak *et al.*, 2023, p. 2520).

Again, Andriole (2017, p. 4) opined in *MIT Sloan Management Review* (Volume 58, Issue 3) that digital transformation necessitates robust backing from top-level executives, emphasizing the pivotal role of senior management in driving organizational change. Beyond merely introducing the concept, sustained and visible support from the senior management team is imperative for the successful execution of transformations.

Based on the insights gained from this study, several key recommendations emerge for both accounting professionals and organizations aiming to successfully navigate the digital transformation of accounting through AI and analytics:

- **Invest in continuous learning and skill development:** Accounting professionals should proactively enhance their technical skills in AI, data analytics, and cybersecurity through online courses, certifications, and workshops. Organizations must invest in comprehensive training programs covering these emerging technologies to ensure that their workforce remains skilled and adaptable.
- **Foster a culture of innovation:** Accountants should cultivate a mindset geared toward innovation and experimentation, embracing new technologies and methodologies. Organizations should encourage an environment where innovation is rewarded by supporting experimentation with AI and analytics tools and creating cross-functional teams to drive digital transformation projects.
- **Enhance collaboration and communication:** Accountants need to develop strong communication and collaboration skills to work effectively with IT departments and data scientists, facilitating smoother integration of AI and analytics into accounting processes. Organizations should promote collaborative efforts between accounting and technology teams through joint projects and regular inter-departmental meetings.
- **Address ethical and regulatory challenges:** Accountants must stay informed about the ethical and regulatory implications of using AI and analytics and understand data privacy laws and compliance requirements to maintain integrity and trust. Organizations should implement

robust governance frameworks to ensure that AI and analytics practices comply with relevant laws and ethical guidelines, regularly updating policies to address emerging challenges.

- **Leverage advanced analytics for strategic decision-making:** Accountants should utilize advanced analytics to provide deeper insights and support strategic decision-making, developing predictive and prescriptive analytics competencies to anticipate trends and recommend actionable strategies. Organizations must integrate analytics tools into decision-making processes, using data-driven insights for strategic planning and risk management.
- **Invest in cybersecurity:** Accountants need to learn cybersecurity practices to protect sensitive financial data, mitigating risks associated with digital accounting systems. Organizations should prioritize robust cybersecurity measures to safeguard financial information, regularly updating security protocols and training employees to recognize and prevent cyber threats.

By adopting these recommendations, accounting professionals and organizations can effectively manage the digital transformation of accounting, leveraging AI and analytics to enhance efficiency, accuracy, and strategic value in their practices. This proactive approach will not only ensure resilience in the face of technological disruption but also position the accounting function as a critical driver of organizational intelligence and growth in the modern era.

Additionally, accountants face numerous challenges beyond digitalization and AI, impacting businesses and organizations. In Society 5.0, a human-centered society emphasizing the Sustainable Development Goals (SDGs), accountants must reimagine their role as integral to the social sciences, reshaping their social image. Consequently, the accounting profession should be elevated, dignified, promoted, and reinvented to meet the demands of this new societal paradigm (Tavares *et al.*, 2023, p. 6).

13. Conclusions

The digital transformation of accounting through AI and analytics signifies a fundamental shift in the profession, profoundly altering how financial information is processed and utilized. These technologies automate routine tasks, enhance data analysis, and offer predictive insights, enabling accountants to move beyond traditional roles and become strategic advisors within their organizations. By reducing the time spent on manual data entry and improving the accuracy of financial records, AI allows accountants to focus on higher-value activities, such as strategic planning and financial analysis. As the transformation of the entrepreneurial mindset is influenced by a wide array of internal and external factors, the full recognition of technology's benefits within the accounting system may require a significant amount of time. Every stakeholder involved in the accounting system is responsible for embracing the elements of Industry 4.0, beginning with acknowledging the opportunities they present and subsequently leveraging them to their fullest potential (Kutnjak *et al.*, 2023, p. 2520).

Moreover, AI and advanced analytics provide robust fraud detection, risk management, and predictive forecasting tools. These capabilities allow accountants to identify and mitigate risks more effectively, contributing to better-informed decision-making and strategic planning. The practical benefits of these technologies are evident in various industries, where companies have achieved significant efficiency gains, cost savings, and improved accuracy. However, integrating these technologies also presents challenges, such as ensuring data quality, maintaining regulatory compliance, and developing the necessary technical skills. Organizations must support their accounting workforce through training, innovation, and collaboration to successfully navigate the complexities of digital transformation.

It is also highlighted by Kroon *et al.* (2021, p. 181) that various opportunities are associated with blockchain technology, proposing that accountants could serve as planners and coordinators for blockchain participants or even administer blockchain networks. They also outline potential tasks for accountants, such as scrutinizing transaction records on a blockchain, innovating audit procedures for blockchain transactions, and ensuring the coherence between blockchain data and real-world items.

The integration of AI and analytics into accounting is crucial for maintaining competitiveness and driving growth in the digital age. By embracing these technologies, accountants can enhance their strategic value, contributing significantly to their organizations' success. The ongoing digital transformation of accounting will continue to shape the profession, positioning accountants as critical players in advancing organizational intelligence and sustainable business success.

14. Implications of the Study

The findings of this chapter analyze the profound impact of digital transformation on the accounting profession, mainly through the integration of AI and data analytics. These technological advancements streamline and automate routine accounting tasks and enhance strategic decision-making capabilities by providing deeper insights through advanced data analysis. The study highlights the necessity for accounting professionals to develop a blend of technical and soft skills to remain competitive and effective in this evolving landscape.

Organizations must prioritize continuous learning and skill development, ensuring that their workforce is equipped to handle the complexities introduced by AI and analytics. This prioritization involves investing in training programs, fostering a culture of innovation, and encouraging collaboration between accounting and technology experts. The study also reveals potential challenges, such as the need for upskilling, job displacement concerns, and ethical considerations surrounding data privacy and cybersecurity. Addressing these challenges requires proactive strategies and a growth mindset among professionals and organizations alike.

By adopting these recommendations, accounting professionals can enhance their resilience and adaptability, positioning themselves as valuable assets in their organizations' digital transformation journeys. Ultimately, this will lead to more efficient and effective accounting practices, driving organizational intelligence and strategic growth in the digital age. The study provides a roadmap for accounting professionals and organizations to navigate the technological disruptions and leverage the opportunities presented by AI and analytics, ensuring sustained success and competitiveness in the modern business environment.

15. Limitations of the Study

While this chapter provides insights into the transformative impact of digital transformation on accounting practices, it is essential to acknowledge certain limitations. Firstly, the scope of the chapter may only encompass some aspects of digital transformation in accounting, as the field is vast and continually evolving. Additionally, the examples and analysis may need to fully capture the diversity of experiences and challenges accounting professionals face in different organizational contexts. Furthermore, the chapter primarily focuses on the benefits and opportunities associated with digital transformation, potentially overlooking some risks, ethical considerations, and implementation challenges that organizations may encounter. Lastly, the chapter's conclusions and recommendations may be subject to individual interpretation and may not apply universally to all accounting settings.

References

Abdullah, S., Nawi, M. N. M., Halim, M. A. S. A., Omar, K., Rosli, N. A., & Harun, A. N. (2024). Digital Transformation for sustainable business performance: A systematic literature review. [Transformation digital para el desempeño empresarial sostenible: Una revisión sistemática de la literatura]. *UCJC Business and Society Review*, 80, 48–83.

Andriole, S. J. (2017). Five myths about digital transformation. *MIT Sloan Management Review*, *58*(3), n/a-22.

Arief, S. (2024). Digital transformation in accounting: The nexus between technology, leadership, and beyond. In: A. Perdana & T. Wang (eds.), *Digital Transformation In Accounting And Auditing*, pp. 29–59. Palgrave Macmillan.

Baltzan, P. (2021). *Business Driven Technology*, 9th edition. McGraw-Hill Higher Education (US).

Bican, P. M. & Brem, A. (2020). Digital business model, digital transformation, digital entrepreneurship: Is there a sustainable "digital"? *Sustainability*, 12(13), 5239.

Davenport, T. H. & Kirby, J. (2016). Just how smart are smart machines? *MIT Sloan Management Review*, 57(3): 21–25.

Fadi, S. S., Abdallah, B. A., Qais, M. O., & Alshurafat, H. (2023). The impact of artificial intelligence disclosure on financial performance. *International Journal of Financial Studies*, 11(3): 115.

Feroz, A. K., Zo, H., & Chiravuri, A. (2021). Digital transformation and environmental sustainability: A review and research agenda. *Sustainability*, 13(3): 1530.

Fülöp, M. T., Topor, D. I., Constantin, A. I., Căpuşneanu, S., Breaz, T. O., & Stanescu, S. G. (2022). Fintech accounting and Industry 4.0: Future-proofing or threats to the accounting profession? *Journal of Business Economics and Management*, 23(5): 997–1015.

Gonçalves, M. J. A., da Silva, A. C. F., & Ferreira, C. G. (2022). The future of accounting: How will digital transformation impact the sector? *Informatics*, 9(1): 19.

Kutnjak, A., Pihir, I., & Vidačić, S. (2023). Shifting towards digital transformation in bookkeeping agency — attitudes pre- and post-implementation of new technologies. *TEM Journal*, 12(4): 2512–2521.

Kroon, N., Maria do Céu Alves, & Martins, I. (2021). The impacts of emerging technologies on accountants' role and skills: Connecting to open innovation — a systematic literature review. *Journal of Open Innovation: Technology, Market, and Complexity*, 7(3): 163.

Lehner, O. M., Ittonen, K., Silvola, H., Ström, E., & Wührleitner, A. (2022). Artificial intelligence based decision-making in accounting and auditing: ethical challenges and normative thinking. *Accounting, Auditing & Accountability Journal*, 35(9): 109–135.

Lombardi, R. & Secundo, G. (2021). The digital transformation of corporate reporting – a systematic literature review and avenues for future research. *Meditari Accountancy Research*, 29(5): 1179–1208.

Malkawi, E. & Khayrullina, M. (2021). Digital human skills form the corporate economy and business development. *Ekonomicko-Manazerske Spektrum*, 15(1): 64–74.

Potrich, L. N., Selig, P. M., Matos, F., & Giugliani, E. (2022). Organisational resilience in the digital age: Management strategies and practices. In: F. Matos, P. M. Selig, & E. Henriqson (eds.), *Resilience in a Digital Age. Contributions to Management Science*, pp. 59–70. Springer.

Raguseo, E. (2018). Big data technologies: An empirical investigation on their adoption, benefits and risks for companies. *International Journal of Information Management*, 38(1): 187–205.

Rikhardsson, P., Thórisson, K. R., Bergthorsson, G., & Batt, C. (2022). Artificial intelligence and auditing in small- and medium-sized firms: Expectations and applications. *AI Magazine*, 43(3): 323–336.

Siekmann, F., Schlör, H., & Venghaus, S. (2023). Linking sustainability and the Fourth Industrial Revolution: A monitoring framework accounting for technological development. *Energy, Sustainability and Society*, 13(1): 26.

Tavares, M. C., Azevedo, G., Vale, J., & Bandeira, A. M. (2023). The accountant in the new era: Renewing the profession for Society 5.0. *2023 18th Iberian Conference on Information Systems and Technologies (CISTI)*, Aveiro, Portugal, pp. 1–6.

Vărzaru, A. A. (2022). Assessing artificial intelligence technology acceptance in managerial accounting. *Electronics*, 11(14): 2256.

Vărzaru, A. A., Bocean, C. G., Criveanu, M. M., Adrian-Florin Budică-Iacob, & Popescu, D. V. (2023). Assessing the contribution of managerial accounting in sustainable organizational development in the healthcare industry. *International Journal of Environmental Research and Public Health*, 20(4): 2895.

https://doi.org/10.1142/9789811296475_0013

Chapter 13

National Information Structures in Science and Technology: Evaluation of the Creation, the Evolution, and the Current Situation in Selected Countries

Lillian Maria Araujo de Rezende Alvares*, Marcel Garcia de Souza†, Washington Luís Ribeiro de Carvalho Segundo†, Edgard Costa Oliveira* and Tereza Raquel Merlo‡

**University of Brasilia, Brasilia (UnB) Brasilia – Federal District, Brazil*

†Brazilian Institute of Information in Science and Technology (IBICT), Brazil

‡University of North Texas, Denton, TX, USA

1. Introduction

The studies conducted by Fritz Machlup since 1933 are the first fragments of what would come to be configured as the Information Society. The requirements were clear, information is an essential input for economic and social progress, and it ushers in a new era, where science and technology occupy a vital space in development. The first documentalists of the 1890s saw their scope of action gradually broadened until, in the mid-1990s, Le Coadic (1996) presented the definition that best fits this work: “Information is the lifeblood of science. Without information, science cannot develop and live. Without information, research would be useless, and knowledge would not exist.”

Yes, information is the circulatory system of an institution. It seeks and provides knowledge throughout the management and innovation process. In science and technology institutions, it is the pre-existing knowledge that is necessary for new research and development. In this scenario, it did not take long for the expression *information in science and technology* or *scientific and technological information* to emerge. *Roughly speaking*, “it designates the knowledge obtained from [scientific and technological] research and development activities. It is an essential input and final product of research and has strategic importance in the development of society” (Pontes, 1990).

Although binomial science and technology have traveled different paths throughout history, today they are inseparable. Longo (1989, n.d.) states the following:

> “Nowadays, more and more technologies are generated from scientific knowledge. Expressions that are current today, such as high technology or advanced technology and state-of-the-art technology, are coined to express those technologies that are intensive in the use of scientific knowledge employed that are at the frontier of science, on the threshold of the unknown in their specific field.”

Currently, this association is widely disseminated and rooted in society, as shown in the essay by Castro (2016, p. 18) in a weekly magazine: “[science] requires a lot of care to prosper and frequent returns to the great productive matrices, from which the most fertile ideas sprout.” The prerequisites, including the provision of information, to meet the respective parties, are different, however. It is necessary to distinguish and characterize scientific information and technological information in order to achieve their main objectives more precisely.

For Aguiar (1991), scientific information is all knowledge that results from scientific research, whose dissemination of new knowledge, above all, ensures the authorship of those who developed it and serves as an input for the next evolutionary stages. Technological information, on the contrary, is “all knowledge of a technical, economic, market, managerial and social nature, which, through its application, favors progress in the form of improvement and innovation" (International Federation for Information and Documentation (FID), 1961). The concept of FID thus encompasses all kinds of information that contributes to industrial, economic, and social development, both at the level of the company and that of a nation.

Among scientific information products, the most prestigious in the international community are articles published in peer-reviewed journals, whose editorial trajectory lends credibility to the research results presented therein. Another example is bibliographic databases that organize and provide access to metadata references for books, theses and dissertations, research reports, and other publications of interest to science. In the other direction, there are the products and services of technological information, characterized mainly by the added value they bring with them, such as environmental monitoring services, mapping of items of interest and patent databases.

The understanding of the relevance of the contribution of specialized information to support the development of science and technology led countries to organize their national infrastructures of scientific and technological information, especially after the Second World War. It is important to briefly record the strategic actions of the United Nations (UN) and its agencies in stimulating and supporting the creation of national information policies in different countries of the world, decisively in developing countries. Silva (1994) showed that UNESCO, in particular, has played a prominent role since its first General Conference in 1946. It influenced the area in the production of different programs and in the creation of theoretical frameworks that still support information activities. Fundamentally, its participation included in its genesis actions in the fields of bibliography and documentation, in the creation of libraries, and in the activities of scientific and technological information itself. Today, UNESCO seeks to strengthen the knowledge society, reducing inequalities in access to information through technology with the Information for All Program (Ifap), created in 2000.

The situation of the basic structure of scientific and technological information in some countries is the objective of this research. In fact, the anticipated result from the beginning is that many countries have organizations of this nature. Therefore, it was necessary to establish selection criteria based on dispersion and geographical representation, on the available information and on the success in obtaining answers to the questions addressed. Initiatives were selected from Asia, Africa, Central America, North America, South America, Western Europe, and Eastern Europe.

2. Methodology

In order to conduct comprehensive research on National Science and Technology Information Frameworks (ICT) in different countries, it is essential to adopt a methodology that allows for effective comparison between different national systems. The criteria for the selection of countries were established considering the geographic diversity, the stage of economic and technological development, and the presence of active government policies in science and technology. The selection aimed at a broad representativeness to illustrate different models and approaches to the management of scientific and technological information.

After the selection of countries, the second stage involved data collection. This phase combined the analysis of publicly available official documents and reports as well as questionnaires sent to the institutions. The combination of primary and secondary sources was vital to gaining a deep and multifaceted insight into ICT structures. The analysis and interpretation of the collected data was the third stage and required dealing with the diversity of the data obtained, in a quantitative evaluation in the context of existing theories on information management and science and technology policy.

3. Support

Science and technology are recognized as essential drivers of modern economic and social development. An in-depth understanding of the structures that support scientific and technological information can provide valuable insights into how different nations capitalize on their knowledge from scientific and technological research and development to promote innovation and growth. Moreover, in a globalized context, where scientific and technological competition and collaboration transcend national borders, understanding these structures can facilitate international cooperation and the exchange of information and knowledge.

Indeed, the study of ICT structures offers an opportunity to analyze how countries face challenges in the organization and dissemination of scientific and technological knowledge and how they promote a more informed and engaged society in science and technology. Additionally, research can contribute by providing rich comparative data that can be used to test existing theories or develop new theories about the management and impact of scientific and technological information.

4. National Institutes of Information in Science and Technology

4.1. *Brazil: Brazilian Institute of Information in Science and Technology*[1]

Initiatives to promote information aimed at the development of science and technology have always been treated as a priority by UNESCO. At its first conference, in 1947, this organization encouraged the establishment of national documentation centers, especially in developing countries. In Brazil, the milestone occurred with the creation of the Brazilian Institute of Bibliography and Documentation (IBBD), in 1954, as an organ of the then National Research Council (CNPq). Its emergence was due to a joint action between UNESCO and Fundação Getúlio Vargas (FGV), which maintained an expressive collection in social sciences and inherited, in 1947, the Cataloging Exchange Service, created in 1942, in the former Department of Personnel Administration (DASP) (Barbosa, 1970). The main activities of IBBD included the National Collective Catalog of Serial Publications (CCN), specialized bibliographies, bibliographic searches, Registry of Research in Progress, Cataloging Exchange Service (SIC), and document reproduction. Part of its actions aimed at training human resources, by creating the first master's program in Information Science in Latin America in 1970; today it also offers a doctorate program, which is recognized as one of the best post-graduate programs in the country.

In the 1970s, the Brazilian government developed public policies for scientific and technological information. The First National Development Plan (PND) of 1972–1974 introduced the National Science and Technology Information System (SNICT), designed to coordinate

[1]This section is dedicated to the researcher Lena Vania Ribeiro Pinheiro, whose passion and dedication to strengthening IBICT were fundamental to the advancement of scientific and technological information policies in Brazil. Her enduring legacy in the field of information science continues to be a source of inspiration and longing for us.

scientific and technological information actions and establish a national cooperation network.

The first Basic Plan for Scientific and Technological Development (1973–1974) aimed to capture, process, and disseminate up-to-date information on science and technology. The second Basic Plan (1975–1979) expanded the space for scientific and technological information, including it among activities to support scientific and technological development.

In 1976, the IBBD was transformed into the Brazilian Institute of Information in Science and Technology (IBICT), reflecting the profound transformations in society, such as the emergence of computers and the automation of information processes. The IBICT assumed a new institutional profile, focusing on promoting and coordinating the implementation of the SNICT.

From 1980 to 1985, the IBICT strengthened its role in scientific and technological information policy, supporting the creation and implementation of information systems. The Third Brazilian Scientific and Technological Development Program (PBDCT) recognized the importance of the IBICT, assigning it the function of decentralized coordination of information activities in science and technology.

At this stage, three important milestones emerged in Brazilian information policy: the Programmed Action for Scientific and Technological Information, the Scientific and Technological Development Support Program (PADCT), and the National Plan for University Libraries (PNBU). The Programmed Action, drawn up in 1984, involved more than 100 information professionals and resulted in a diagnosis of needs and guidelines for the area.

The PADCT supported priority areas, such as biotechnology, geoscience, mineral technology, chemistry, instrumentation, and scientific information. Notable projects included the creation of the ANTARES network, which established service stations throughout Brazil to promote decentralized access to databases.

The PNBU of 1986 focused on the modernization and enrichment of university libraries, by promoting the planned acquisition of collections and the training of librarians. The National Science and Technology Strategies emerged as successors to the development plans, highlighting the National Research and Teaching Network, created in 1989 to build RNP — National Research Network, or the national academic internet infrastructure.

In addition to the IBICT, other institutions also played significant roles, such as the Regional Library of Medicine (BIREME), founded in 1967, which was a network model in Latin America, promoting access to scientific health information. It is also worth highlighting the Brazilian Agricultural Research Corporation (Embrapa), created in 1973, which developed information systems for Brazilian agriculture, as well as the Nuclear Information Center (CIN) of the National Nuclear Energy Commission, which became a center for the generation of knowledge in nuclear sciences.

In 2002, the IBICT created the Brazilian Technical Response Service (SBRT) to expand micro and small companies' access to technological knowledge. In 2005, the Brazilian Manifesto in Support of Free Access to Scientific Information was launched, joining the international open-access movement. In the wake of the open access, the IBICT has developed competence in building open-access repositories and creating free software tools for processing and disseminating information.

The Brazilian Digital Library of Theses and Dissertations (BDTD), with more than 2 million documents, is one of the institution's main initiatives, integrating information systems for theses and dissertations from all over Brazil into a single portal, adopting technology sharing and interoperability. IBICT's participation in international initiatives, such as Latindex and La Reference, reinforces its importance in the dissemination of Brazilian scientific production.

The IBICT also developed other information services, such as the Brazilian Portal for Open Access to Scientific Information (oasisbr), today with almost 2 million scientific articles, 6,000 research datasets, and 64,000 books and book chapters; the Brazilian Network of Digital Preservation Services (Rede Cariniana), a digital preservation system based on the distributed network model, which monitors and provides subsidies to other Brazilian projects that need to preserve authentic digital materials certified by recognized institutions. It is important to highlight that in 2018, the IBICT developed a digital repository model, Hipátia, which aims to create an interoperable technological platform to ensure the security and access of digital documents, minimizing the vulnerabilities and potential risks of cyberattacks, which could compromise the integrity of their data; and BrCris, the Brazilian Scientific Research Information ecosystem, an aggregating platform that allows retrieving, certifying, and visualizing data and information relating to the various actors working in scientific research in the Brazilian context.

IBICT's editorial line is intense, with the publication of scientific journals, such as *Ciência da Informação*, *Inclusão Social*, and *LIINC em Revista*. The magazine *Ciência da Informação*, launched in 1972, became electronic in 2004 and continues to publish advances in information science research. In fact, the content of this journal represents much of Brazilian research in information science and a fraction of the development of this field in Ibero-America. It has a Brazilian Thesaurus in Information Science, developed at the Institute itself for indexing and retrieving information about its products.

In line with the social inclusion policy of the Ministry of Science, Technology, and Innovation (MCTI), the IBICT began to develop actions in this line of scientific dissemination or popularization of science, in which it gained prominence with Canal Ciência, a scientific dissemination portal to support scientific education, which offers digital content and face-to-face educational activities. The main function of the Portal is the dissemination of Brazilian research developed by universities, centers, and research institutions in the areas of science, technology, and innovation. The Canal Ciência team rewrites research results in an easy-to-understand language — aimed at non-specialized segments of society — and disseminates them in multiple formats.

The trajectory of the former IBBD, now transformed into IBICT, demonstrates its fundamental role in the promotion and organization of scientific and technological information in Brazil. From the creation of information systems and networks to the modernization of services with emerging technologies, the IBICT has been a pillar in the democratization of access to knowledge, by supporting the country's scientific and technological development, reflecting its ongoing commitment to innovation and inclusion.

4.2. *Canada: Canada Institute for Scientific and Technical Information (CISTI)*

In North America, the Canada Institute for Scientific and Technical Information (CISTI) is one of the world's leading references for information in science and technology, with an emphasis on health sciences. It is subordinate to the National Research Council (NRC), emerged as its library (1924), and evolved into the National Science Library in 1957[2]. In 1974, its designation was changed to CISTI to reflect a new, broader mission than the previous one. It is located in Ottawa, the country's capital.

Establishing, operating, and maintaining the Canada National Library of Science constitute, in fact, a key part of CISTI's activities. Due to its historical support for health sciences-related topics, it is also the leading institution providing information and specialized services to Canada's medical community. Among its accomplishments in the area, the CISTI was responsible for coordinating access to MEDLARS and DOCLINE, both products of the United States National Library of Medicine (NLM).

The Institute operates on three fronts: the National Science Library; NRC Research Press, Canada's foremost scientific publishing house, founded in 1929; and Information Intelligence Services (IIS). The NRC Research Press publishes 16 journals, including *Genome* and several others, as well as 15 journals on behalf of scholarly societies. Due to the good results achieved, it became a private initiative and is currently no longer linked to the CISTI.

IIS is the latest service, whose purpose is to provide information analysis and scientific and technological information services in support of Canadian research, offered by a national network of experts located in the information centers of the various institutions linked to the NRC across Canada.

In addition, the CISTI has recently joined the global effort to organize open data for scientific research. This and other activities make up the three strategic objectives of the CISTI. The first, *developing and fostering information infrastructure that enables the access, use, and preservation of Canadian research outputs*, is based on (i) PubMed Central Canada (PMC Canada), in partnership with the Canadian Institutes of Health Research (CIHR) and the US NLM with a view to providing free access to the results of research in science, technology, and health, (ii) and The National Research Council Publications Archive, in order to provide access to more than 50,000 publications, including 8,000 full-text publications contained in the largest institutional repositories in the country.

---

[2]In fact, it became the National Science Library officially in 1967.

The second, *accelerating discovery and innovation,* is achieved through (i) *sharing knowledge on a global scale,* an alliance of several nations to create a single portal to access global scientific databases, accelerating the innovation process, and (ii) collaborating to *develop knowledge discovery tools* (CISTI Lab), a laboratory that collaboratively studies and develops tools and services for applications in next-generation libraries and electronic publications.

Finally, the *collaborating to expand access to digital science, technology, and health research information and data* through the (i) Research Data Strategy Working Group, whose goal is to ensure that Canada's research data are accessible and usable for current and future generations of researchers; (ii) *DataCite*, an international collaboration of libraries to improve access to research data; (iii) the Federal Science *eLibrary* (FSeL), whose objective is the partnership between the six most representative entities of science and technology to improve the information infrastructure; (iv) the *Canadian Virtual Health Library* with a view to connecting health information networks across the country and ensuring access to available knowledge; (v) and finally, *the Canadian National Committee for Codata*, which aims to improve the quality and accessibility of scientific data, as well as to promote and share knowledge on the importance of collecting, organizing, and using data to advance science and technology.

In the effort of national and international cooperation, the CISTI is affiliated with the Association of Research Libraries (ARL), the Canadian Association of Research Libraries (CARL), the Canadian Library Association (CLA), the International DataCite Federation, the International Council for Scientific and Technical Information (ICSTI), and Research Data Canada.

4.3. *China: Institute of Scientific and Technical Information (ISTIC)*

The Institute of Scientific and Technical Information (ISTIC) is a government institution founded in 1956 and subordinated to the Ministry of Science and Technology of China (MOST). Its main function is to support government agencies that develop science and technology activities, providing information to universities, industries, and research institutes. It is an academic, research and development unit and is also responsible for the dissemination of information technology.

To carry out these duties, it has seven functional divisions, six operational centers, and three corporations. The main activities include analysis of scientific and technological information, organization and representation of scientific documentation, dissemination of new information technologies, management of the electronic information platform in science and technology, training in information science, management of some scientific societies, and publication of books and scientific journals. In addition, the ISTIC has under its management the National Library of Engineering and Technology. Of the staff, 46.5% of the professionals have a bachelor's degree and 36% have a master's or doctorate.

The ISTIC collection is composed mainly of national and international journals, with themes focused on science and technology policies, theoretical and methodological studies in information science, sharing and management of science and information technology resources, and knowledge of linguistic technologies.

It is worth mentioning the Resource Sharing and Promotion Center (RSPC), a unit linked to the ISTIC responsible for basic research on scientific and technological information resources and applications for MOST and other entities of the federal government and the business sector that promote research and development in the field of IST. As a priority, the RSPC seeks to facilitate the integration and sharing of S&T resources, support studies and applications of competitive intelligence, induce technology transfer, and disseminate patents and standards.

Its graduate program in information science began in 1978 at the master's level, for studies in archival science, library science, and information science. From 2002 onward, doctoral and post-doctoral courses also began, being the first extra-university initiative authorized to grant high-level certification in information science. With the consolation of graduate studies, the ISTIC initiated a series of projects to enable the achievement of the master's degree with part-time dedication and the internship program with university students, such as Peking University, Nanjing University, Zhejiang University, Wuhan University, and Jilin University, with a view to conducting research in information resource management. With these initiatives, it became a national academic and training center in the field of scientific and technological information.

Regarding scientific information, it should be noted that, as of 2010, the Institute gathered 1.5 million national theses and dissertations, 220,000 foreign theses and dissertations, 100,000 conferences in foreign languages, and 60,000 annals of national congresses. It has also collected 1.23 million U.S.

government reports published since 1958 and more than 4,000 titles per year from foreign journals. It has approximately 300,000 reference books published abroad and has made available 18 electronic platforms for scientific research, including Web of Knowledge and INSPEC, among others.

Still on the organization and availability of scientific information, the ISTIC has created 33 full-text databases, covering more than 7,500 titles of digitized open-access journals. In addition to the above resources, there is a collection of about 4,000 monographs donated by more than 1,000 researchers from the Chinese Academy of Sciences and the Chinese Academy of Engineering. Of the digital collections contained in the Institute, national and international abstracts have reached 45 million, with an annual increase of up to 3.3 million entries.

In recent years, the Institute has been awarded 19 major projects funded by the National Social Science Foundation of China, the National Natural Science Foundation of China, and the Postdoctoral Fund. Initiatives were made to develop technologies for a variety of S&T systems, including the scientific-technological documentation system, the scientific-technological terminology system, and the DOI system, and these efforts have led to the creation of several patents, software copyrights, tools, models, and innovative methodologies that facilitate studies in scientific and technological information.

The country's openness has also influenced the field of ICT, causing the ISTIC to represent China in several international organizations, including UNESCO (in the IFAP Information for All program), the International Commission on Information Science and Technology (ICSTI), and the Asia Pacific Information Network (APIN). It has consolidated cooperation with research institutes in more than 30 countries, including Canada, the United States, and Japan, making it an important space for the exchange of scientific and technological information. Also noteworthy are the partnerships with the following: (i) Thomson Reuters to conduct the Scientometrics Laboratory, (ii) the Millennium Institute in the United States to conduct a research center, and (iii) the Japan Science and Technology Agency (JST) and KISTI South Korea Institute of Science and Technology Information for regular cooperation, including exchange mechanism.

Regarding the International Conference on Cooperation and Promotion of Information Resources in Science and Technology (COINFO) sponsored by the ISTIC for many years, the Institute has been successful in holding the event with good repercussions in the Science and Technology

Information community, as demonstrated by its permanence since 2006, in partnership with several universities, such as Zhejiang University (China), University of Southern Queensland (Australia), Beijing Institute of Technology (China), Beijing Jiaotong University (China), and Beijing University of Posts and Telecommunications, among others.

4.4. *Cuba: Scientific and Technological Information of Cuba (IDICT)*

In Central America, the Institute of Scientific and Technological Information of Cuba (IDICT), linked to the Ministry of Science, Technology and Environment (CITMA) and initially instituted as the Institute of Documentation and Communications of Cuba. InformationCientífica y Técnica em 1963,[3] aims to ensure that the Executive Branch and some priority industrial sectors have access to scientific and technological information. It was created with the objective of organizing the National System of Scientific and Technical Information (SNICT), elaborating it, and verifying the implementation of the National Information Policy.

It was in 1976 that the national alliance was consolidated, with the creation of units linked to 12 cities, initially called Multisectoral Centers for Scientific and Technical Information (CMSICT) and now as the Center for Information and Technological Management (CIGET). It is home to the IDICT Central Library (which evolved for the National Library of Science and Technology (BNCT) and the BioMundi consultancy.

The BNCT, inaugurated in 1988, is one of the most ambitious projects of the IDICT because from the organization of the decentralized collection that it promoted among the libraries of the SNICT, it allowed to give the country the condition to quickly access updated information in science and technology. The collection is mainly focused on the areas of medicine, biology, electronics, public health, and higher education.

Biomundi Consulting was created to support the country's development in the fields of biotechnology and the pharmaceutical industry. Inaugurated as Biotec, its characteristic activities are focused on business intelligence in partnership with the Instituto Superior de Tecnologías y Ciencias Aplicadas

---

[3]At the time of its creation, it was linked to the Comisión Nacional de la Academia de Ciencias de Cuba (ACC).

(INSTEC). The results achieved were also applied in Mexico, Venezuela, and Brazil.

IDICT's main services include information analysis, auditing of business information, and access to and search for documents, including access to Cuban and foreign databases, periodic dissemination of information, translation and certification of documents, and development of portals, and is also the national provider of internet connectivity, among others. It prepares publications, especially on the topics of information technology, business management, quality management, biotechnology, and genetic engineering.

Globachev and Muñoz (1983) stated that access to foreign databases, particularly, required heavy investment in computing, telecommunications, and automatic information processing. To this end, it had the decisive support of CAME member countries,[4] and in fact, the first experiments in the 1980s were in databases in Russia and Bulgaria, part of the International System of Scientific-Technical Information (SIICT) of CAME.

Regarding Internet access, the IDICT, through its National Center for Automated Information Exchange (CENIAI), has provided connectivity to the federal government, numerous research centers, embassies, hotels, and other organizations. The resources from this exclusive activity in the country help the Institute financially.

To meet the requirements of professionals in library[5] and information science, the Institute offers training programs at the undergraduate, master's, and doctoral levels, as well as short-term events in this area. It has 500 professionals, most of whom have higher education in different specialties. It should be noted that at the beginning it also received support from Soviet professors from the Institute for the Elevation of the Classification of Information Workers (IPKIR) to deepen knowledge in information science methodologies.

With regard to scholarly communication, especially serial publications, the Institute has a series of activities that strengthen decision-

[4]The Economic Council for Mutual Aid (CAME), which brought together the countries of the bloc, was led by the former Soviet Union and was responsible for the master plan for the long-term development of the economic and technical-scientific activity of the member countries.

[5]In Cuba, as in most Spanish-speaking countries, the current term for library science is librarianship.

making on the acquisition of journals. Based on bibliometric studies and considering certain indicators, the recommendation for purchase is made and where they should be made available. In addition, it has the efficient Catálogo Colectivo de Publicaciones Seriadas, which allows the location of periodicals throughout the country. It publishes the Revista Ciencias de la Informaci6n which is processed by various information services, such as Lisa, Compendex Plus, Inspec, Clase, and Cubaciencia.

By the way, the Cubaciencia database contains approximately 30,000 records, including summaries of Cuban information sources, theses defended by Cubans inside and outside the country, and the annual awards granted by the Cuban Academy of Sciences, among others. In scientific dissemination, the National Portal of the Forum of Science and Technique stands out, which brings together the full text of nationally awarded works. To date, 1,192 awarded works are available on the Portal.

Among all the products and services, the one that stands out in the Ibero-American scenario is the Congreso Internacional de Informaci6n (INFO). Starting in the mid-1980s, the proposal to create the event came to promote the discussion about librarianship and information science among information professionals in this region. The success of the event has ensured that INFO has been held biannually in more than 15 editions to date.

Following INFO's trajectory, another prominent event is the International Workshop on Business Intelligence and Business Knowledge Management (IntEmpres), dedicated to sharing experiences in the field of business intelligence and knowledge management with a view to business competitiveness in Latin America. Two of the editions were held in Brazil (2004) and Venezuela (2006). Since 2004, the INFO and IntEmpres events have been held jointly.

4.5. *France: Institute for Scientific and Technical Information (INIST)*

In Western Europe, the Institute for Scientific and Technical Information (INIST) is located in France, linked to the Direction de l'Information Scientifique et Technique (DIST) of the Centre National de la Recherche Scientifique (CNRS). DIST's strategic vision is the continuous improvement of knowledge sharing. In addition to the INIST, it has two other linked units: the Centre pour la Communication Scientifique Directe

(CCSD) and the Perseus Platform and the Scientific and Technological Information Correspondent (CorIST).

The INIST is the closest to the objectives of this research. Created in 1988, it aims to facilitate access to the results of scientific and technological research carried out in France. It is characterized as a documentation center whose mission is to collect, process, and disseminate the results of scientific and technological research from all over the country and is responsible for the production of three bibliographic, multilingual, and multidisciplinary databases: Pascal, Francis, and Doge. It is based in the town of Vandœuvre-lès-Nancy.

Since 1973, the Pascal database has covered scientific and technological literature. Its database has more than 17 million records, almost all of which are abstracts of journal articles (88%). The rest are dissertations, books, patents, and reports. Francis, on the contrary, is a database focused on humanities and social sciences, and Doge encompasses research papers on business management. It is produced in collaboration with the Institut Européen de Données Financières (Eurofidai). All of them comprise the majority of European production. Together, they represent one of the largest collections of science in Europe.

The services with the greatest added value of INIST are the solutions to carry out the monitoring of scientific and technological information, supporting digital scientific publications and the construction of scientific portals. It works in close coordination with the Digital Scientific Library (BSN),[6] whose objective is to serve the teaching and research communities and give greater visibility to scientific and technological results in France.

The INIST maintains close cooperation with numerous institutions, including the Correspondent for Scientific and Technological Information of the Institut des Sciences Humaines et Sociales (CorIST-SHS). The correspondents are professionals selected in each CNRS institute to disseminate information and good practices and inform the challenges that arise. At the moment, the correspondents are at the Institut de Chimie (INC), Institut de Physique (INP), Institut des Sciences Biologiques (INSB), Institut des Sciences de l'Information et de Leurs Interactions (INS2I), Institut des Sciences de l'Ingénierie et des Systems (INSIS), Institut des Sciences Humaines et Sociales (INSHS), Institut Écologie et Environnement (INEE), Institut National de Physique Nucléaire et de

[6]Digital Scientific Library.

Physique des Particules (IN2P3), Institut National des Sciences de l'Univers (INSU), and Institut National des Sciences Mathématiques et de Leurs Interactions (INSMI). With CorIST-SHS, the objective is to disseminate good practices in information science itself, strengthen relationships, unite and break the isolation of STI initiatives, facilitate the sharing of information and experiences, gather skills, practices, and tools, locate experience and find answers to challenges, and promote and improve information actions and functions in STI products and services.

With the very large research infrastructure (TGIR) focused on research in humanities and social sciences (TIGR Huma-Num), the cooperation aims to support the set of services for the storage, processing, visualization, communication, dissemination, and preservation over the research of research data in the digital environment in the long term in humanities and social sciences. That is, it follows the different phases of the digital data lifecycle, thus becoming a digital curation initiative.

Via EPRIST, the cooperation is to contribute to the discussion between those responsible for scientific and technological information of public research institutions in France. The objective is to promote the exchange of experiences, with a view to facilitating inter-institutional reflection on the evolution of the field to contribute to the definition and implementation of scientific and technological information policies. Secondly, it seeks the joint acquisition of information resources, compares the performance of ICT management tools, promotes bibliometric practices, assists in the organization of unique author identification, and supports the evaluation of the best resources for institutional archives.

With the Association des Directeurs et Personnels de Direction des Bibliothèques Universitaires et de la Documentation (ADBU), it discusses policy for university libraries in France and Europe. The ADBU operates through five commissions, which deal specifically with action with government, education, the profession and the professional, research, and the digital environment. It holds specific high value-added events and an annual conference.

The Unité Régionale de Formation à l'Information Scientifique et Technologique (URFIST) plays a prominent role in partnership with INIST. Being a decentralized training initiative in the field of information in science and technology, it is vital for the French STI framework. There are seven universities aimed at disseminating modern documentation practices in the academic community: Université de Bordeaux, Université Lyon 1,

Université de Nice, École Nationale des Chartes, Université Rennes 2, Université de Strasbourg, and Université de Toulouse. The scope of activities ranges from digital literacy and information literacy to building skills in the digital age for monitoring, prospecting, and bibliometrics.

With 24 million queries in 2010, the Agence Bibliographique de l'Enseignement Supérieur (ABES) receives a prominent place as an information resource for higher education and research in France, and therefore, cooperation with the INIST is a priority. The ABES was created in 1994 to implement the Sudoc catalog, a set of all higher education library catalogs. Inaugurated in 2001, today, there are 1,419 libraries with more than 10 million bibliographic records. With this mission, the ABES is also responsible for the acquisition of electronic resources, which brings it closer to the Couperin consortium, responsible for acquiring digital information resources in the best conditions, seeking to integrate these resources and ensuring the best distribution for users. It brings together more than 200 members, including universities, colleges, and research organizations, among others.

A product resulting from the DIST, and of special interest for this research, is the Perseus Platform, inaugurated in 2005, which is a portal for the dissemination of complete collections of scientific publications, mainly in humanities and social sciences. The oldest document dates from 1840. It currently has approximately 170 collections, with more than 530,000 full-text and open-access documents. The portal receives an average of 25 million visits per year. It offers several options for the analysis of information by users, such as indexing of articles, export of bibliographic references (BibTex, RefWorks, and Zotero RIS), detachable screens, cross-references, and unrestricted access to all portal services, among others. For authors, it offers above all digitization, dissemination, and archiving of publications, referencing of documents, and visibility on the web (search engines, bibliographic databases, and discovery tools). For libraries, it offers metadata (MARCXML, mods, DC) via OAI-PMH and Z3950, query statistics, and long-term preservation.

4.6. *Ghana Institute for Scientific and Technological Information (INSTI)*

On another continent, the Republic of Ghana, a West African country, is one of the few African countries to observe specific scientific and technological information actions in support of research and development. To realize the vision of the future of science and technology in the country, the Institute for Scientific and Technological Information (INSTI), a government entity linked to the Council for Scientific and Industrial Research (CSIR), was created. Located in the country's capital, Accra, the Institute seeks to develop national capacity in information products and services with a view to helping organize and disseminate the results of scientific and technological research, at home and abroad, to the public and private sectors and to the CSIR itself.

The Institute operates in three segments: library and documentation; scientific publishing and printing; and thematic mapping. The scientific information services, developed in the library and documentation segment, include reference services, selective dissemination of information, organization and representation of information, questions and answers, and documentary research, among others. It also includes the following online resources: Access to Global Online Research in Agriculture (AGORA), Health InterNetwork Access to Research Initiative (HINARI), Online Access to Research in the Environment (OARE), Journal Storage (JSTOR), and Essential Electronic Agricultural Library (TEEAL). In addition to these, it has national S&T information resources such as Ghana Science Abstracts (GHASAB), Ghana Agricultural Research Information (GHAGRI), Directory of Science Experts in Ghana (EXPERT), and AGRIS database and Science and Technology Theses in Ghana (S&T).

The thematic mapping segment is the one that adds the most value, whose objective is to collect data for the design and construction of thematic maps that portray in cartographic form data related to the socioeconomic characteristics of Ghana (education, poverty, health information, tourism, infrastructure, physical and environmental conditions, population, and industrial and agricultural activities) from Geographic Information Systems (GIS). It also directly addresses the specific demands of specialized maps.

Additionally, established at the CSIR is the Ghana National Scientific and Technological Information Network (Ghastinet), whose focal point, of nine sectoral nodes, is the National Science and Technology Library and Information Centre (Nastlic). Ghastinet's main objective is to provide broad access to scientific and technological information through its own methodologies to a target audience composed of government officials, private companies, researchers including professors and students, and micro and small industries. By the way, just as the CSIR established Nastlic, it also organized libraries and documentation units in several of its institutes, with professionals specialized in processing, storing, searching, retrieving, and disseminating information (Villar, 1996).

The Network also aggregates international information resources, such as CAB International Abstracts, Agris, TropAg and Rural, and the Maize Germplasm Databank, all focused on agricultural research, given that the country is predominantly agricultural and whose export of agricultural commodities is particularly based on cocoa. In fact, the provision of information in the solution of agricultural problems such as low yields in the cultivation of local varieties and vulnerability to pests requires the organization of forms of transfer of appropriate technologies. Considering the context of the illiteracy of most farmers in rural areas, strategies should consider the dissemination of information associated with technical communication and technological extension.

4.7. *Russia: All-Russian Institute of Scientific and Technical Information (VINITI)*

In Eastern Europe (and Eurasia), the Russian Academy of Sciences (RAS) began the new project of creating the Institute for Scientific Information in 1952. Among the 400 research institutes of the RAS, it receives special attention for supporting the scientific and technological development of the Union of Soviet Socialist Republics (USSR 1922–1991). Almost immediately, it expanded its functions and received in 1955 the new designation, All-Russian Institute of Scientific and Technical Information (VINITI).

Both on the occasion of the USSR and now for Russia and for The Commonwealth of Independent States (CIS),[7] VINITI is a world leader in scientific and technological information (YASHUKOVA, undated). It is also the institution responsible for the Russian State System of Scientific

[7]Regional organization created in 1991 during the dissolution of the Soviet Union, whose participating countries are some former Soviet republics: Armenia, Azerbaijan, Belarus, Georgia, Kazakhstan, Kyrgyzstan, Moldova, Russia, Tajikistan, Turkmenistan, Ukraine, and Uzbekistan. Estonia, Latvia, and Lithuania declined to participate. Today, the political conflicts between Russia and Georgia, as well as between Russia and Ukraine, prevent us from determining the current status of the CIS.

and Technical Information (GSNTI) and has remained the largest information center in Eastern Europe for more than six decades.

The creation of VINITI coincides with the "golden age" of the Soviet Union when scientific and technological research took priority over the development of Cold War military technologies. According to Maruskova (2012), even Eugene Garfield pointed out in his speech honoring the 50th anniversary of VINITI that he was the inspiration for the creation of the Institute for Scientific Information (ISI) in the USA. The same author informs that for more than three decades, the Institute was led by Alexander Ivanovich Mikhailov (1905–1988), an important researcher in information science, whose work subsidized studies in the area around the world.

The purpose of the institute is to provide information support to basic and applied research in the country, especially for those implemented by the government's higher education and research centers. Its priority is the development of information and communication technologies, methodologies, and tools for the construction of information systems and the availability of scientific information products and services to support federal and regional programs and projects for economic, social, and national security development.

To continue the activities, it conducts research in the following lines: theory, organization, and representation; automatic retrieval; scientific communication, giving rise to a graduate program in information science. Furthermore, in the effort to train them, it promotes several events for information professionals and librarians. It publishes the monthly peer-reviewed journal *Scientific and Technical Information* — Series 1: Organization and Methodology of Information Service and Series 2: Information Processes and Systems. Both are translated into English and indexed by Springer and Scopus. Another publication, quarterly and peer-reviewed, is the *International Forum of Information.*

Among VINITI's first activities is the analysis of the world's scientific and technological literature with a view to publishing abstracts. This work resulted in VINITI's[8] JA (VINITI's RZh),[9] one of the Institution's main products since then. The abstracts produced are the result of intense analytical research of the data flows obtained from the information sources of more than 100 countries in 60 languages, resulting in approximately 1 million documents per year. Per year, therefore, there are 28 volumes

[8]VINITI's Journal Abstract.

[9]Also, in VINITI's e-RZh electronic format.

with 224 issues in total. The fields of study are astronomy and space science; biology, biotechnology, and biophysics; chemistry; civil defense; economics and management; electronic technology and energetics; environmental science; geography and geophysics; informatics; mathematics and computer science; mechanical engineering; metallurgy; physics; publishing; radio, electronics, and computer technology; and transport.

Another product of the greatest relevance is the VINITI Database RAS, the largest database in Russia with bibliographic information on proceedings, conferences, regulatory documents, books, patents, journals, and theses. The national content makes up 30% of the total number of documents. In fact, the VINITI Database RAS and VINITI's RZh are the Institution's main information products.

With the large collection available at VINITI, it is only natural that they have been members of the Executive Committee of the Universal Decimal Classification Consortium (CDU) since 2000. The Institute has exclusive rights to the publication and dissemination of the CDU in the country, in Russian print and electronic versions.

The VINITI has a wide range of products and services, such as robust information retrieval services, the deposit of scientific papers, reference services, and the publication of scientific rankings. To this end, it also has the Center for Research and Information Services and more than 800 information professionals, trained in various academic disciplines and fluent in several languages.

5. Final Thoughts

The research on National Science and Technology Information Frameworks (ICT) in various countries reveals that, although each nation adapts its approaches to its specific needs and contexts, there is a consensus on the crucial importance of these infrastructures for scientific and technological development. A comparative analysis demonstrates that strategies for managing scientific information vary significantly, influenced by economic, political, and social factors. The diversity in approaches — from highly centralized and government-led to more decentralized and based on international collaborations — shows that there is no single model for success. However, the effectiveness of ICT institutions seems to be directly linked to their ability not only to respond to the immediate needs of their national contexts but also to anticipate and influence future directions in science and technology.

The results, however, were sufficient to establish a comparative basis and to ascertain in which direction the institutions are paving the future. It can be said that the main choices fall on the economic priorities of the nations. For example, the Institute for Scientific and Technological Information (INSTI) of Ghana and its entire S&T framework have chosen to cater to agricultural research, given that the country is predominantly agricultural. The CISTI, in turn, followed the tradition in health sciences, which, since the end of the 1950s, has invested in its National Library of Sciences primarily focused on this area. China, with its extension and entrepreneurial vocation, opted for engineering, and Cuba, whose results in biotechnology and public health are internationally recognized, reflects the vocation in ICT activities.

It is worth noting as well the date of creation of the institutes: Most of them are research institutes linked to national science and technology bodies and the main foundation dates are from the 1950s. They were all founded and then had transformations and expansions of their mission in the 1960s and 1970s, apart from France that only founded the INIST later in 1988. This difference can be explained by the composition of the French scientific and technological information system, which is decentralized, dispersed, and numerous. Certainly, among the activities of the Centre National de la Recherche Scientifique (CNRS) and the national research system, some of which are reported in this work, are dates of creation much earlier than the 1980s.

Another dimension that stands out is politics. It is easy to see that Cuba, a member country of the CAME, received decisive help from the USSR (1922–1991). Their ties of cooperation were described in the article "20 años de relaciones VINITI-IDICT." Naturally, proximity established the same priority in the development of activities, that is, the analysis and cross-referencing of information. The All-Russian Institute of Scientific and Technical Information has in VINITI's JA its most complex and important product, aimed at serving both the scientific information community and the information technology community. On the contrary, the Institute of Scientific and Technological Information of Cuba (IDICT) has managed to stand out in business consulting services, based on its collection and access to available information.

Another aspect that deserves attention is culture. The Institute of Scientific and Technical Information of China (ISTIC) stands out for its concern about processing large amounts of information and delving into products and services in terminology. The numbers, in fact, are eye-catching and not just because of the size of the country. The most recent survey reports that the country has gathered 1.5 million national theses and dissertations, 220,000 foreign theses and dissertations, 100,000 foreign language conferences, and 60,000 national congress proceedings, and has collected 1.23 million U.S. government reports and more than 4,000 foreign journal titles/year. It has approximately 300,000 reference books published abroad and has made available 18 electronic platforms for scientific research. But, roughly speaking, Chinese production will only be processed in the international community if it is in another alphabet and foreign production will only be processed domestically in its fullness if it is in Chinese language.

Other common segments that stand out are the occurrence of training programs in all of them, some of which are high-level, offering master's, doctoral, and postdoctoral courses, such as IDICT, ISTIC, and VINITI, respectively. Likewise, most of the institutes maintain national science and technology libraries linked to them, as it is the case of Canada, China, Cuba, and Ghana.

In an endeavor to aid knowledge sharing, many of them publish their own publications in information science, such as the *IDIT Journal of Information Sciences*, *Scientific and Technical Information* — Series 1: Organization and Methodology of Information Service, and Series 2: Information Processes and Systems, and VINITI's *International Forum of Information* and *Ciência da Informação from IBICT*.

At the forefront of the initiatives are France and Canada in the theme of open data, scientific research, and data curation, which aim to ensure access to research data at a global level. In fact, such an initiative is the new paradigm of science and requires a powerful infrastructure for storing, processing, and preserving what gave rise to and sustained scientific research or technological development. In this segment, France has gone even further, not exactly in the heart of the matter, but in the adjacent issues, such as the participation of humanities and social sciences, which also carry out research, but do not have the appropriate training to deal with data technology. Using the terminology *digital humanities*, it has its own initiative to deal with this issue. In fact, all the scientific and technological information initiatives reported here are strongly supported by technology, the fundamental aspect for the evolution of science, which in turn is essential for the economic and social progress of humanity.

Finally, the research reaffirms the need for robust government policies that support the development and maintenance of these infrastructures, ensuring that they are aligned with national development priorities and capable of competing and collaborating in an increasingly interconnected global landscape. The exchange of experiences and practices among different countries provides a valuable foundation for the continuous evolution of ICT structures, strengthening each nation's ability to maximize its scientific and technological potential.

References

Aguiar, A. C. (1991). Informação e atividades de desenvolvimento científico, tecnológico e industrial: tipologia: proposta com base em análise funcional. *Revista Ciência da Informação,* 20(1): 7–15.

Castro, C. de M. (2016). Ciência poderosa e frágil. *Revista Veja*, 18.

Globachev, O. I. & Muñoz, E. M. (1983). Veinte años de relaciones VINITI-IDICT. Actualidades de la Información Científica y Técnica. *La Habana* 14(4): 29–39.

INSTI (The Institute for Scientific and Technological Information) (2016). Retrieved January 12, from http://csir-insti.org/.

ISTIC (Institute of Scientific and Technical Information of China) (2016). Retrieved January 12, from http://www.istic.ac.cn/English/.

Longo, W. P. (1989). Ciência e tecnologia: evolução, inter-relação e perspectiva. In: *Encontro Nacional de Engenharia de Produção, Enegep*, 9. Porto Alegre: Universidade Federal do Rio Grande do Sul.

Markusova, V. (2012). All Russian Institute for Scientific and Technical Information (viniti) of the Russian Academy of Sciences. *Acta Informatica Medica*, 20(2): 113–117.

Pontes, C. C. C. (1990). Bases de dados em ciência e tecnologia. *Transinformação,* 2(2): 33–42.

Silva, L. A. G. da. (1994). Políticas e programas de informação e documentação da unesco e fontes para seu estudo. *Informação & Sociedade* 4(1): 68–84.

Villars, J. A. (1996). The Ghana National Scientific and Technological Information Network (GHASTINET) Project. In: *Bridge Builders: African Experiences with Information and Communication Technology*. Washington, DC: National Academy Press.

Yashukova, S., All-Russian Institute of Scientific and Technical Information of the Russian Academy of Sciences (VINITI RAN) (2016). PPT Presentation. Retrieved February 5, from https://www.academia.edu/116106775/All_Russian_institute_for_scientific_and_technical_information_viniti_of_the_Russian_academy_of_sciences?sm=b.

https://doi.org/10.1142/9789811296475_bmatter

Index